The American Sharpe

The Adventures of an American Officer of
the 95th Rifles in the Peninsular and
Waterloo Campaigns

The American Sharpe

The Adventures of an American Officer of
the 95th Rifles in the Peninsular and
Waterloo Campaigns

Gareth Glover

Frontline Books

THE AMERICAN SHARPE

The Adventures of an American Officer of the 95th Rifles in the Peninsular and Waterloo Campaigns

This edition published in 2016 by Frontline Books,
an imprint of Pen & Sword Books Ltd,
47 Church Street, Barnsley, S. Yorkshire, S70 2AS

ISBN: 978-1-84832-777-1

CIP data records for this title are available from the British Library

For more information on our books, please visit
www.frontline-books.com, email info@frontline-books.com
or write to us at the above address.

Printed and bound by CPI Group (UK) Ltd, Croydon, CR0 4YY [TBC]

Typeset in 10.5/12.5 point Palatino

Contents

Introduction

A number of journals and collections of letters have already been published by members of what is undoubtedly the most famous British regiment of the Napoleonic wars, the 95th Regiment[1] of the Line (Rifles); more commonly known as the '95th' or 'the Rifles', although the latter does ignore the fact that the regiment was not the only unit of the British Army of that time to be armed with a rifle rather than the smoothbore musket carried by most of the infantry.

It does seem that the members of the 1st Battalion 95th Foot were particularly adept at keeping journals, with over half of the published journals from this three-battalion regiment actually emanating from the 1st Battalion.

Now yet another is published for the first time, some two hundred years after the events it describes. This set of journals and the accompanying letters form a fascinating and very extensive view of the life of a rifle officer, just like Bernard Cornwell's fictitious character Richard Sharpe, but what makes them even more fascinating is that they have the added twist of the fact that the author was an American by birth!

James Penman Gairdner served in the Peninsular War without a break, from the siege of Ciudad Rodrigo in January 1812 until the end of the war in 1814 and then continued with his subsequent experiences during the Waterloo campaign and the ensuing occupation of France for the next three years. He was also wounded three times during his active service.

Three surviving hand written journals, written generally on a daily basis, in ink, in small leather bound pocket books have survived, although occasionally, at times of heightened activity, it can be seen that he has caught up with events a little later; or paradoxically during periods of acute boredom he skips rapidly over the dates. But what they do offer are truly contemporary accounts of occurrences, full of the honest description of actions he experienced and saw with his own eyes, but also with the inevitable confusions and misunderstandings of events outside of his personal knowledge. But beyond everything else, it is refreshingly untainted by the dreaded hindsight which inevitably creeps almost imperceptibly into the narratives of those who edited their journals in later years for publication. There are feint hints that at times James has revisited odd sections of the journals, but these are rare and do not materially affect the immediacy of his narrative.

Despite the fact that these journals are preserved with the greatest care by the National Army Museum, at Chelsea in London, some parts of the journal have faded almost to the point that it is impossible to read the writing. Luckily I was able to obtain images of these pages with which I have used some special techniques that I have developed to draw out the little remaining ink, allowing me to transcribe them in full. It has been a high priority of mine to complete this project because it will not be long, literally months, before the ink has deteriorated beyond the possibility of ever being transcribed, particularly with reference to parts of the 1815 journal, which have certainly taxed the vision of this editor.

But a very interesting aspect of his journals and letters is the relationship of the now fully independent Americans and their family still in the 'Old Country'. It is clear that their relationships were still strong and in fact their loyalties remained fluid in many situations, family often being more important than country. These exchanges, particularly with his father, make for very interesting reading in this regard and throw valuable light on this confusion of identity for many, including even those born in an Independent United States.

It astonishes me that such valuable source material has been virtually ignored for so long and it is high time that they were published and I am very glad that I am able to do so now.

Gareth Glover
Cardiff, 2016

---

[1] The author knows of published accounts by eleven members of the 95th, Private Edward Costello; Lieutenant Robert Fernyhough, Bugler William Green; Private John Harris; Captain John Kincaid; Captain Jonathan Leach; First Lieutenant George Simmons; Captain Harry Smith, Private George Walton, Private Thomas Knight and Quarter Master William Surtees. Of these, six served in the 1st Battalion 95th Foot.

Acknowledgements

I cannot fail to start by offering my heartfelt thanks to Dr. Alastair Massie Head of Academic Access, Collections, at the National Army Museum, Chelsea, London and his staff for their help in providing me with suitable images of the letters and journals to work from and permission to publish the completed text.

I have received a great deal of help and advice from both Mrs Eleanor Hoare, the college archivist at Eton, who confirmed that James did not attend there, despite family claims to the contrary; and Miss Joanna Badrock, Archivist and Records Manager at Harrow School, where he almost certainly did attend, which does this time agree with the family histories.

But without doubt I have received great encouragement and a mass of invaluable information, which has certainly enhanced this work very materially from surviving descendants of James. This support has been very ably coordinated by Sue Martin, a descendant of John Gordon and a severely overworked tax accountant in America, who however has made the time to supply me with copies of copious documents and obtained even more, including a further set of letters, from other branches of the family (the Blackmores) who reside in Australia. I must therefore also thank Greg Blackmore who generously granted permission to utilise all of the information he had gathered regarding James and his family.

Thanks must also go to Christa Hook who kindly allowed me to reproduce her portrait of James Penman Gairdner in this book.

I must also offer my thanks to Robert Burnham and Ron McGuigan who answer all my incessant and probably inane questions with such good humour and grace. Finally I must as always offer my grateful thanks to my wonderful wife Mary, who could not be more supportive of my efforts and now knows more about Napoleonic warfare than she ever wanted to!

Chapter 1

The Gairdner Family

The story of James Penman Gairdner is very much one tied up in the history of the Scottish traders who traded with the Southern states of America and where many of them found their homes and indeed their graves. This had been common practise for decades and does not seem to have been interrupted at all by the American War of Independence. Indeed even after the American states became a unified nation, the Scottish merchants continued to trade and live harmoniously in the Southern states whilst still trading with Britain.

The Gairdners were slightly late to this trade, but seem to have made up for this quite quickly, to establish themselves rapidly within the upper echelons of Charleston society.[1]

James Gairdner, the father of our man James Penman Gairdner, was of Scottish descent[2], but very soon after the end of the American Revolution he moved out to Charleston where he traded as a merchant in a company set up with his brother Edwin, the firm being known simply as James & Edwin Gairdner. This mercantile company was located at 114 East Bay Street, Charleston and existed throughout at least the first two decades of the 19th Century. He also seems to have run a separate shipping company with his brother Gordon, which owned a number of trading ships.[3]

Around 1802 his brother Edwin was made a bankrupt in America, although he continued to own large plantations in Jamaica and then appears to have branched off into administering landed estates as an attorney for Penman, Shaw and Company. In this role he had sought and received assurances that he would be sent the powers of attorney to administer the estates of those who died in debt to Penman, Shaw and Co. He had apparently carried out this role previously on the estate of a Mr Manly and he seemingly performed his duties to everyone's satisfaction.

1

But this changed completely in the case of the estate of a Mr Shiras. In this case, Edwin was apparently on the brink of bankruptcy again and despite the fact that he produced very questionable accounts stating that Shiras had died owing him nearly $7,000 it became clear that he had used his position to procure this money for himself over his obligations to Penman, Shaw & Co and may well have passed other bills to himself against Shiras's estate.

Penman, Shaw and Co. looked to Edwin's guarantors, Moodie & Black by name to cover his losses. This eventually led to a court case with Moodie (his brother-in-law) & Black (a friend) arguing that Edwin had acted for Penman, Shaw & Co. and that they were therefore entirely responsible for his losses, not themselves. But they lost this court case brought at Charleston in February 1812 and Edwin and his guarantors were held liable to cover the losses.

An appeal however was held on 7th March 1812 and the decision was overturned in favour of Moodie & Black which put the losses squarely back on Penman, Shaw & Co. No further appeal was allowed.[4] The comments in James Penman's' early letters regarding his Uncle Edwin Gairdner and Aunt Moodie[5] all refer to the arguments between the two parties before the court case came to pass. Edwin however survived all of these machinations and continued to own extensive plantations in Jamaica where he eventually died.

Our man, James Penman Gairdner, was actually born in Charleston, the son of James Gairdner and Mary Gordon[6] and was baptised on 15 July 1792 at the Independent (Circular) Congregational Church in Charleston. It is certain that James had two sisters, Elizabeth, who married a Colonel Foster, and Margaret. It is probable that James had further siblings; Edwin Gordon, whose birth is unknown but died in 1791, and Mary Catherine, born in 1794 and who died 29 September 1800.[7]

In 1804, aged around twelve, James was sent to England to stay with his aunt and to receive his formal education. He appears to have been a boarder at Harrow from 1804 until 1809 and in his first year may indeed have been Lord Byron's 'flunkie'.[8]

But the merchant trade does not seem to have enamoured our James, who decided to join the army as an officer without purchase in the even then famous 95th Rifle Regiment.

He became a Second Lieutenant vice Austin who had become a 1st Lieutenant vice Macleod[9] deceased.[10]

Two years later James gained promotion to First Lieutenant but did not rise any further in rank during his army career.

James saw a great deal of active service during the final years of the wars against Napoleon. Having arrived literally just in time to be involved in the capture of the fortress of Ciudad Rodrigo in January 1812, he was then present at the final bloody siege of Badajoz where he was wounded, the battles of Salamanca, Vitoria where he was wounded again, this time more severely, the Pyrenees, Nive, Nivelle, Orthes and the final battle of the war at Toulouse in 1814.

After some tense correspondence with his father regarding the terrible possibility of him, as an American, being posted to America to fight against the country of his birth in the War of 1812, he instead found himself fighting in the Waterloo campaign where he was wounded once more and then formed part of the Army of Occupation for the next three years.

But the prospect of years of a boring life in some garrison town, with little or no opportunity for advancement or action seems to have convinced James to abandon his army career and return to America, where he married, raised a family and saw out his days as a plantation owner.

Chapter 2

Enlistment and Training

James Penman Gairdner was sent from Charleston, South Carolina, to England at the age of twelve, for his education at Harrow, but it was not long before his youthful fearlessness and innate sense of adventure caused James to turn his back on a future in the mercantile trade and instead to obtain a commission in the British Army.

It may perhaps appear odd, to say the least, that a young American lad should wish to join the British forces, so long after the American war of Independence. However, his father had been born in Scotland and although James had been born in Charleston, it is clear that family ties were still strong with the 'Old country' and loyalties were clearly riven. Indeed, a number of years later, James' father summed up their confused loyalties, by stating that his son could continue to serve in the British Army as long as he never fought against Americans.

Although his father had become wealthy by trade, it is not clear whether his father had offered to provide any money towards purchasing a commission in the army or whether influential relatives were acting to gain the favour of a free commission. Whatever attempts were made, it is clear that they did eventually succeed in 1810 in securing James Penman a commission 'without purchase' as a Second Lieutenant (equivalent to an Ensign in line regiments),[1] in the 2nd Battalion of the 95th Foot, later to become famous as the Rifle Brigade.

The use of rifled weapons, already commonplace for hunting, had been experimented with by many European armies since the 1750s with limited success, its proven accuracy often thought to be severely outweighed by its cumbersome loading, hence slow rate of fire.

In 1800 an Experimental Corps of Riflemen was set up under Colonel Coote-Manningham wearing a green uniform and armed with the new Baker Rifle. This corps was formalised in 1802 as the 95th Foot, it was expanded to two battalions in 1805 and a third was added in 1809. All three of the battalions regularly fought abroad, often operating at company level, being individually attached to different brigades of the army. When James joined he was initially allocated to the 2nd Battalion which then had only three companies serving at Cadiz, and hence James actually joined the remaining seven companies at their depot for instruction.

To James Gairdner esquire, Augusta, Georgia[2]

London, Sunday 10th September 1810[3]

My dear father,
I take the opportunity of writing by a Mr Campbell who is going to Georgia and is to see yourself. When I wrote you last I was beginning to despair about my commission, but last Saturday I was to my great joy gazetted a 2nd Lieutenant in the 95th Regiment of Foot & which I must join in three weeks, as only one month is allowed from the day an officer is gazetted and I have been gazetted a week.[4] You will doubtless have heard before this will reach you, the unfortunate state of the Gairdner's [Edwin's] affairs, we have not heard lately how they are coming on, they talked at first as if they would be able to accommodate matters, but Mr Gibbon thinks they must become bankrupts. Mr Harvey suffers by it so much so that when my aunt wrote to him requesting him to pay £200 of yours which was in his hands for my use, which of course we particularly want at present. He wrote word that he could not pay it at present without great inconvenience on account of the loss he had sustained through the Gairdners. My aunt wrote him immediately stating my appointment to a lieutenancy in the 95 [th] so that I hope it will be forthcoming. They say they have more goods in Trinidad than sufficient to cover all my Uncle Edwin's affairs with them, so far lucky. My aunt will doubtless have written you that my uncle having sent over bills to the amount of £1,500 had fortunately consigned them to Mr Gibbon. My Aunt Moodie's[5] sudden arrival in England astonished us all, my aunt is very much vexed and grieved at her arrival under such circumstances as well as my Uncle Gordon. She is living at present with my uncle, she seems perfectly contented with her situation and entirely unconcerned at the state of her affairs. I dined with the Gairdners yesterday, they seem in much better spirits than I have seen them in since their present embarrassments. I sincerely wish they may be able to recover their affairs, although by all accounts Mr Graham,

one of their creditors is very much incensed against them as they have it is said, behaved very shabbily to him. My aunt has been very much advised to go out of town[6] this summer on account of her own health and her son's. She has made several attempts but has given up all thoughts of it now, she is however going down to Mrs Gibbon for a week to a place they have near Epping Forest for the summer and is going to leave her children under Mrs Bell's care while she is away. I think it is a pity she could not go somewhere and stay longer, for her health certainly requires it. I am very busy at present, I have but three weeks left of the month I am allowed to equip myself. I am learning dancing every day for it will never do for an officer not to be able to dance. I have been learning drawing in which I think I have greatly improved. I do not know whether I ever heard anything with so much pleasure as when I heard that the long expected commission was come at last. My real wish is to distinguish myself, of which I have no doubt I shall do if I have but an opportunity. I belong to the second battalion, some of which are abroad and some a[t] Hythe on the coast of Kent. As I am the junior officer I shall have to join those that are at Hythe but there is no knowing how soon I may have to [go abroad?] which of all things I ardently desire. It is a regiment that sees an immense deal of service as it is the only one of the kind in this country. I will let you know all the particulars of it when I join. In the mean [time] believe me my dear father, your dutiful & affectionate son, James P. Gairdner.

His father replied in early 1811, offering sage advice on controlling his finances and avoiding debt. He acknowledged that James would be unable to live entirely upon his army wages of 4 shillings and 5 pence per day[7] and arranged to supply funds which he could access through his aunt, but he cautioned against profligacy. He enquired about his regiment and how he was settling in and also put out a tentative offer to supply the funds to purchase a first lieutenancy (equivalent to lieutenant in the line regiments). This would require the sum of £550 to cover the official purchase price, however his second lieutenancy could be sold for £400, therefore the sum required for the step in rank would actually only amount to £150.

He also encouraged James to undertake lessons in French, Greek and Latin, to aid both his education and his linguistic abilities when abroad. Finally his father mentioned the tensions already building in the United States against Great Britain despite the constant loss of American shipping to French privateers. The 'Louisiana Purchase[8]' by which Napoleon agreed to sell 828,000 square miles of territory for fifty million

Francs ($11.25 million) and the cancellation of debts worth a further 18 million Francs ($3.75 million)[9] had eased relations with France. Napoleon's Berlin decree of 1806 now restricted neutral ships trading with Britain or her allies. Given that the Royal Navy ruled the oceans it had little real effect; but the British retaliatory 'Order in Council' of 1807 forbidding neutrals trading with Napoleon's Empire was enforced with much greater rigour; added to which the Royal Navy's habit of searching American crews for British nationals, and given the difficulties of determining between British and American nationals only a few decades after they had been one, led to many Americans being forcibly enlisted into the Royal Navy. This caused severe aggravation for American shipping and eventually led to war in 1812 despite the Order in Council having been belatedly revoked two days before.

Light infantry rifle training was, as presumed by his father, markedly different from that of the line infantry. No long lines of red coats standing shoulder to shoulder and marching in formation here; the rifles were taught to fight in pairs, they skirmished in front of the line infantry, one firing whilst the other remained loaded. Their role was to prevent the enemy skirmishers approaching the British line and breaking up the cohesion of enemy attacks by picking off their high value targets with accurate long distance fire. The severe losses of officers, N.C.O.s, buglers and drummers would seriously degrade the command and control of enemy units. This was their role, requiring independent thinking, in a highly dangerous and rapidly changing situation.

20th February 1811[10]

To Lieutenant J P Gairdner, 95th Regiment, Hythe Barracks, Kent

My dear boy,
Since writing you [on] 1st November I have received your favours of 10th September & 15th October [the latter no longer extant] & am very happy to hear you are so much pleased with your profession & that your brother officers are so agreeable. Hythe must be a pleasant station I should suppose in summer, it is not a great way in a direct line from your old residence at Broadstairs. The exercise in your regiment differs I suppose considerably from those of the line, are you practised to fire at a mark? What is your uniform and arms? As money is very scarce with me at present [I] am glad to hear you find living cheaper than you expected in the army & that £100 will answer in addition to your pay.[11] The mess of a regiment must indeed be managed in a very frugal manner as there are many officers in the

army that have nothing whatever but their pay to subsist on. I shall however send by the present opportunity to your aunt (as you may have been removed) a bill for £150, but there is no occasion for you to spend it all in the year but let the £50 remain for next year for fear of remittances not coming in time as you *must not* get into debt. You must also recollect that I cannot send you a remittance until about this time of the year when my crop gets to market. I hope as my land is now getting into good order to be able in 2 or 3 years to allow you whatever you wish without any inconvenience. I must endeavour to have money ready to purchase for you a first lieutenancy I suppose, what will it cost?

At all events it is better to begin frugal, but by no means mean or stingy, depend on it my son, that it is a very difficult matter for a person to retrench his expenses, many a one is turned by being too expensive at the outset in life, goes on because he is ashamed to retrench. Make it a point *never to borrow* money, or lend it if possible, it is a common & a true saying that a man often loses his money & his friend by lending. You are young and must be very particular in your conduct. Let me know how the mess is managed, what it costs & everything regarding you or your manner of living is interesting to me. Your aunt writes me that you was very fond of the flute, it will be an amusement particularly in the long winter nights. I do not know whether you understand French or not, if you do not, I should wish you to learn it as soon as possible, you ought also to look into your Greek & Latin books now & then that you may not forget altogether what you have been so long learning.

I have not heard anything of Robert Walker[12] lately, where is he & what ship is he in? Adam you would hear long ago got married, he lives about 4 miles from me, is well and doing very well.[13] Public matters are not going on well at all, the ruling party are entirely in the French interest although Bonaparte has been plundering, seizing & burning all American property he could lay his hands on for some years, they want to involve this country in a war with Great Britain if possible. Let me hear from you often. I remain, my dear boy, your most affectionate father, James Gairdner.

James replied to his father in February, acknowledging that he had made the right decision becoming a soldier. The pastimes of the officers were more refined than perhaps would be expected, playing the flute and chess being two popular activities. Regarding purchasing a further step in rank, James explained to his father how the system worked. A two week leave of absence, which he hoped to extend, had allowed him to visit his aunt in London and he updated his father on family news.

To James Gairdner esq, Augusta, Georgia[14]

[Undated but probably written mid February, and marked 'Answered 26th May 1811']

My dear father,

I am now in London on leave of absence which I obtained for a fortnight, and am staying with my aunt in Northumberland Street. I continue to like the army and to rejoice more & more every day that I chose it for a profession. The greatest part of the 95th is in Portugal and the second battalion to which I belong has seven companies at home, the other three are in Portugal and the seven that are at home will most likely be sent out early in the spring. I sincerely hope they may, there is nothing I would like so much as to be sent to Portugal, or indeed on any active service whatever. The officers are all pleasant gentlemanly men and I am never at a loss for amusement when with the regiment. I practise the flute a good deal, I began to learn it about a year ago, I have had no lessons or assistance of any kind, I have made I think considerable progress. I also play at chess which is a very military game and which I am very fond of, there are many of the officers that play pretty well, Colonel Wade[15] plays very well.

I wrote this morning to ask Colonel Wade to extend my leave of absence another fortnight. The tenth of March is the day on which the general leave of absence expires and all officers must return by that day and during the whole summer no officer is allowed to go on leave of absence except on particular business. If we are not sent on service before the summer which I hope and believe we shall be; General Murray[16] who commands the garrison of Hythe will have pretty frequently field days at Shorncliffe[17] which is about two miles from Hythe, at least that was the case last summer, he is very fond of military show and parade. My aunt wishes that I would inform you of all the regulations concerning purchasing of commissions. There is a quarterly return made to the War Office by the commanding officer of the regiment of all officers who are able to purchase and where their money is to be had when called for and whatever step is open for purchase cannot be sold out of the regiment if there is anybody in it who has given in his name for purchase. The senior officer whose name is down for purchase of course gets the step. The price of my next step is one hundred pounds and as the money that Mr Harvey has of yours is not forthcoming immediately, Mr Gibbon has drawn a bill upon [you] for the money and I will at the next

9

quarterly return give a reference to Mr Gibbon. The next step after that, which is to be a captain of a company I must have been in the army three years before I can be promoted to it; the purchase of that is one thousand pounds. The regulations with regard to that are similar to those above mentioned. The promotion in the Ninety Fifth has been for the last two years very quick, there is a talk of raising another battalion to it[18], if that happens it will be a great help to me.

My friends in London much the same as usual, my Aunt Gairdner is not very well, she talks of going out of town this summer, I hope she may be able to accomplish it for she as well as her family stand very much in need of country air and exercise. My Aunt Gordon has been confined to her room for some days with a cold. My Uncle Gordon is I think better than when I saw him last. The Gairdners are rather in low spirits but good health. I have not heard from Scotland lately, my grandmother and the family at Wooden[19] were very well when I heard last. [In] your last you gave good accounts of your crops which I am happy to hear. In my last which I hope you have, I mentioned that I did not require such a large allowance as I at first expected. Remember me to all friends and believe me my dear father, your dutiful son, James P Gairdner.

Six months later and everything had changed. Because of his rise up the seniority list following losses in the war, James had been transferred into the first battalion which was serving with Wellington's army in Spain and it was not long before he was ordered out to the peninsula to join them.

Chapter 3

Journey Out to the Battalion

James eagerly prepared his field kit and camp equipment for the hardships of campaigning in Spain and Portugal. The 1st Battalion 95th had been involved in the Peninsular War since the early days, arriving in Spain as part of Sir John Moore's corps in 1808. It had participated in the advance into Spain and subsequent dreadful retreat in winter blizzards to Corunna, where a pyrrhic victory allowed the army to embark on ships to sail back to Britain in early 1809. It returned the following summer and as part of Brigadier General Robert Craufurd's famous Light Division, and was force-marched to Talavera, where it unfortunately arrived only just too late to participate in the British victory. However, although victorious in battle, the British army was forced to retire by superior French forces threatening to cut off their line of retreat. The battalion had then fully participated in the slow retreat of 1810 towards Lisbon including serving with distinction at the Battle of Bussaco and then moved behind the impenetrable chain of forts known as the Lines of Torres Vedras, whilst the superior French army of Marshal Masséna slowly starved outside. During the subsequent retreat of the French, the 1/95th played a significant role in harassing them back into Spain.

Reinforcements for the French army stemmed the rot and a cagey war of manoeuvre led to the bitterly fought battles of Fuentes d'Oñoro in the north and Albuera in the south. The campaigning season of 1811 ended with Viscount, later Duke of, Wellington's army poised on the Portuguese border but with almost all of the major border fortresses in French hands and a large French army in its front.

It was whilst both armies rested in their quarters during the winter of 1811 and prepared for the upcoming campaign that James Gairdner prepared to sail with a cadre of reinforcements for the battalion. But far more importantly for our understanding of James' personal war, he thankfully began a daily journal, which he kept up with an almost religious fervour for the next five years.

November 1811

14th[1] Having been removed from the 2nd Battalion to the 1st and having obtained leave to join that part of the 1st Battalion in the peninsula,[2] I embarked this day on board the *Leopard* 50 guns, Captain Dillon, for Lisbon. Joined the lieutenants' mess.

15th Went on shore [in Portsmouth] to make some purchases & returned on board the same evening.

16th Remained at anchor at Spithead.

17th Got under weight [*sic*] about three o'clock this afternoon, we sailed in company with the *Diadem* 60 under Captain Phillimore[3] who was commodore of the squadron & four frigates of which I forget the names.[4]

18th – 25th We continued making very good progress all the time. The weather was fine & the wind for the most part fair & plenty of it.[5]

James was blessed with a very short passage of only nine days to Lisbon, but the voyage was certainly long enough to convince him that a career in the navy would not have suited him at all.

26th Anchored this day about three o'clock p.m. in the Tagus opposite the packet stairs Lisbon. I had an opportunity during this voyage of learning more of the life, manners and habits of a sailor together with their interior discipline and economy than ever I should have learnt by books or conversation.

The power of the captain on board his own ship is arbitrary and almost unbounded, their punishments, two or three of which I was witness [to], at the will of the captain and limited solely by him. Upon the whole judging from what I saw I should never [be] happy as a sailor. I was at this time a red hot soldier who was fond of my profession & from the little I had seen of it, and who did not find one single objection to it. I have since seen almost all the vicissitudes of a soldier's life though in a short space of time and neither the fatigues, dangers or want of comforts to which a soldier on service is exposed have in the least disgusted me with it. There is one and one only objection that I have to the army, viz the subordination of the junior ranks and the power that a commanding officer has to annoy, if he pleases to act unlike a gentleman. To the navy this objection exists and in a greater degree, for both the subordination of the junior ranks and the power of the commanding officer are greater and more unlimited.[6]

27th   I landed this day at the packet stairs and after taking lodgings (not being able to get accommodation at Cairns' Hotel, the place I intended to put up at) went on board the *Leopard* again and brought my luggage on shore. Dined at Cairns' ordinary and went to the theatre in the evening with an officer who dined there also.

28th November – 4th December *Blank*

One week after his arrival at Lisbon, James was ordered to proceed with a detachment, presumably partly of men having recovered from illness and wounds, returning to their units from the General Hospital.

December

5th   Having reported myself to the commandant at Belem I was yesterday afternoon ordered to parade at Belem at 5 o'clock with a detachment of the Light Division with which I embarked this morning at daylight for Figueras[7] on board the *Argus* transport lettered M.E. There were several other officers on board in charge of detachments.

6th – 24th *Blank*

The route taken up country was rather unusual, most soldiers record sailing up the Tagus, landing in the vicinity of Santarem and marching from there. On this occasion the detachments sailed up the Atlantic coast of Portugal and disembarked at Figueira de Foz near Coimbra. The advantages of landing the troops further north are obvious, but were more weather reliant.

The reason for the delay in sailing is not made clear, but was probably because of storms or contrary winds. They eventually disembarked nearly three weeks later at Buarcos.

As they marched up country, the party would quarter in villages along the route each night. They had no tents; the officers found a room, often shared, in the few houses, no matter the state of disrepair, the men slept in the open no matter the weather.

25th   Landed this day at about 12 o'clock at Buarcos in boats and marched to Figuera [da Foz] which is a nice little town. We had excellent quarters.

26th   Remained all day in Figueras, rainy.

27th   The whole of the detachments under the command of Captain Percival of the 9th Regiment[8] marched this morning at 9 o'clock to Montemor [o-velho] 3 leagues. The baggage and such men as were unable to march went up the Mondego in boats. The day was fine, although the roads were bad from late rains and the country was very beautiful.

28th   At the same hour we marched to Tentugal 3 leagues.[9] Good quarters, the people exceedingly civil.

29th   To Coimbra 2 leagues, rainy weather, it was a long time before the men got into quarters or the officers got billets. Dined with Stokes[10] & Coane,[11] the former here on command,[12] the latter sick.

30th   Halted all day, bought a baggage ass for 18 dollars.

31st   The detachments under the same officer set off at 9 o'clock this morning for Chao de Lamas.[13] It was a very long march but through a most beautiful country. We did not get into Chao de Lamas until after dark, there is only one inhabited house in the place, all the officers were in it; very cold night hard frost. My baggage did not come in tonight, felt the want of my boat cloak and provisions.

January 1812
1st   Marched to San Miguel de Poiares through [via] Miranda [do Corvo], met my baggage on the way, fine frosty weather.

2nd   To Moita [da Serra] a wretched little village.

3rd   To [Vendas de] Galizes, the head quarters of the Waggon Train[14] being here and the place full of them I went to Vila Pouca [da Beira] a village about 2 miles English to the right of the road, where I got a very good quarter. It is a very nice little village with a convent of nuns in it.
    Captain Percival with his detachment left us here to join his

14

regiment, the division being about 60 miles from here,[15] the next senior officer was Lt Fraser of the 79th.[16]

4th   Halt, rainy.

5th   To Maceira[17] 3 leagues.

6th   To Sao Paio 3 leagues on the march, I shoved on before the detachment and missing my road went through Gouveia a nice looking town situated on the side of the sierra which is a branch of the Sierra d'Estrella, got good quarters at Sao Paio though a poor village.

7th   To Celorico [da Beira] a dirty uncomfortable village, it being full of sick & of officers on command, I was glad to get into a wash house.

8th   Halt.

The party was now approaching their various regiments and they split to go their separate ways.

9th   The 79th[18] & 26th[19] Regiments having been sent from the 1st Division to Viseu on account of being sickly, Lt Fraser the officer commanding the detachments went back to join his regiment, each officer got an independent route here. I with my party marched this day to Guarda, a more fatiguing march on account of the mountain on which Guarda is situated being so steep. It is the coldest place I ever was in and is I believe reckoned the highest *city* in Europe. The weather is now clear and frosty.

It now became clear that they were nearing the front line and that the army had moved out of winter quarters and had suddenly moved to snatch the fortress of Ciudad Rodrigo from the French before their main army could react to this unexpected attack.

10th   To Pega,[20] a small village, I today heard cannonading and heard some report of Lord Wellington besieging Ciudad Rodrigo.

11th   To Sabugal, I here heard for certain that Lord Wellington is besieging Rodrigo. Since I marched in here, part of the 7th Division being General Alten's headquarters have arrived here.

15

12th   Through Alfaiates & Forcalios to Casillas de Flores on the frontier of Spain, a very long march. The troops in Sabugal & General Alten's headquarters marched to Alfaiates. My baggage did not come in tonight.

13th   My baggage came in this morning about 9 o'clock, just as I was about to move off. Smith[21] and Grey[22] rode in to the village and we went on together to El Bodon where we found the 2nd Brigade of the Light Division and General Craufurd's headquarters. Lord Wellington was at this time besieging [Ciudad] Rodrigo with the 1st, 3rd, 4th & Light Divisions, each division taking the duty for 24 hours, in turn. Our division had just come home. I was appointed to Captain Uniacke's[23] company the same day.

Chapter 4

Two Sieges in Four Months

Wellington had been making preparations to besiege the fortress of Ciudad Rodrigo, which commanded the northern route into Portugal, for months. Siege guns, cannon balls and gunpowder were stockpiled surreptitiously and the troops quietly prepared fascines and ladders in readiness for the coming assault.

The divisions were put in motion in early January when Wellington judged the French army to be too dispersed to interfere within twenty-four days. By 5 January his forces were in place and despite the wintry weather, the fortress was fully invested by the 8th and the Redoubt Renaud was stormed that night.

14th The batteries opened on the town this day at 5 o'clock.

15th *Blank*

16th It being the turn of our division to take the trench duty this day, we marched in the morning before day break to relieve the 4th Division. The 1st Brigade went into the trenches in the morning and we relieved them about 5 o'clock. I was sent with the command of a party to fire into the breach[1] and this night was the 1st time I ever saw a shot fired [in anger].

General Craufurd went in today with a flag of truce to the governor, summoning him to surrender, to which he returned a bravadoing [sic] answer that 'he would be buried in the ruins first' or something to that effect.

17th Marched home again to El Bodon. We this evening received an order to hold ourselves in readiness to march tomorrow to the trenches. All the ladders in this place have been embargoed today.

18th   Did not march today but received an order to march tomorrow to the Convent of La Caridad and halt there until further orders.

The company James' belonged to mounted the breach and turned right in an attempt to clear the ramparts of the enemy and reach the main breach which the 3rd Division was busy attacking. This movement was achieved successfully, but the explosion of a mine at the main breach changed everything.

19th   Marched before day break to La Caridad where we remained for some hours. The officers and men of the forlorn hope and storming party volunteered here[2]. We then moved on to the camp ground near the trenches where we remained until dark, soon after dark we moved up to the convent close to the town from whence we moved on to the breach. There were two breaches, one was stormed by our division, the other by the 3rd Division, the division on duty in the trenches at the time. Poor Uniacke was blown up by a mine that was sprung near the larger breach.[3] We remained in the town all night, which like every night was dreadfully cold. General Craufurd received a dangerous wound tonight[4] and General Vandeleur a slight one.[5]

The rushed siege caused heavy losses at the storming. The Light Division suffered one officer and eleven men killed and eleven officers and ninety men wounded. The 95th, of which all three battalions had contingents present, suffered two thirds of this loss.

Private Edward Costello recorded the devastation at the main breach the following morning. 'The sight was heart rending in the extreme. The dead lay in heaps, numbers of them stripped. They displayed the most ghastly wounds. Here and there, half-buried under the blackened fragments of the wall, or reeking on the surface of the ruin, lay those who had been blown up in the explosions, their remains dreadfully mangled and discoloured. Strewed about were dissevered arms and legs.'[6]

20th   Marched back to El Bodon, met the 5th Division on our way, marching to Rodrigo.[7]

21st – 23rd   Blank

24th   Heard today that poor Uniacke died this morning early.

25th Marched with the company and band to Galegos [de Arganan] to attend poor Uniacke's funeral.

26th Received an order this evening to march tomorrow morning to Fuenteguinaldo.

27th Marched at 8 o'clock this morning, I was on baggage guard. Rained very [hard] and all day.

28th *Blank*

29th Were obliged to quit our quarters (Smith & myself) on account of the rain coming in through the roof.

30th – 31st *Blank*

Whilst encamped at Ituero, a court martial was held at Nave de Haver on 12 February on eighteen British soldiers who had deserted and were captured in Ciudad Rodrigo. The execution by firing squad took place soon after. The division formed three sides of a square, the fourth side formed by a large trench, in front of which the convicted men were arranged and shot by a firing squad. It is clear from the evidence of many that it was bungled and that many did not die instantly. It required the firing squad to reload to finish them off and the provost finished by discharging a pistol into each head. The bodies were then tossed into the mass grave and the men of the division marched past.

February
1st – 25th We remained all this time at Guinaldo and lived very well, the weather was for the most of the time fine and frosty. We had no marching or bother. The only time that we marched out of the place was one day that the division was ordered to assemble at Ituero [de Azaba] to be present at the execution of 9 men who had deserted to the enemy from this division and who were condemned to be shot.[8] They were taken in Ciudad Rodrigo on the 19th of January. Colonel Beckwith[9] joined the division during this period, and also a detachment from England for the 1st Battalion with the following officers, viz Austin[10], Bell[11] and [Jos?[12]]. The 1st Battalion were at this period in Espeja, Ituero [de Azaba], Campillo [de Azaba], Castillejo de Azaba & El Bodon.

Wellington now felt that the defences of Ciudad Rodrigo were repaired sufficiently that he could order the bulk of his army southward in an attempt to capture the significantly stronger fortress of Badajoz, which guarded the southern route from Spain into Portugal.

26th   Received an order last night to march by a route which ends at Castelo do Vide. Marched this morning at daylight through Casillas de Flores and Forcalhos to Alfaiates 3 leagues, General Vandeleur here also.

27th   Marched through Nave, Vila Boa & Sabugal to a small village called Vale Mourisco[13] about a league beyond Sabugal which our regiment alone occupied.

28th   Marched through Sortelha (an old Moorish fortification of very romantic appearance and situation) to Casteleiro 3 leagues. Sortelha is situated on the side of a steep rocky mountain, there is in it a castle of very romantic appearance, the country all about it is exceedingly wild rocky and uncultivated. We had good quarters at Casteleiro, having lost our mess mule at Guinaldo. We bought a mule here for 56 dollars. 52nd & head quarters at Sortelha.

29th   Marched to Capinha 3 leagues, a good village.

March

1st   Marched to Alpedrhina. I went on before the regiment to tell off quarters and the guide took me across the country without keeping any road. On reaching the top of the sierra which surrounds the immense plain in which Castelo Branco stands, I was delighted with the view which burst on me all at once, at a distance was seen Castelo Branco. The side of the sierra is well wooded and the whole plain exhibits a contrast of wildness and cultivation. I passed through a very good looking town called Val de Prazeres about 2 English miles from Alpedrinha, which is a very good town (we had excellent quarters there) and most beautifully situated. The whole brigade here.

2nd   Marched through Lardosa to Alcains 2 leagues, the brigade marched together and were all in Alcains. I saw here for the first time a Portuguese funeral and a more barbarous unfeeling sight I have seldom seen.[14]

3rd   The brigade marched to Castelo Branco 2 leagues, the 1st Brigade which had been since the commencement of the march moving on a different road marched in here today.

4th   The 2nd Brigade halted all this day in Castelo Branco, the first brigade marched this morning, it is a dirty uncomfortable town. There is the ruin of a castle on the highest part of the place. There is also a bishop's palace & garden.

5th   Marched this day to Retaxo where our regiment was alone (2 leagues), head quarters & 52nd at Sarnadas [de Rodao].

6th   Marched to Nisa 5 leagues, crossed the Tagus by a bridge of boats at Vila Velha [de Rodao]. The road is very bad indeed and the pass of Vila Velha is I should think very formidable in a military point of view.

7th   Marched to Castelo de Vide 3 leagues, the place our route ended at. When we arrived there 3 companies forming the left wing were halted and distributed in quintas[15] about Castelo de Vide. The other 3 companies and the head quarters of the regiment went on to Escusa a village about 2 miles[16] from Castelo de Vide.

Whilst here a court martial was held on Private Joseph Allman, who had been captured by Spanish guerrillas whilst attempting to cross over to the enemy near Salamanca. Private Costello was actually one of the guards watching over the prisoner the night before his planned execution. Allman drew his outstanding pay and bought wine for himself and his guards and swapped his shoes with another guard whose shoes were worn out saying 'They will last me as long as I shall require them'. He was executed on the morning of 10 March by firing squad. Marching up to his grave in heavy rain, he discovered it to be already waterlogged, when he stated 'Although a watery one, I shall sleep sound enough in it' and declined a blindfold from the provost with 'There is no occasion, I shall not flinch'. Having given a kind word to each of those destined to be his executioners, they fired and his body slumped into the watery pit. Although James makes little mention of this event, it is clear that it had a bad effect on the ordinary soldiers of the regiment.

8th – 13th We remained at this time at Escusa, a very nice little village where we had excellent quarters and were very comfortable indeed. We marched to Castelo de Vide one day to see the sentence of death put into execution on Joseph Allman of our regiment, who was sentenced to be shot for desertion to the enemy.[17]

I also walked frequently to Castelo de Vide which is a good town and clean for a Portuguese town, there is not however a very good market or any good shops and it has been an old fortified town, its situation however is not good. It has on one end of it a citadel cut off & fortified from the town itself, there are some old pieces of cannon lying dismounted on the ramparts, but none mounted in any part, the walls are breached and in ruins in many places. There is also a town called Marvao about 2 miles from Escusa very well worth seeing, indeed it is situated on a steep rocky mountain, on one side the mountain is very high and almost perpendicular on the other viz the side looking towards Spain. The ascent of the mountain though high is not so much so, or so perpendicular as the other, but the ground is so rocky that to make a trench would be next to an impossibility. There is in the highest part of the town a castle which completely commands the town and is in itself inaccessible (except on the side that opens into the town) from the situation of the mountain. On the part in which it is built the place appears to have been lately repaired, there are several pieces of cannon mounted, most of which are brass and have been brought from Campo Maior. Marvao is not however a regular fortification, there being no bastions, outworks &c (except in that part of the town which is most accessible, an outer wall with cannon mounted on it).

It is however from the peculiarity of its situation in my untutored opinion impregnable. It is garrisoned by a regiment of Portuguese militia. On entering the town we were taken by the guard up to the governor's house to obtain by permission to visit the place, he gave orders that the British officers should be admitted everywhere. There is from the castle a most extensive view.

I walked from Escusa to this place several times, it is a very beautiful walk and the place itself a great curiosity. We received a mail from England while here with the account of the capture of [Ciudad] Rodrigo], I received while here the 1st letters I have received since I left England.

14th   Being Orderly officer today, I went out at 10 o'clock with the bat men for forage and on my return at about 2 o'clock I found that the regiment had marched to Portalegre. There were orders left for me to bring on the baggage to Portalegre, I got off at about 3 o'clock but did not get into Portalegre until after dark. I had an adventure on the road with two rascally Portuguese peasants. I remarked that the Portuguese begin to trim their vines about this time. Portalegre is a very fine town but on account of coming in so late at night and marching out so early the next morning I did not see so much of it as I wished. General Vandeleur who since the capture of Rodrigo has been suffering much from his wound & the rheumatism stopped here, the command of the division devolves on Colonel Beckwith.

15th The division marched soon after daylight to Arronches 4 leagues. Arronches is a dirty uncomfortable town, it has formerly been fortified but its situation in a military point of view is very bad.

16th The division marched to Elvas, 4 leagues, we here understood that some divisions were already encamped in front of Badajoz and that we are to march tomorrow morning for that place. Elvas is a beautiful fortification and the town itself well supplied with everything.

17th The division marched off at about 8 o'clock this morning to the neighbourhood of Badajoz, we crossed the Guadiana by pontoons and found the 3rd and 4th Divisions encamped near the town. The 1st and 6th divisions are in front under General Sir T. Graham[18] and the 2nd & 7th under General Sir R. Hill,[19] the 5th Division have not come from the north yet. We understood that we should get tents on the ground, we however have seen none yet. Towards evening the weather which since the commencement of our march has been very fine, changed and commenced raining. Balvaird[20] was the only officer in the regiment who had a tent which every officer not on duty crowded into. Working and covering parties were warned early in the evening and the ground was broke as soon as it was dark. The garrison did not fire at all.

18th – 25th Everything went on as well as could be expected until the 25th on which day our batteries opened on the town. The weather was very bad and the duty pretty frequent, it came to my turn to be on duty on an average twice in five days. Colonel Beckwith (who at the time we marched from Elvas was not able to come with us from illness) came in the same evening and was carried off again (the next day in a car so that the command of the division devolved on Lt Colonel Barnard,[21] Major O'Hare[22] also who at the time we marched from Escusa was very ill and followed us slowly joined on the 19th. The officer's got tents the 2nd day, the men some days after. On the 19th the enemy made a sortie in the morning but were repulsed with loss. On the night of the 19th Freer[23] of ours who was on duty in the trenches was wounded. On the 25th our batteries opened on the town at about 11 o'clock in the morning, the same night the outwork called Fort Picurina was stormed. It was carried but with some loss. I was on duty in the trenches the next day and went into the fort, it is wonderfully strong.

26th – 30th *Blank*

31st   The 5th Division which arrived soon after the commencement of the siege and was posted on the other side of the river was about this time ordered to the front. The 48th, Richard Ellwood's[24] regiment arrived during the siege.

April
1st – 3rd *Blank*

4th   The town is ordered to be stormed tomorrow.

5th   The following are the heads of the orders relative to the storming of Badajoz which is ordered to take place at 9 o'clock tonight. The Light Division will storm the breach in the flank of the bastion of Santa Maria. The 4th Division will storm the breach in the face of the bastion of La Caridad. The 3rd Division will escalade at the castle. The 5th Division (which had been sent to the front but had returned) will extend down to the waterside and attract the attention of the garrison by firing. About 5 o'clock in the afternoon the order for storming was countermanded and the usual parties for the trench duty were warned.

The storming of Badajoz was set for the night of 6 April, the 3rd Division would attempt to escalade the castle walls, the 5th Division would cause a diversion near the Olivenca gate and the 4th and Light Divisions would storm the main breach. The breach, defended with mines and topped with wooden beams encircled with razor sharp sword blades sticking out in all directions known as *chevaux de frise* proved impassable. For five hours the divisions sought to break through without the slightest glimmer of success. 'Individual officers, forming up 50 or a 100 men at a time at the foot of the breach, and endeavouring to carry it by desperate bravery; and fatal as it proved to each gallant band in succession, as fast as one dissolved, another was formed,' wrote Johnny Kincaid.[25]

The castle being taken, the French ceased defending the breach and the town was taken and turned over to a disgraceful night of rape and pillage. The 1st Battalion 95th lost three officers, three sergeants and twenty-four men killed, with a further nine officers, fifteen sergeants and 139 men wounded, including our James, who was hit three times early in the storm, none of which was serious. Being evacuated, he escaped the dangers of lying at the foot of the breach for hours, where many wounded succumbed to further grenade attacks and the incessant musket fire.

6th Our company was sent to relieve a company of the 52nd on picket near the river at about 12 o'clock, this day. At about 6 o'clock we were ordered to come in and join the regiment at dark as the town is to be stormed tonight. A third breach has been made since yesterday. At about 8 o'clock we paraded in rear of the 52nd and our regiment was directed to put itself under the orders of Lt Colonel Elder[26] who was to command the reserve and who had orders to remain in some quarries till further orders, he however neglected those orders and followed the column to the breach and brought his reserve into action with the main column.

The defence of the garrison is universally allowed to have been very good. I received three wounds early in the attack, viz one in the right leg very slight, one in the left arm and one in the chin and after lying on the ground was at last helped off by a sergeant of our company and with the assistance of some of the 52nd band who were coming with bearers carried to the hospital tent where my wounds were dressed and I was then put into a tent for the reception of wounded officers[27]. The firing continued for a long time after I was carried off, at last as I have since understood the 3rd Division having got into the castle, the enemy deserted the breaches and ours and the 4th Division got in without further opposition.

7th I remained in the tent until the afternoon when I was removed to our camp ground.

Chapter 5

Recovery

James was forced to remain at various hospital stations whilst he recovered from his wounds. During the time he languished in these dull towns, the army returned north to drive the French forces under Marshal Marmont away, which had made an incursion into Portugal whilst the army was occupied with the siege of Badajoz. To help the regiments recruit their strength, each battalion was authorised to incorporate fifty Spaniards but in the first month the First Battalion only managed to enlist eight men.

8th   An hospital for the wounded being established in Badajoz I was removed there this afternoon and got into a very good house. Fitzmaurice[1] who is wounded in the leg is also in the house, Johnston[2] who is wounded in the arm has another house but comes here to meals.

9th   Johnston finding it very inconvenient to come here to meals and go home again, came here this day to live in the house altogether.

10th – 14th We remained here until the 15th doing very well. There were 12 nuns in the house who came daily to see us, they were however almost all of them *ancient*. The army commenced moving northward on the 10th on which day our division marched to Campo Maior.

The wounded were transported to hospitals at Elvas.

15th   We were removed in a spring wagon to Elvas, got into a pretty good house.

16th April – 17th May. We remained here all this time doing very well. 2 or 3 days after my removal to this place I was able to walk about a little and after that I gained strength every day and gradually extended my walk. I went two or three times up to the Fort La Lippe which is a most beautiful fortification.[3] It is reckoned the most perfect fortification (I have heard) in Europe and is I believe impregnable except by mining. To breach it is impossible for example being situated on the top of a high mountain, the walls are not visible except either at a great distance from it or close to it within a few yards of it. The shape of the work is like that of most forts viz four bastions & four curtains, it has besides outworks of various kinds and is a complete masterpiece of fortification. Fort La Lippe is situated on the left of Elvas as you look towards Badajoz, there is another fort on the right of the town called Fort Santa Lucia, it like Fort La Lippe consists of four bastions and four curtains. Its situation is not so commanding, nor has it the same outworks, it is however very strong. The town of Elvas itself is a very fine fortification.

The south side of the town (or what I before called the right of the town as you look towards Badajoz) is the part most accessible with respect to the nature of the ground. But on this side is Fort Santa Lucia, a strong work which could not be taken without a regular approach and which must be taken before the town could be approached on the south side and there were small outworks building beyond Fort Santa Lucia at the time I was at Elvas. On the north side the ground is so steep and perpendicular that it would be impossible to breach these; besides that any breach dug there would be raked by the guns of La Lippe. On the east side there are stony outworks, besides the ground is fully commanded by La Lippe and partly by Santa Lucia. On the west side the ground is steep and unfavourable to an approach, the works of the town itself are very stony and defended by many outworks within the ditch. Elvas is situated on the side of a hill, on the highest part is a sort of castle or rather battery whose guns command all the lower part of the town.

Elvas at the time I was there was garrisoned by Portuguese Militia, the governor was a Portuguese Marshal named Victoria[4]. There is a telegraphic communication between the town & La Lippe as there also might be with Santa Lucia. On the west side of the town there is an aqueduct which extends a great way into the country, is built of stone and plastered.

I also rode one day to Badajoz which is 3 leagues from Elvas.

The breaches were repairing very fast, it appeared to be a very nice town and very well supplied.

The Army of Portugal under Marmont during the siege of Badajoz taking advantage of the absence of the British from the north, entered Portugal, laying waste the country and sent parties as far down as Castelo Branco & Vila Velha, the besieging army however proceeding northward after the capture of Badajoz compelled them to retire. By letters received from the division while we're here, we learn that the army are cantoned. Our regiment is at Ituero [de Azaba] the rest of the division in those villages on the frontier of Spain.

18th   There being an order that all the sick and wounded should remove to Estremoz as soon as sufficiently well to go. Johnston, Fitzmaurice and myself set off this day, but thinking it too far to be able to travel in one day in the state we were, we determined to make two stages of it and went this day to Borba a very nice village two leagues from Estremoz and three from Elvas. Johnston & myself rode, Fitzmaurice went in a spring wagon. The country through which we passed was very beautiful. This place is renowned and I think very justly for good wine & pretty women.

19th   Went on to Estremoz this day, good into indifferent quarters.

20th   There is a medical board sited here, 3 times in each month, this being one of the days, we appeared before it. Johnston and Fitzmaurice got 2 months leave to England. I got 3 weeks leave to this place.

21st May – 5th June. I remained all the time here doing very well with respect to my injuries, but very bad off for money. When Johnston & Fitzmaurice went away, which was I believe on the 23rd I messed with Worsley[5], he went off to join the regiment on the 28th, I lived the rest of the time by myself. Estremoz is a nice town, very clean for a Portuguese town and I should think admirably adapted for an hospital station as there are many very large convents and large airy squares. It has formerly been a fortified town, it has on the highest part of it a castle or rather citadel and there are the remains of two small forts outside the walls of the town. The walls are however now going to decay, they are broken down in many places, there is nevertheless a guard of militia at every gate as if it were a regular garrison. The country about Estremoz is remarkably beautiful, towards the south on a ridge of romantic looking mountains on the top of one of which is situated Evora Monte. Towards the west as far as the eye can reach is a level plain, highly cultivated with all kinds of corn particularly *bearded wheat*, the other points are equally beautiful & thickly wooded with olives, with which the province of Alentejo abounds. The women of this place have a peculiar way of dressing, they have a sort of black silk cloak fastened to the waist and brought over the head and shoulders like a hood, almost all the women of this place dress in black.

Only a few letters from James survive from the Peninsular, but given that he rarely mentions having corresponded it is likely that he wrote only infrequently. Here he begins a correspondence with his cousin Laura, who was Edwin Gairdner's eldest child.

Elvas, 25 April 1812

To Miss Gairdner

Albermarle Row, Clifton, England

My dear Laura,

My aunt writes that you are to become my correspondent during her illness but there is no reason why either my letters or your answers should be confined to that period, and as you have more leisure time and more convenience for writing than I have (except during my confinement while away from the regiment on account of these wounds) I shall expect to hear pretty regularly from you. I have very good quarters and am very comfortable, having been wounded on the evening of the 6th of this month in the storming of Badajoz where our regiment and indeed every regiment involved suffered exceedingly, I was the 2nd day after, viz the 8th, taken into Badajoz where I and two other wounded officers got into a very good house and were pretty comfortable. There were 12 nuns living in this house, some of them Spaniards, and some Portuguese, who were very attentive to us, they came up to see us every day and told us all the news. Their convent had been taken from them and turned into a hospital for the wounded soldiers. After staying there for a week we were removed to this place and a few days ago I was allowed to get up and walk about a little which I now do every day. I was heartily tired of being confined to my bed, but now that I can walk about I can wait patiently until I am perfectly recovered. I was wounded in the face, the left arm, and very slightly in the right leg, which last is now so far recovered that I have the use of it as well as ever. There is no news here, the army are marching to the north to try to catch the French, who of course have very good intelligence of their motions and will take good care to be off in very good time.

You must when you write tell me everything that is going on at home in England, for everything is interesting to a person that is in a foreign country. You must let me know everything as well concerning yourselves or concerning all our friends both in England and Scotland. I understand that Ebenezer[6] Gairdner with his wife and children are at Clifton, of course you see them very often, remember them particularly to me. I did not see Mrs Gairdner when I was in London last, she was then at some place a little way out of town, and I had fixed with Eben[ezer] upon a day to go out to see them, but was too late for the coach, we fixed upon another day but before then I left town for Portsmouth. Their son ought to be a fine boy by this time, I suppose he can walk and talk quite well now. The other if I recollect right is a daughter. You were one of the party in the journey to Scotland, how did you like Wooden, and the Scotch people in general? I am very happy to hear that you are getting on so well in the musical way. I hear that the old maid and Mrs Mallet are making wondrous progress, in a short time you will be able to perform anything amongst you, duets, trios, concerlantas, in fact nothing will be too grand for you. You ought to invite Gordon[7] and then you will be complete, but I dare say he would prefer any other amusement just now to hammering at a flute gamut. I suppose you had plenty of reel dancing when you were in Scotland; I recollect one evening when I was there when they were dancing reels as usual just before supper, my grandmother prevailed upon me to stand up for one reel, and I will be bound to say that nobody present nor indeed anybody in Scotland ever saw a reel danced in that manner in all their lives before. It was Rebecca of Mellendean[8] who asked me first to dance and I will be bound she repented it, for after jostling her, treading on the other lady's toes, and I believe almost knocking the gentlemen over I thought it high time to give up, and sat down after having performed a reel to the astonishment of everybody. I had not certainly been under the skilful hands of our friend Mr Denzies whose well known talents I hope I should not now disgrace by such an awkward exhibition. We have sometimes when we are quiet for any time in a town or village, dances, the Portuguese, but particularly the Spanish girls are very fond of dancing and dance very well. I think you told me before that you have nothing of the kind at Clifton. I had a letter from my Aunt Gordon on the 17th February, she says in that, that our Aunt Moodie is still in Scotland in very indifferent health. I hope by this time that she is well. I also hear that your brother in law Mr Mallet has been very unwell, how comes it that his wife remains at Clifton during his illness as if quite unconcerned about his welfare?

This part of Portugal is very fertile and is the best part of the country for fruits, vegetables and corn of every kind, but it is not so beautiful as the north, nor is it reckoned so healthy, but I believe there is little difference in that respect, however I would prefer spending the summer in the north, because it is much cooler.

You must remember me particularly to all friends. Is Mrs Bell with you now? If so remember me to her, if not remember me when you write. Remember me also to Emily, Jane[9] and Gordon and believe me my dear Laura, yours affectionately James P. Gairdner.

I expect to hear from you very soon and very often.

6th   Having got a bill on England cashed, I bought a black pony from Manners[10] for 40 dollars to carry my baggage, my baggage as having been stolen the 2nd day after I came here and Leach and myself set off this day to join the regiment, we went this day to Fronteira 4 leagues, a very good town in which we got a good billet. Leach[11] has one of the Spanish Bulldogs who killed a leveret today. I met with a curious instance of the ignorance of the Portuguese peasantry today. When we were about 2 miles on our road we asked a peasant how many leagues it was to Fronteira, he told us one, about a league further on, on asking another, he said it was two leagues, about a league further another said it was three leagues off, and when we were within an English mile of it, another fellow told us we were four leagues from it.

7th   We went on this day to Alter do Chao 3 leagues, it is an hospital station.

8th   Through Crato and Flora de Rosa [&] Alpalhao.

9th   To Nisa 3 leagues.

10th   To Vila Velha [de Rodao] 3 leagues.

11th   Halted all this day in Vila Velha, a miserable little village. Bathed in the Tagus today. The view from Vila Velha is very extensive, but the most cheerless uncultivated looking country I ever saw. The weather is now remarkably hot.

12th To Castelo Branco 5 leagues through a miserable country covered with gum cistus.

13th Halted all day. Castelo Branco is a dirty uncomfortable town. Felt the heat very oppressive here. We heard here that the army had broken up from its cantonments and were marching on Salamanca.

14th Through Alcaceres [Alcains?] to Lardosa where we dined and after dining went on to Alpedrinha, when I passed through this place on our way to Badajoz I thought the situation beautiful, but it is now that the trees are in full leaf, doubly so.

15th Wishing for variety sake to halt in towns we had not been in before and having heard that Covilha was a good town, Leach and myself set off this day for that place. Alpedrinha is situated on the side of a sierra which is a branch of the Sierra de Gata, the road from it to Covilha is very beautiful especially that part which runs over the sierra. It is thickly wooded with principally chestnut trees, also wild cherry and other trees. We passed through a [straggling?] village[12] of which I forget the name about half way down the sierra on the other side and Fundao, a good town, at the bottom of it. We halted and dined at an uninhabited quinta about 3 leagues from Alpedrinha and after dinner went on the Covilha, we got an excellent billet on a house outside the walls of the town.

On this day but unknown to James he became a First Lieutenant in the 95th Rifles vice Croudace,[13] killed in action.[14]

16th We halted all this day in this place. Covilha is situated on the side of the Sierra d'Estrella, its situation is exceedingly beautiful, the entrance to it particularly so. It has formerly [been] a fortified town, it has still a wall all round it and the remains of an old castle in the highest part of it. But there are a great many houses outside the walls inhabited principally by Jews (for this place is noted for abounding in Jews) and which are far the best houses. Covilha is renowned for its cloth manufactories, inside the town are many good shops well supplied with everything. The country about it is exceedingly beautiful and it is by far the nicest place I have seen in Portugal.

The Portuguese tell some curious stories about a lake situated on the top of the Sierra d'Estrella which in the 1st place, they say is bottomless and communicates with the sea, and which has the power to turn wine into vinegar almost immediately. The French were in this place for two days when they entered the country during the siege of Badajoz.

17th We passed through Caria this day to Sortelha an old Moorish fortress. I thought when we passed through this place in February last, that it was a very nice place but the houses are very poor and all the country about is miserably barren. Its situation and appearance are notwithstanding very romantic, there are one or two pretty good quintas outside of the town, in one of which we were billeted.

18th Went on this day to Sabugal, but it being a poor place and much crowded, as soon as we drew our rations we went on to Vila Boa about a league further[15]. There are a great number of beggars in all these villages, reduced to this state I suppose by the last invasion of the French during the absence of the army from this part of the country while employed at Badajoz.

19th Through Nave and the outside of Aldea da Ponte to [La] Albergueria which is in Spain, we dined here and went on in the evening to Fuenteguinaldo[16]. This is not the direct road, but it being an old quarter of ours, we made this detour to see some old friends. From various circumstances and for various reasons I felt a sort of melancholy pleasure on entering this place again that I shall never forget.

20th We dined here and after dinner went on to El Bodon.

21st Went to Ciudad Rodrigo, drew rations and went on to Sancti Espiritus. Overtook Grey & Travers[17] here also Duncan Stewart[18] who is marching a detachment. The breaches of Rodrigo are not half finished nor the forts either. The inhabitants are the sulkiest, most uncivil set I ever saw. Although it is six months since the siege I saw unburied human skulls and bones lying in the streets contiguous to the breaches. Catillejo de [blank - Yeltes].

22nd To [Huebra?] 3 leagues where we dined and went on in the evening to Castro [Enriquez], the road hitherto from Rodrigo has been woody but as we drew near Castro the country became one open corn country.

23rd To a village called Calzada de Don Diego where we dined and in which we overtook Worsley and Wilkinson of the 43rd[19] and after dinner went on to La Rad[20], a place consisting of 3 houses, we passed through fine corn country this day, saw a great many peasants ploughing and there is throughout this part of the country every appearance of industry and tranquillity.

24th Went on to a wood about a league from Salamanca where we found the baggage and commissariats of some of the divisions, we here learnt that the French have fortified a convent in Salamanca in which they have left a garrison and some sick, that the 6th Division were in the town besieging this fort,[21] that the 1st, 3rd, 4th, 5th & Light Divisions are in position in front of the town and that Marmont's army are close to them. We also heard that the 6th Division made an attack on the fort last night and were repulsed with loss. After drawing rations here we crossed the Tormes and went to a quinta on the bank of the river where we dined. At the ford we met the baggage of our division going to the rear. After dinner we sent our baggage to join that of the division, keeping our riding horses and boat cloaks and set off to join the division. We went into Salamanca which is a very fine town, the square and cathedral are beautiful. After staying in the town about half an hour we set off to join the division. We found the army in position on a range of heights called St Cristobal [de la Cuesta]. The 2nd Brigade of the Light Division to which our battalion belongs is detached in front to the village of Aldealengua close to the river. The division is now commanded by Major General Charles Baron Alten[22], an officer of the German Legion. The right brigade by Lt. Colonel Barnard & the left by Major General Vandeleur who joined as the division marched through Portalegre on its march from Badajoz.

Chapter 6

Salamanca

James returned to his battalion to find it forming the advance guard of the army covering the city of Salamanca. Marshal Marmont sought to manoeuvre Wellington out of his chosen defensive position, whilst the Duke remained determined to capture the three fortified convents which the French still maintained within the city.

25th   The division as is usual on these occasions gets under arms an hour before daybreak. There is an hill near where our brigade is which commands a view of the enemies camp. There is an officer on duty there for an hour at a time with a prospect glass to observe their motions, I was on duty there today. The baggage came up today.

26th   Rain. We were last night in consequence of a false alarm given, that our picquets were attacked, obliged to get under arms in the middle of the night.

The forts surrendered and Marmont retired.

27th   The convent was set on fire this day by red hot balls being fired into it, whereupon the garrison surrendered. I remarked both yesterday and today that many cannon were fired by the enemy, which as no part of the army were engaged must have been signals to the garrison.

28th   The enemy retired last night, we marched this day at about 12 o'clock to Castellanos de Moriscos, a village close in front of the position we had occupied and in which the 7th Division were one day engaged with the enemy, I saw several dead bodies on the road. The other brigade at a village close by called Moriscos. There is a grand ball given to the army this night at Salamanca.

29th Marched to Parada [de] Rubiales about 3 leagues and bivouacked in a wood near the town. There are very curious wine cellars on the outside of this place. It is said that the enemy are retiring in three columns by different roads and that we are following them in the same manner. It was in General Orders when the army broke up from its cantonments on the other side of the Agueda [note by Gairdner – which was on the 11th of this month] that the Light Division & the 1st German Hussars form the advanced guard of the army.

30th Marched to Castrillo [de la Guarena] and bivouacked near the town, we have no cover as in our last bivouack and the [weather] is excessively hot.

July

1st Marched through Alaejos (a good looking town with the remains of an old castle) to La Nava del Rey. The enthusiasm of the people in these two towns surpasses everything I have seen before in the country, the towns themselves are also far superior to what I have hitherto seen in Spain, the enemy passed through there this morning and in La Nava del Rey they ordered 30,000 rations of wine to be produced in the market place at a certain hour, which was nearly arrived when our advanced guard of cavalry appeared in the town and they made off without their wine. I am very unwell with the dysentery. We with the cavalry and General Pack's Brigade occupied the town. Our company on inlying picquet in the market place, our company's mess disposes itself here, Lister[1] and myself mess together now.

2nd To Rueda when we arrived near the town, we halted and remained there for a long time, at last we marched close to the town where the men bivouacked, the officers got into houses. The enemy are at Tordesillas which is on the other side of the Douro[2] and is about two leagues from this.

3rd Marched to some hills opposite Tordesillas and in sight of it, where we halted in contiguous columns of brigades the whole of the day. Observed a cannonading a considerable way to our left which I understand was occasioned [by] some part of the army attempting to force the river in that part and I suppose we were brought up to the ground we occupied the whole of this day to be a check on those of the enemy at Tordesillas, for we could see them very plainly bivouacked on the outside of the town. Towards evening we marched back to our old ground near Rueda and I got into the house I occupied yesterday. There are here besides ourselves, General Pack's Brigade head quarters, the 14th Light Dragoons & the 1st Hussars K.G.L. and some artillery.

The 2nd Hussars, the 11th, 12th & 16th Light Dragoons are at La Seca about a league from here.[3]

4th   My dysentery still continuing I took some physic [medicine] today. There is an order for one officer per company to lie out with the regiment.

5th – 8th *Blank*

9th   There is an order given out this day, that the Light Division and Pack's Brigade may come into the town to cook but remain no longer than necessary.

10th   *Blank*

11th   The division orders of this day say that the troops need not be under arms at day break and that the baggage need not be sent away at night.

12th   Our company for inlying picquets this evening.

13th – 14th *Blank*

15th   It being the turn of our brigade to lie out on the left of the road to Tordesillas yesterday evening, when we were relieved on picquet we joined the brigade and lay out with them. Got under arms before day break, the 1st Brigade, Pack's Brigade, the 14th Light Dragoons, 1st German Hussars and head quarters moved from here this afternoon. The 2nd Hussars, 11th, 12th & 16th Dragoons moved from La Seca here. It is reported that General Bonnet joined the Army of Portugal on the 8th and that they have made a movement to our left towards Toro & Zamora. The houses occupied by the 1st Brigade were consequently given up to our brigade, we will occupy them tomorrow morning. Sir S. Cotton and staff are here.

News arrived that Marmont had reinforced his army and was now on the advance once again. Marmont however did not seek to take Wellington on directly, but to manoeuvre onto his line of communications, forcing him to retire. This led to days a manoeuvring at very close range across the plains around Salamanca.

16th We lay last night on our original ground outside the town. Got under arms this morning before daybreak and at about 7 o'clock marched into the town & occupied the quarters of the 1st Brigade. I joined Leach's company's mess this day. Formed as usual on the old ground at 6 o'clock in the evening, but instead of laying out we were allowed to sleep in quarters but ordered to assemble on the ground before day break. About 9 o'clock there was an order given for the brigade to assemble right in front immediately on the road to Tordesillas, baggage on the reverse flank of the column. Commenced marched at about 10 o'clock, marched all night and halted at about 7 o'clock near a village called Castrejon [de Trabancos], found the 1st Brigade of our division, Pack's Division & the 4th Division here.

17th Remained here all day, baggage sent to the rear in the evening to Torecilla de la Orden.

Threatened by the numerous French cavalry, Wellington ordered his army to retire in columns or squares to avoid being overrun by them.

18th Soon after day break the enemy's cavalry commenced skirmishing with ours, the village of Castrejon is situated under a ridge of heights between the ground we occupied and the heights. Our 1st Brigade was sent [to] occupy the heights. I observed a great many infantry crossing a marshy plain in our front and moving to turn our left in a straggling irregular manner, who when they had crossed the plain, formed regularly. Soon after this a very strong force of cavalry and some infantry advanced on our left, some charges then took place between these cavalry & ours, they then brought some horse artillery to our left and commenced cannonading our columns. Lord Wellington rode up and desired us to retire.

    We retired accordingly to some heights in front of a village called Canizal, the enemy moved along some heights in a parallel line with us, the whole way cannonading us at intervals but without doing any harm. They took up their position on a ridge of heights opposite those we occupy, there is a small river between us. When we took up this position the enemy wished to possess themselves of part of the ground occupied by the 4th Division. The 40th & 27th charged and defeated them, there was a French general officer taken on this occasion.[4] The day is excessively hot and we are badly off for water. At night we moved about five hundred yards to the rear of the ground we at first halted on. Three companies of the 1st Battalion of which ours is one are sent on in front a little way. 2 companies of the 2nd Battalion lately arrived from England joined the division on the march from Castrejon to this position.

The weather was so very hot today and water so scarce that a great number of men, particularly Portuguese, died of fatigue and heat.

Rifleman Edward Costello records an incident involving James Gairdner. 'Pratt, a fine, young fellow of the 14th Dragoons and a townsman of mine, brought in a French dragoon on his horse. The poor Frenchman, who had lost his helmet and had a severe cut on his cheek, seemed exceedingly chop-fallen, but declared with much vehemence that the Englishman could not have taken him had he possessed a better horse. Lieutenant Gardiner[5] of our company who spoke excellent French, repeated this to Pratt.

"Then by Jasus, sir," Pratt answered, "tell him if he had the best horse in France, I would bring him prisoner – if he stood to fight me."

The words caused roars of laughter from all but the prisoner who, patting the goaded and smoking steed exclaimed affectionately, "My poor beast has not had his saddle off for the last week."

And such appeared to be the case because, before the house was sold, the saddle was removed and part of the flesh that had become a sore, came away with the saddle-cloth. In this condition, the animal was sold to Lt. Gardiner for five dollars.'

19th　We remained quiet all the morning, we were making batteries in different places. I saw a body of the enemy apparently about 1,000 men moving to our right. About 3 o'clock in the afternoon the enemy got under arms and commenced moving to our right, we moved also, our division occupied a hill to our right and in front of our original position. The enemy were in force on a hill near us with a small valley between. As soon as we advanced to the brow of our hill they commenced shelling and cannonading us, which our artillery not being heavy enough to return, the division retired immediately leaving some men in extended order on the brow of the hill.

Because of their losses, the battalion was reduced from eight companies to six and James joined Captain Leach's company along with Private Costello when the brigade remained at Getafe for three months.

20th   Got under arms before day break. Soon after day break saw the enemy moving to our right. We soon after commenced moving in the same direction. Soon after the commencement of the march we entered a fine wood and saw nothing more of the enemy this day, they were however moving in a parallel line to our left and we heard cannonading in that quarter. In the afternoon we halted for a short time near a village where the following arrangements took place in the 1st Battalion. The 8 companies being ordered into 6, Mc Dermid's[6] & Smyth's[7], the company I belonged to were broken up. Leach's company (to which I am now attached) Greys' & Stewarts' are attached (with head quarters of the battalion) to the 1st Brigade, the other 3 companies viz Balvaird's, Crompton's[8] & Beckwith's remain in the 2nd Brigade. After halting for about an hour here we moved onto another village about a league further on near which we bivouacked. The whole army are here.

21st   The army began to move off by divisions last night at 9 o'clock. Our division moved off the last at about 3 o'clock this morning. We arrived at and halted outside of the village of Moriscos (the village the 1st Brigade occupied on the 28th of June when we broke up from the position of St Cristobal) at about 12 o'clock. Weather very hot. At about 5 o'clock in the evening we marched again and crossed the Tormes at a ford near the village of Cabrerizos, halted on the opposite bank, for about 2 hours it commenced raining. Marched on then about a league to some ground where some other divisions were bivouacked, we halted here for the night.

Wellington's stunning victory over Marmont began with the Duke spotting that the French army was strung out too much on their line of march and vulnerable to be defeated in detail. This is exactly what Wellington succeeded in doing. But the memoirs of the 95th are largely silent about this great victory, because they were hardly involved in this action.

22nd It rained very hard last night with a great deal of lightning and some thunder. Heard a good deal of firing in our front all the morning, at about 11 o'clock we were moved forward and understood then that Lord Wellington had determined to attack the enemy. The attack began about midday, those of our regiment in this brigade viz our three companies and the 5 companies of the 3rd Battalion were detached on the left of the position to watch a part of the enemy [note by Gairdner – General Foy's Division] that were on a hill opposite to us. Our division was not engaged until the close of the action and then very little. Neither was the 1st Division engaged, those engaged were the 3rd, 4th, 5th, 6th, and part of the 7th. The action lasted until dark and the defeat of the enemy was most decisive. We followed them this night to a village nearly opposite to Aldealengua. Marmont has been wounded.

Following the retreating French, the 95th came upon the scene at Garcia Hernandez, where Bock's Heavy Cavalry Brigade broke through two formed squares and captured some 1,400 men.

23rd We commenced marching again this morning before daybreak. Crossed the Tormes by a ford, halted a few minutes on the bank, given to understand we were to halt half an hour, marched off suddenly. Soon after this arrived on the ground, where General Bock's Heavy German Brigade of cavalry had just made one of the most dashing charges ever (I believe) known, on the enemy's rearguard of infantry. We marched over the ground just after the charge, it was made up an hill, arms and accoutrements were lying in every direction, in one place near the top of the hill where they charged and broke a square. The form of the square might be seen by the arms and accoutrements &c lying as if they had been charged in columns of sections. We continued following them until towards afternoon (their rearguard in sight all day) when we halted near a village.

24th Marched again before daybreak through Penaranda [de Bracamonte] a good looking town (or rather city, for it is what they call a ciudad) to Flores de Avila where the division bivouacked in two woods outside of the town, the officers got into houses. The people in Penaranda received us very well, they told us that Marmont was about to have had his arm amputated[9] when the advanced guard of the army appearing, he was obliged to make off. Our company on picquet, head quarters here.

25th   Our baggage which we have not seen since it went to the rear on the night of the 17th came up today, halted here all day.

26th   Through 3 different villages to Aldeaseca, head quarters here bivouacked outside of the town, could not get houses. Weather very hot.

27th   Through Arevalo, a curiously situated town (situated between two rivers it has been a Moorish fortress, it is a good looking town) to Mantega de Vaca[10], we were quartered in the village of Mantega de Vaca.

28th   To Olmedo a good town, where the division are quartered in a convent, the officers are to take whatever houses they think proper but are given to understand that head quarters will be here and that they are liable to be turned out of their quarters. Many have been turned out, however I got into a pretty good house with a stable and have been lucky enough to keep it. The French General Ferey[11] who was wounded on the 22nd has been buried here and dug up again by the inhabitants, I saw his body. He was buried again by our division. The people here received us very well, a priest met our division as we marched in with fireworks which is a token of rejoicing among the Spaniards. Olmedo has formerly been fortified, it is surrounded by a wall with small round towers at about every hundred yards.

29th   We marched this morning at about daybreak , we understood we were to march to Portillo which is a town situated on a mountain when we were in sight of Portillo and about a league from it, we were halted for a considerable time, at last we marched to a village to the left of it called [La] Pedraja de Portillo. The division bivouacked outside of the town, the houses of which there were very few were told off to the officers.

30th   Marched before day break and forded the Douro, halted on the right bank of it in a pine wood, about 6 miles English from Valladolid. The 1st Division halted on the left bank. About one o'clock an order was given that all except one officer per company might go to Valladolid. I rode in together with Hopwood[12], Layton[13] and Leach, it is a fine city, the entrance to it is very fine, it is a larger place than Salamanca but I do not think it so handsome a city, the plaza or square (which is the part of a city or town in which the Spaniards pride themselves more) of this place is large but by no means handsome, it appears to be a very old place. The French having been here so long, the place is completely Frenchified and the inhabitants did not seem over glad to see the English. There are good shops & coffee houses here, the latter of course established by the French for I never saw any in the country before except at Badajoz which place also the French had possession of for a long time. The enemy left behind them here some sick and some British prisoners[14]. I saw a man of the 3rd Dragoon Guards here and a more wretched figure I never saw. He said however that he had not been ill treated, but that he got rations very irregularly but he believed it was not their fault for their own sick were in the same way.

31st Halted all day in the same ground as yesterday. I have a very bad toothache.

August

1st Received an order last night to march at daybreak this morning, marched accordingly to Tudela de Duero about a league & a half from where we bivouacked, the whole division are quartered here, pretty good quarters. Had a tooth drawn by Jones[15].

2nd There is I believe some prospect of remaining quiet for a little while and I sincerely wish we may, for we have had hard work for the last 6 weeks. Tudela is a pretty good town, It is situated on the right bank of the Douro, there is a bridge here, one of the arches of which the French have destroyed. The country about here is very beautiful.

About 5 o'clock this evening we received an order to march immediately to Aldeamayor [de San Martin]. In consequence of the bridge being destroyed, we were obliged to ford the river, the ford is a very bad one and caused considerable delay before the division could march off from the opposite bank. I was on duty to bring up stragglers. Got to Aldeamayor about 9 o'clock, our brigade bivouacked outside the town, the other quartered in the town.

3rd The officers of our company got a house in town. The men are ordered to change their ground by day to a wood and return to the old ground at night on account of the wood being damp.

Rode this evening to Portillo, about a league from here, it is situated on the top of a mountain & has been a Moorish fortress, it is a curious place and put me much in mind of Guarda.

Leach being given charge of the three companies attached to the 2nd Brigade, his company transferred with him.

4th   The 1st Brigade marched this day to Pedraja de Portillo. Balvaird having gone to England on account of ill health, Leach as senior captain is now attached with his company to the 2nd Brigade in order to take command of the 3 companies.

        The 2nd Brigade to which we now belong, remains at Aldeamayor. Drew a bill on England for £25. Rode this evening to a village beyond Portillo, head quarters are at Cuellar.

5th   Rode over to Pedraja where the 1st Brigade are to receive the money for the bill I drew. I was acting as adjutant this evening at a flogging match[16] and was blackguarded by old Vandeleur like a pickpocket. Received an order this evening to march tomorrow morning.

Wellington now left Clinton's 6th Division to pursue Marmont, whilst he turned his army south to take the political prize of Madrid.

6th   Marched before daybreak and bivouacked in a fine wood on the left bank of the Caya near the village of Alpino[17], this day's march was through a fine corn country. There is a General Order that the officers see regularly 1/3 water mixed with the rum.

7th   Marched before daybreak & bivouacked in a pine wood on the banks of the Piron near Puente de Roble[18]. 1st Division are encamped near us. Fine level corn country. Rode to a village a little off the road on this day's march and bought some turkies [sic] very cheap.

8th   Through Carbonero [el Mayor], a very good town and Yanguas [de Eresma] to the bank of the Eresma where ours and the 1st Division encamped.

        I stopped in Carbonero to forage for the mess, the people in this place have a very peculiar way of dressing, the way in which the women dress their hair is particularly curious and they are altogether the wildest looking set I ever saw. In Yanguas they are much the same. Query, is this the same Yanguas in which Sancho Panza was taped in a blanket?[19]

9th   To the park of the Pallacio d'el Rio Frio where we found several other divisions bivouacked, it is about a league from Segovia. I went into the palace which is a large square building of stone, plastered on the outside & coloured brick. There is no furniture inside nor any ornaments except about a dozen pictures, I do not know what it might have been but in its present state it is not worth walking an hundred yards to see. After breakfast I rode into Segovia, it is a very fine old city, better worth seeing I think than either Salamanca or Valladolid, the entrance to it is beautiful. The most remarkable things in it are the cathedral which is uncommonly beautiful, especially the inside of it. There are some very fine painted glass windows. The castle or towers of Segovia (which is made honourable mention of in Gil Blas[20] and in which they show what they call Gil Blas' cell) is a very curious place. It is excessively strong by nature, being built on a rock, very high and perpendicular on every side, but that which looks towards the city, and even in front of that part of it runs a very deep ditch cut out of the rock over which there is a draw bridge. The Spanish government have always used it as a state prison, but the French have used it as a fort and mounted some guns on it. The French when they left the place rendered useless all the artillery they left here, the ditch above mentioned is full of gun carriages, guns, mortars &c. I saw in the courtyard in the interior of the building a small English brass mortar with GR and a crown on it laying spiked. The view from the top of the tower is very fine, on the one side a fine corn country and on the other that immense ridge of mountains which runs from the rock of Lisbon across the whole peninsula and which in this place divides Old from New Castille. There is also a very handsome stone aqueduct said to have been built by the Romans. The town has a very ancient appearance but is clean and pleased me very much.

10th   Marched about a league & a half and encamped in a field near a village called I think [Otero de] Horreros. I today saw the first league stone I ever saw in the country, on it was inscribed Madrid 11 leagues.

11th   Marched this day across the Sierra de Guadarrama which divides Old from New Castille, the road of the pass paved with stones. At the top of the sierra is a stone pillar with a lion on the top of it, which marks the boundary of the two Castilles. Just at the beginning of the pass we passed through the small village of San Rafael, the church of which the French have made a temporary fortification of and is very curious. The view of New Castille from the top of the sierra is very wild and cheerless, the face of the country being entirely burnt and uncultivated. On gaining the bottom of the mountains we passed through the village of Guadarrama, part of which is fortified in the same manner as San Rafael we halted and bivouacked in the park of the far famed Palace of Escorial. After breakfast I rode to Escorial it is (though now apparently much destroyed and deserted) a very good town, it is built entirely of stone and is by far the most uniformly built town I have seen in either Spain or Portugal. In the palace itself I am I confess rather disappointed, however I saw it to great disadvantage, the French having plundered it of everything they could carry away worth taking, the chapel however is very beautiful and the mausoleum or sepulchre of the sovereigns of Spain which is underneath the chapel is the most magnificent thing of the kind I ever saw, the paintings on the ceiling over the principal staircase together with those in that of the library is very beautiful, but there is not a book left in the library. All that I saw of what was formerly the inhabited part of the place was entirely plundered but it had not the signs of having ever been grand, for I did not see one room that could have conveniently dined 20 people. In this place also the French have been obliged to make little fortifications at the end of every street leading out into the country.

12th Halted here all day, I rode again to Escorial, saw Fraser of the 79th.[21]

13th Received an order last night to march. Marched accordingly this morning at about daybreak along a very fine road called the Carmino Real, with regular league and half league stones. To Las Rozas, [note by Gairdner - 1st Brigade to Majadahonda, the Portuguese cavalry the other day behaved very ill at this place, they actually ran away from some French cavalry and deserted some guns they ought to have defended. Some German cavalry also were in Las Rozas charged, obliged them to leave the guns & behaved exceedingly well.] A small village about a league and a half from Madrid. Even in this small place though only six

English miles from the metropolis, the church and all the entrances to the place are fortified. It is almost deserted, many houses are quite uninhabited. After breakfast I rode with Leach, Pemberton[22] & Hopwood into Madrid. I had heard that Madrid for a capital was a small place and the idea I had formed from what I have seen of some of their towns and cities fell far short of what it really is, it is really a beautiful city. There were preparations going on at the time I entered to proclaim the new constitution which was done that afternoon, there were a great many processions parading the streets, the houses as is usual on public occasions were hung with tapestry &c and the windows crowded with women. I am very much mistaken if I did not see in one of the windows one of the nuns that was in the house I was in at Badajoz after I was wounded. After riding about the streets for [a] short time we went to the *Fuente d'Auros* an excellent coffee house where we dined. After dinner we walked out, the 5th Division was just marching out, having been relieved here by the 3rd. The streets through which they passed were crowded with people and I never saw such real enthusiasm in my life as they showed. I was seized hold of and kissed by men, women & children, old & young. After this we went to the play, the house is small but very neat, there is one thing remarkable with respect to their prompter, he is seated in a sort of trap door in the middle of the lamps with his face towards the stage with a sort of cover or canopy over him. Slept at the *Fuente d'Auros*, our horses are at a public stable.

14th Went after breakfast to see the palace, it is a very fine building outside, but not finished. The inside is the most beautiful magnificent thing I ever saw. Every room is hung & furnished different from the others, they are all full of pictures which are of course first rate performances. There is one of Napoleon Bonaparte crossing the Alps of which I have seen prints in England. Soon after coming out of the palace we met an officer of the 3rd Division who told us that they were just about to storm the Retiro[23], which the French have fortified & left a garrison in. when Lord Wellington sent in some message by Lord F. Somerset[24] & the garrison surrendered. He told us that they were to march out at 3 o'clock, I went to see the garrison march out, they I understand surrendered on condition that they should march out with the honours of war, that the officers should keep their baggage & the soldiers their packs. They piled their arms before they came to the outer gate and then marched out. They were uncommonly fine men, a great many Germans among them, they were almost all drunk & complained of their head having surrendered. After this went to the Fuente d'Auros and dined.

15th   Went to see the Retiro. The principal fortification is a large square building called *La China* formerly a china manufactory which building is surrounded by a line of fortifications of earth in the regular form of bastions, curtains &c with the banquettes, ditches &c & which is very complete [&] strong indeed. There were a great quantity of horses taken in La china. After this I went to see the museum, it is exceedingly well worth seeing indeed. There is in it a perfect skeleton of the *mammoth* which is I believe the only perfect one in the world, and there is among the specimens of sculpture a Venus & Cupid cut out of a solid block of blue and white marble with which I who know nothing about [with] these things was very much pleased.

After this I rode to Villaverde, a village about 3 miles from Madrid in the direction of Toledo, where the division are & to which place they marched from Las Rozas & Majadahonda on the 14th. On my way to Villaverde I crossed the Manzanares by the beautiful bridge of Toledo. The more I have seen of Madrid the more I am pleased with it, very much crowded at Villaverde.

16th   The 1st Brigade moved to Getafe, a village about 3 miles from here.

17th   Rode into Madrid returned to dinner. Even in this place the streets leading into the country are fortified, this is what the French call having quiet possession of a country.

18th   Not very well.

19th   The 1st Brigade moved to Madrid.

20th   In consequence of the complaints of the badness of the water here, our brigade moved this morning to Getafe, very good quarters. 14th Dragoons here.

21st   Very unwell.

22nd – 30th *Blank*

31st   There is a grand bullfight given in Madrid this day to Lord Wellington & the army.

Marshal Marmont had been replaced by General Souham. He rapidly reorganised his army and began to put pressure on Clinton's covering force. Wellington took the majority of his army northwards in an effort to defeat Souham, but he retired and the Duke was forced to carry out a siege at Burgos with hopelessly inadequate means.

The Light Division, however, remained near Madrid for ten weeks until the combined armies of King Joseph and Marshal Soult appeared. They were initially ordered forward to face this threat but on hearing of Wellington's retreat from Burgos, they were forced then to retire as well.

September

1st   Lord Wellington has left Madrid today and gone northward. General Clinton who was left with the 6th Division and several regiments lately arrived from England in the north when we marched for Madrid and whose head quarters were at Cuellar has been obliged to retire to Arevalo. Lord Wellington has taken with him the 1st, 5th & 7th Divisions. The 3rd Division is in Madrid, the 4th at Escurial, the 2nd are in the neighbourhood of Toledo.

2nd September – 20th October. During most part of the time I have been here, I have been very unwell, add to that I never had money, for the army has never been worse paid than since we have been here, so that I have not had much pleasure to boast of having enjoyed in the capital of Spain. Notwithstanding all this, I like it better than any quarter I ever was in as a soldier.

21st   We received an order this morning at about 5 o'clock to march at 8. The brigade marched accordingly, passed through Villaverde, crossed the Manzanares by a very bad ford (in which there was a great deal of the baggage apart, mine among the rest) passed through the town of [Villa de] Vallecas and went on to a place called Rivas [Vaciamadrid] which consists of a convent and two or three houses. [Note by Gairdner – Saw a division march from Madrid towards Pinto as we crossed the road, it must have been the 3rd Division. The 1st & 2nd Battalions of our regiment with

49

the officers of the 1st Battalion in the convent, the officers of the 2nd Battalion in a house near the convent, the rest of the houses occupied by head quarters of the brigade. The 1st Cacadores are at Vaciamadrid the 52nd marched on. The situation of this place is most romantically beautiful, it is situated on the right bank of the River Uresma, which bank is uncommonly steep & bold while the other bank is quite flat and the country on the other side for a considerable extent is a flat plain. It must be an excellent sporting country, we bagged about twenty wild pigeons here.

I saw in the convent garden what I never saw before, out of England, viz *hops*. 1st Brigade at Vallecas, saw the first green corn I have seen this year on this day's march.

22nd   Marched at about 7 o'clock back again and halted at the village of Vicalvaro, a village about a mile & [a] half from Vallecas. Part of the 1st Brigade occupied this place yesterday and marched out to Vallecas as we marched in. General Alten has been desired to remain in Madrid & General Vandeleur commands the division pro tempore. Madrid is about 5 miles English from here.

There is in this place a large building which the French have used as a cavalry barrack, it is fortified, that is to say there is a ditch cut round with a sort of draw bridge at the entrance and all the window shutters loop-holed.

23rd *Blank*

24th   Received an order this evening at about 5 o'clock to march tomorrow to Alcala de Henares.

25th   The division marched accordingly about 7 o'clock, I set off at the same time for Madrid. Rode out in the evening to Alcala. Passed the Urema by a very handsome bridge, passed also through the village of Torrejon [de Ardoz].

26th   Halted here all day. Alcala is a very nice town indeed, it is situated on the right bank of the Henares. It is about 4 leagues from Madrid from which place to Alcala there is a Carmino Real. It has the appearance of a very ancient town, it is surrounded by a wall in most parts and has the remains of a castle. There are several convents in it and a college, a very fine building with a very good library, which I went to see several times and with which I was much amused. The houses a[re] built for the most part in a different way from the generality of Spanish houses, but they are exceedingly comfortable. I have not seen a place in Spain I would sooner pass the winter in than Alcala, the country about it must I am sure abound in game.

27th Received an order at about 10 o'clock to march immediately to Arganda [del Rey]. The division marched accordingly, crossed the Henares by a bridge about half a mile from Alcala. The opposite bank of the river is excessively steep and bold and there is a pass to ascend which is very short, but is for its size the most steep and formidable I ever saw. Passed through a fine country, saw Rivas on our right hand on the march and arrived at Arganda at about 3 o'clock. Pretty good quarters, the people very civil, I never saw anything like the quantity of onions in this place, every house & yard is full of them. Just as I was going to bed we received an order to march back to Alcala immediately, baggage to precede the column. Marched accordingly and arrived at Alcala just as day was breaking.

28th Immediately on our arrival we halted outside of the town in close column & sent out picquets. We remained here until about 8 o'clock when we were ordered to march into town & occupy our old quarters but to assemble again in the same manner in one hour. Went in, got some breakfast & came out again to the same ground where we remained until about 2 o'clock when the old general (Vandeleur) having finished his sleep came out and sent us to our quarters, I went to bed immediately, got up at about 5 o'clock & dined.

There is an order given out that the division shall lie in the streets under the piazzas (which are in most of the streets) and that the officers may occupy the houses in rear of their respective companies I in consequence slept in rear of the company this night, but left my baggage &c in my old billet.

29th General Alten arrived this day and took command of the division again. Soult is said to have crossed the Tagus last night.

Chapter 7

Retreat

The retreat from Madrid started with the aim of retiring slowly to rejoin Wellington's army, which was retiring from Burgos, and to concentrate near Salamanca.

30th   An order was given at about 9 o'clock to march at 10 to the opposite bank of the Urema which is between this and Madrid and there encamp. Just as the order was given, it commenced raining very hard. I on baggage guard. When we arrived on the opposite bank of the river the division halted, the baggage was ordered to proceed in front of the column to Aravaca about ½ league on the other side of Madrid and about 6 & ½ from Alcala. Passed close to Madrid, I rode into it, it look[ed] miserably melancholy, the rain ceased at about 5 or 6 o'clock, did not get to Aravaca until some time after dark. We bivouacked on the roadside. We are I hear to march to Arevalo. It is reported that Massena has arrived with reinforcements and taken command of the army of Portugal. 2nd & 3rd Divisions lay near us this night.[1]

31st   Marched down close to Madrid directly opposite the palace where we remained the whole day. Skerret's detachment from Cadiz and also the 4th Division came in from the front while we were here. Skerret's troops have had some skirmishing lately, 2 companies of our 2nd Battalion who were at Cadiz have had an officer (Budgeon) wounded[2]. A great quantity of stores of every description were destroyed today in Madrid for want of conveyance to carry them off. I was sent into the town to bring out stragglers. Rode to the Retiro (the building of La China is blown up at the angles, but the ramparts by which it is surrounded are not at all damaged. Moved back in the evening to the ground we occupied yesterday evening, the 2 companies of the 2nd Battalion [95th] lately from Cadiz joined the 2nd Brigade this evening & the 3 companies of the 1st Battalion went back again to the 1st Brigade & now the 1st Battalion is together again. The 20th Portuguese Regiment of the line from Cadiz joined the 1st Brigade, they are very strong. An order was given this night that the baggage move off tomorrow morning at 3 o'clock, the column at 6.

November

1st   Commenced our retreat from Madrid this day and never have I left a place in the peninsula with so much regret for various reasons. It is the most beautiful city without exception I ever saw, in situation it is little superior to London, being in a very flat country, but as to the city itself, it surpasses in beauty every other I ever saw, the number of elegant, or rather, magnificent public buildings and dwelling houses of the nobility is amazing.

The beauty of the streets & fountains (particularly the fountains in the prado or public walk, which is I believe the most beautiful promenade in Europe) is superior to anything either in London or Edinburgh. I was also much surprised at the excellence of the coffee houses, they have however been brought to that by the French. The coffee houses are during the summer abundantly supplied with ice. Madrid is entirely surrounded by a wall which evidently was never intended for a wall of defence, nor can I conceive the intention of it unless it is to prevent smuggling. In the wall are several gates all of which are very beautiful[ly] executed and form very principal ornaments to the city. The markets are abundantly supplied with meat, vegetables and fruit. It is without exception the most delightful quarter I ever was in, out of Great Britain.

The civility of the people from first to last was beyond anything I have seen in the country, their enthusiasm on our first entrance I shall never forget and even on our leaving them unprotected to those oppressors from whom they had fondly believed we had delivered them forever, there was not a grumble or word of reproach. I felt sincerely for them.

We marched this day to [blank – Las Rozas according to Simmons] and bivouacked on the right bank of the Guadarrama, all the cavalry ordered on except the hussars. I saw Watts of the 3rd Dragoons[3] today, the baggage is at Galapagar & is ordered to precede the army with the exception of one animal per company which animal is to precede the regiment every day on the march. It is reported that Soult is to join Massena.

2nd   Marched at sunrise to a field near the village of Guadarrama, the guns moved this day in rear of the division with three companies of our battalion of which ours was one in their rear.

Just as we arrived at our bivouack a wild boar & sow were started, the sow was killed by one of the 52nd, our heavy baggage was on the ground when we arrived but moved on immediately. One company was on picquet this evening at [the] porter's lodge of La Escorial park. There were a great quantity of stores passing our piquet the whole night. We got a cask of rum that fell out of one of the cars.

3rd   Crossed the Sierra de Guadarrama by the same passed [sic] by which we crossed before and marched through the village of Navas de San Antonio to Villacastin, 6 leagues. The country through which we passed until we came close to Villacastin was very barren. I saw a great quantity of horses destroyed at the top of the sierra. There was an immense number of sick fell out today on the march. It is reported that Don Carlos d'Espana[4] has been discovered to be a traitor.

4th   Through Velayos and another village to La Vega [de Santa Maria]. The first part of the road was uncultivated with green oak, the last part a fine corn country. The hussars in our rear have reported that 4 French regiments of cavalry & some infantry crossed the mountains of Guadarrama today. It is said that Massena has crossed the Douro with loss, also that we are to march to Salamanca not Arevalo. Our heavy baggage was here when we halted, received a letter from England.

5th   The heavy baggage went off very early this morning, I was on the light baggage guard for the brigade today, the light baggage preceded the column about an hour. We marched through the villages of Villanueva de Gomez & San Pascual to Fontiveros 5 leagues. When I arrived there with the light baggage the 2nd & 3rd divisions were there, they moved on immediately, the 4th Division marched today immediately in front of the light. The heavy cavalry bivouacked here also. The heavy baggage was here when I arrived but moved on immediately.

6th Marched this day to some hills between Flores de Avila and Penaranda [de Bracamonte], on which the whole of General Hill's army viz 2nd, 3rd, 4th & Light Divisions, lay this night. Just as we commenced the march it began raining very hard but gave over towards the afternoon.

7th Marched this day to some hills about a league from Alba de Tormes, where we lay all night. All the baggage, light & heavy, is sent across the river, consequently we have neither tent nor provisions except a little mutton that was issued, rained very hard all night.

Arriving at Salamanca, Wellington hoped to end his retreat here and the troops were allowed some rest for a few days.

8th Marched to Alba de Tormes & halted for about 2 hours just outside the town, during which time quarters were taken up for our division, but the intention of putting us into the town was given up, all this time it continued to rain tremendously. I rode into the town, it is almost deserted, but has been a very fine town, it is situated on the right bank of the Tormes and has a castle which commands the bridge, everything indeed. Don Carlos was ordered out [of] the line of battle of Salamanca to occupy this place, he evacuated it in a very suspicious manner.

  The town has a fine romantic appearance, after halting about 2 hours as before mentioned we crossed the bridge and moved on to a wood in the neighbourhood of Calvarrasa de Arriba and not far from the celebrated field of action on the 22nd of July. It gave over raining towards the afternoon. As we passed over the bridge of Alba de Tormes there were some of the Staff Corps mining an arch of the bridge and some of the 2nd Division going into the town to take up quarters for their division met our light baggage on the ground we lay on.

9th Halted here all day towards evening, the heavy baggage came in and I found that every article of mine, animal and all lost, through the negligence & drunkenness of a rascally bat man.

10th Marched this morning about an hour before daybreak into Salamanca. The whole division are quartered in the Irish College[5], a very fine building. The officers have billets and very bad ones (the place being full of sick and officers wounded at Burgos).

There is an order given that every officer shall appoint an alarm post for his own company and that the division shall march out tomorrow morning before daybreak to the alarm post of the division. Part of the 7th Division are in Salamanca.

11th   Marched to the alarm post before day break which is just outside of the gate of the town. When we had been there about half an hour, we heard a heavy firing of musketry. Lord Wellington rode out to reconnoitre just at this time and ordered us to move on, we marched accordingly up to the position of St Cristobal, on which are encamped some divisions of the army. When we arrived here we understood that the firing was by General Pack's Brigade who are at Aldealengua. Lord Wellington said that as the division are here, they may as well remain until 3 o'clock when they may if all is quiet return to Salamanca, returned accordingly at 3 o'clock. The division is ordered to march out every morning before day break to the alarm post.

12th   Marched to the alarm post at the usual hour, four [in the] morning, marched in again at about 7 o'clock. The effects of poor Crampton[6] (who died at Rodrigo) were sold by auction this day, I bought his gun and several other things.

      Salamanca is not half so nice a place as when I was in it in June last; it was then very clean & the people were very civil indeed. The inhabitants are now quite changed, and the whole town beastly dirty, that however is not much to be wondered at, as it has been for a long time a depot for sick. The cathedral[7] is very beautiful, especially the inside, the plaza maior[8] is the most beautiful I have seen in either Spain or Portugal, the houses in it are built uniformly and are four stories high. The ground floors are all shops and very good ones. It is entirely surrounded by a piazza, the pillars of which have each a stone bust of the sovereigns of Spain. There have been a great many very fine public buildings in this city, but they are now most of them, in ruins. The bridge over the Tormes is very handsome, Salamanca is surrounded entirely by a wall.

13th   Marched to the alarm post as usual & returned. Firman[9] who was on orderly duty last night in going round the quarters in the convent fell down stairs and is dangerously hurt. I am on orderly duty today. I went to the play this evening, the admittance is *four vintems*, but the boxes are all hired by the box. We got into a box with great difficulty occupied by a sulky scoundrel & his wife. This performance is very poor and the theatre itself no great things. The prompter as at Madrid takes his post in front of the stage. There is one thing peculiar here viz above the upper tier of boxes is a sort of gallery for the admittance of *women only*, such women as go alone go there.

George Simmons witnessed Firman's fatal accident: 'In the evening, being orderly officer, I went at eight o'clock to see the lights out and that the men were present. I met Lieutenant Firman, who was upon the same duty for our 3rd Battalion. Finding the stairs very slippery and the place very dark, I observed, "If you will wait, I will go in search of a candle", as I knew there were open spaces in the balusters a person in the dark might walk through. I left him, got a candle from a neighbouring house, and returned. I went up three or four stairs, when I heard a slip and in a moment, poor Firman fell through. In his progress downstairs his feet repeatedly struck one side and his head the other. He came with tremendous force to the bottom, which was a flagged pavement in the cellar. I directly retraced my steps and found him almost dashed to pieces, his skull frightfully fractured and several ribs broken. I had him removed to his billet. He remained for two days in a state of insensibility and died.'[10]

14th Got cash for a bill on England of £27 10s from a company of accounts of the name of Hayward, a very gentlemanly man. About 10 o'clock there was an order given for the division to march immediately across the bridge, on the road to Calvarrasa de Arriba.

Just after crossing the bridge the division halted for a short time, I then went up to our commander Lieutenant Colonel Cameron[11] and explained to him that I had just got some money and as I had lost *my* baggage, requested leave to return to Salamanca for a few hours to purchase some clothes & other necessaries, he after a great deal of needless and ungentlemanly blustering, gave me leave. I had not gone an hundred yards towards the town when the adjutant came and told me that it was the colonel's order that I should go on command with the sick to Tejares in place of Lieutenant Macnamara[12] whose turn it is (Macnamara is the senior 1st lieutenant and I the junior but two with the battalion). I returned to the colonel and requested that he would not put me on duty out of my turn, the only answer I got was 'you may think it a hard case and maybe it is, but if you think

57

so, do the duty first and make your complaint afterwards'. This is *military* justice.

For the first time in my life, though I have before experienced both its hardships and dangers, I cursed a service, in which a low-lifed boute [French; boot] can with impunity annoy an officer, even though he does not fail in one point of his duty, merely because he has a command. That Cameron dislikes me I know, but his reasons for so doing I am perfectly ignorant. I went back (after this answer) to Salamanca but could not find the sick, they were all off. After some time I followed them to Tejares, a village about 2 miles from Salamanca, I found them there together with the commissariat of the division, they had orders to move always with the commissariat.

I got into a wood house and remained comfortable enough all night. The division I understand moved on this evening towards the *Arapiles*. The 2nd Division were engaged this evening. The reason of the army moving across the Tormes is because the French have crossed the river above Alba de Tormes. There is a Spanish garrison in Alba de Tormes.

Wellington was forced into ordering a further retreat towards the Portuguese border. But what to date had been a relatively orderly retreat soon changed greatly in character. The commissariat collapsed completely during this relatively short retreat and this coupled with long forced marches led to the breakdown of discipline in the army. Wellington wrote a scathing criticism of this retreat and the lack of discipline shown but which completely overlooked the exceptionally trying marches the army endured without any regular supplies.

15th   It commenced raining very hard today early. At about 12 o'clock Molloy[13] came to relieve me on this duty. The colonel I understand pretends to be vexed that I was sent out of my turn. Molloy told me that the division had not moved since yesterday evening and that there was no talk of moving when he left them. Just as I left them, the commissariat stores and sick got orders to move. I set off immediately to join the division, attended by my servant and the little baggage I have got, carried on the pony I used to ride. I went into Salamanca to buy some things and saw Captain Smith[14] who told me he had been advised to make the best of his way out of the town for that the French will shortly be in it. I accordingly took my departure & set off to find out the division. I was very soon informed by different stragglers that the army had commenced its retreat, but nobody could inform me in what direction I was likely to find our division, accordingly from this time I wandered at a hazard and was just as likely to walk into the French lines as the English. It continued to rain all this time tremendously. At about four o'clock in the afternoon I passed just at the flank of a line of our cavalry and the French, cannonading each other, there were a great number of people, cars &c in my rear, most of which must I am sure have been taken. I wandered in this uncertain manner (without knowing whether I was going right or wrong, and of course very uneasy, fully at times expecting to walk in among the enemy) until about an hour and a half after dark, when I came up to a house, at the door of which I saw a great many horses and soldiers. I went in and saw an excellent fire and two or three officers who I understood afterwards to be paymasters.

I determined to go no further this night, but brought in my pony & baggage, got some meat cooked, dried myself and lay down in my boat cloak before the fire, I had not lain down 5 minutes before there was a great firing of musketry heard at a distance, all the paymasters cut & run, I not thinking it quite safe took my departure also. Close in rear of this house, between it and the fires of a camp I saw at a distance, which I understood to be the English camp, was a small river, but which was so swollen with the rain that it was impassable. I walked down the bank for about a mile, fording every now and then to find a place shallow enough to bring the pony & baggage over. Not finding any such place I turned back & went up the river, again fording every now & then as before asked. After walking about half a mile above the house, I at last brought the pony over myself & servant holding up his head. The stream was so deep & rapid that I fully expected to have lost him and all the baggage. After crossing I made direct for the lights of the camp and to my great joy walked into the Light Division camp, found out our company tent and heartily tired & wet through, lay down to sleep, this ended the most uncomfortable day I ever passed in my life.

16th   The division marched at about 7 o'clock, with the baggage on the reverse flank of the column about 3 leagues and encamped in a wood. The roads are dreadfully bad, I got up to my knee at almost every step, it rained at intervals all day, the weather is also very cold. In consequence of the badness of the roads we did not get to our bivouack until after dark. The firing that started me last night from the house was by the soldiers firing at pigs. There were a great many stragglers on the flanks, at the same thing the whole of today. Lord Wellington has ordered 2 or 3 to be hung[15]. I bought a piece of pig from a Portuguese soldier on the march today, it rained at intervals all night. The whole of the country through which we marched today was a thick wood of green oak.

17th   The baggage was ordered off some time before the column moved. The column moved at about ½ past 7. The roads as they were yesterday, miserably bad, the weather very cold. We had not moved on far before we were halted, that is to say, the 1st Brigade, the companies equalised to be ready to form a square, our company was sent to the front to look out. After about half an hour we moved on again for about a mile and made another halt for nearly an hour. All this time the enemies [sic] cavalry skirmished with ours. We then moved on after some time, the enemies cavalry and ours still skirmishing in our rear, we perceived some of the enemies cavalry on our left flank. Part of our company was out as a flank patrol, they fired some shots at the cavalry. Some of their cavalry rode in upon the column of the 7th Division which was just in our front & fired into them, they having no flank patrols. They also charged some sick and baggage who were between us and the 7th Division and took several. Lieutenant Cameron[16] of our 2nd Battalion who was in charge of the sick was taken, they rifled his pockets, took away his horse & shoes & let him go again. Lieutenant General Sir E. Paget[17] who was 2nd in command to Lord Wellington was taken prisoner about the same time. Soon after General Erskine[18] told General Alten that it was necessary one brigade of the Light Division should halt to cover the retreat of his cavalry across the River Huebra which was just in our front. Our brigade was accordingly halted and while General Alten was remonstrating with Erskine, Lord Wellington very luckily for us came up and ordered us to retire immediately.

We were hard enough pushed as it was, if we had retired 5 minutes later, God knows what would have been the consequence. At this time we thought that they had nothing up but cavalry, they however pushed on their infantry just as we approached the river. The ground on the immediate bank of the river is quite flat, there is a ridge of very commanding heights on the right bank of the river, on which the enemy planted their artillery immediately on our quitting them and commenced cannonading us as we crossed the ford, they killed and wounded some of our men. We found the artillery of our division drawn up on the left bank of the river returning the enemy's fire, also our and the rest of our division & the 7th Division drawn up in columns. They continued shelling and cannonading our columns & they sent a great quantity of infantry to our left and down towards the river, 2 companies of the 1st Battalion viz Grey's and Macnamara's[19], were sent out to skirmish down to the bank of the river, the other four companies of the 1st Battalion were sent down towards the river and formed in line. Some of the 52nd companies were out skirmishing & poor Dawson[20] (whose company was one) was killed. Ridout of the 43rd[21] was wounded by a cannon shot which was thrown into the column. There were several other officers of the division wounded, but none of our regiment. We continued cannonading and skirmishing until dark. We lay all night on the ground on which we formed line, the 2 companies remaining in front (where they had been skirmishing) as a picquet. It rained very hard all night, we of course had no baggage, there was a little beef issued. By great good luck I got Leach to carry my boat cloak when the baggage was sent off this morning, otherwise I should have had nothing to lay in. Independent of the rain it was a bitter cold night.

I am convinced that if we had not made those 2 long halts at the commencement of the march we should have crossed the ford without interruption.

Leach records that the commissariat delivered cattle still on the hoof at the end of their day's march which were instantly butchered. However, the incessant rains precluded any possibility of maintaining a fire and they were forced to go without and simply lived off the few acorns they could scavenge off the ground.[22] The retreat continued, but luckily the French pursuit ended this day.

18th It was intended that we should get off before day break, the divisions in our front however, not obeying their orders, we did not get off until 3 hours at least after daylight & even then on account of the road being so blocked up, we made but little way. We thought as did Lord Wellington himself that the enemy would follow us this day as usual and it was expected that our division which always formed the rear guard would be terribly cut up, as indeed it would if they had followed us. They however did not attempt it and we proceeded to a wood in the neighbourhood of Sancti Spiritus without interruption where we bivouacked. The country through which we marched this day was not so thickly wooded as formerly, but the roads were equally bad. I saw a great many Portuguese soldiers lying dead in the road today. We had our light baggage with us this evening, we are I understand to be quartered in Rodrigo tomorrow, that will be luxury indeed.

A deserter from the enemy who came in today says that Soult commanded in person, the troops that followed us and that they have gone back to Salamanca for want of provisions. It rained very little today.

19th   We marched this morning before day break, before all the other divisions, to Ciudad Rodrigo. I saw Watts on the march, he told me that their brigade of cavalry was to have covered our retreat on the 17th, but they missed their way & when we arrived at Rodrigo we halted outside of the town for a long time. We were informed that it was impossible to quarter any troops inside of the town and the suburbs being only capable of containing one brigade, the other is to go to the Convent of La Caridad. It was agreed that as the 1st Brigade had the choice at Madrid, the 2nd Brigade should occupy the suburbs and ours go to La Caridad (however they might as well have let us stay where we are as La Caridad is entirely unroofed and affords no shelter whatever). The brigade stopped here some time for biscuit which was served out, in the meantime I walked in to Rodrigo and satisfied my hunger which was most ravenous. After the biscuit was served out, we marched to La Caridad & bivouacked. Thus ended this retreat, one of the most fatiguing and annoying, miserable retreat, for the time it lasted the British army ever made, for though the marches were not long the roads were shockingly bad, the weather for the season of the year very cold and rainy and the want of provisions very great, much more so than from the nature of the case it ought to have been.

It is calculated that the army have lost in prisoners, who were through fatigue & illness unable to keep up, more than 4,000 men, the loss in stores &c &c is immense. I here talk of the retreat from Salamanca to Rodrigo alone, for we never saw the enemy on the retreat from Madrid to Salamanca and the weather was for the most part, fine. Today a fine day.

20th   It commenced raining last night and remained all today.

21st   Rained all day with cold wind. There was an order given this evening for the brigade to march tomorrow morning to Saelices el Chico, a place which I understand affords no more cover than that the place we are at now. General Alten however said that it is but fair that the other brigade should take a spell of lying out and accordingly has ordered that they march tomorrow morning to Saelices el Chico and we march & occupy their quarters in the suburbs.

22nd Last night was a miserable, cold rainy night, our tent was blown down twice. Marched this morning into the suburbs, got into very good quarters, a gloomy windy day.

23rd A fine clear frosty day, Leach and I went up the Agueda with our guns, saw a great number of ducks, could not however get at them.

24th Head quarters left this place today for Freineda, fine day, the breaches are not repaired yet and are getting on very slowly, nor are the forts finished.

25th The 1st Brigade (with the exception of the 43rd Regiment which remain in the suburbs) marched this morning to the following places; 1st Battalion 95th to Villa del Puerco[23], artillery & 1 company 3rd Battalion to Sexmiro, other 4 companies 3rd Battalion to Martillan, 20th Portuguese Regiment to Barquilla. We are very much crowded at Villa del Puerco. There were however in it before we came, a brigade of the 5th Division, some artillery and some of the 12th Light Dragoons, they all marched out as we arrived to make room for us.
        A fine frosty day. We crossed the River Azava by the bridge of Marialba and passed through Gallegos, a fine corn country about Villa del Puerco.

26th A fine day.

27th *Blank*

28th Walked over to Martillan & bought some things at poor Firman's sale, who died at Salamanca in consequence of the fall he got. I brought the man that lost my baggage to a court martial, today he was flogged.

29th I went out shooting today, we saw some ducks & killed one, went as far as Villar de Cuervo, got some bread and wine there. It is a very nice village, there are no troops there.

Chapter 8

Winter Quarters

Finally, the army was placed into winter quarters in Portugal to rest and recuperate after the devastating retreat. To while away the inevitable hours of boredom, races, tennis matches, balls, shooting parties, walking clubs and plays were organised. James' irritation with Colonel Cameron's nitpicking continued however.

30th   Marched this morning at about 7 o'clock to [La] Alameda [de Gardon], about 3 miles, it is to be our winter cantonment. Colonel Cameron not forgetting his old pique, took every opportunity of finding fault with me and with the company because I commanded it today, dirty low lifed work! General Alten and the staff of the division are here, his quarters are not very good. Today being St Andrew's day we all dined together, had a very fair dinner.

The 43rd are at Gallegos, 52nd Nave de Haver, 2nd Battalion 95th Espeja, 1st & 3rd Cacadores & Vandeleur at Fuentes d'Onoro, other regiments where they were before, viz Sexmiro, Martillan & Barquilla.

I rode with Leach & Doyle[1] to Almeida, 4 leagues from here, it is a small but very neat fortress, the works which the French destroyed are repairing very fast, all the earth work is finished and the facing of stone is getting on very well. The town itself is a filthy dirty miserable place, there are however very good shops in it, much better than in Rodrigo. We went by way of Vale da Mula which is in Portugal close on the bank of the small River Turon which divides Portugal from Spain. On the Spanish side of the Turon just opposite to Vale da Mula is Fort Concepcion[2], a very beautiful fort which has been destroyed by the French & English. Coming through Vale da Mula on our way back, we were entreated by a woman of the place to make some Portuguese

Cacadores assist her in burying the body of an English soldier who had died in her house, which these brutes though sitting at their ease in the market place refused to carry 20 yards to a grave that was ready dug. We arrived at home about dark.

December
1st   It is in contemplation to have a regimental mess, I do not think it will answer.

3rd – 5th *Blank*

6th   Walked today to Fort Concepcion, it has been a beautiful fort, the fort itself consists of four bastions & four curtains, the only ground that is not completely commanded by the guns of the fort is on the left of it as you look towards Portugal and here are two outworks in a line with each other and the fort. The first is a circular work with a passage through the centre of it, the outer work is what I believe is called a ravelin, it is in the shape of a fleche. They are both of stone, the outer work is connected with the inner one by a covered way, which is connected with the inner work in like manner.

There is one thing here which I never saw in any fortification before viz on the covered way or crest of the glacis of the outer work or ravelin are stone walls loop holed. All the works are completely destroyed having been blown up by both the French & English. In the main work are many human skeletons & bones. Came home through Aldea del Obispo & Castillejos de Dos Casas.

7th   There being no straw nearer than Barba del Puerco[3] and it being my tour of duty to go for forage, I rode with the bat men of the regiment there today, it is full four leagues there from Almeida. In passing through Villar de Ciervo, General Victor Alten, who is quartered there with the 1st Hussars told me he had that morning sent a party to bring all the forage away and advised me not to go there, I however went on and found plenty. The country between Villar de Ciervo & Barba del Puerco is rocky & uncultivated with a good deal of wood. Barba del Puerco is a nice village, it is situated on the left bank of the Agueda on the opposite bank is *St Felices de Los Gallegos* as it is down in the map but I have generally heard it called *St Felices Grande*.

There is a bridge across the Agueda at this place, the banks of the river are most tremendously steep and this pass is the most formidable without exception I ever saw, for even if there were no opposition it would be impossible to get cannon up or down, yet the French attempted to carry it when our regiment was there about three years ago.

The arch of the bridge nearest Barba de Puerco has been destroyed, the arch is not repaired again, but a passage carried on to the bridge from on one side. As a proof how little confidence the Spaniards place in commissary's Vals[4], when I offered the owner of the straw the Val, he was sitting among a great many women, they all burst out laughing and he said it was very good paper for segars [sic] but worth nothing more.

8th   The regimental mess commenced this day, the pay master has agreed to advance the money which is to be stopped from the officers at each issue.

9th – 12th *Blank*

13th   The mess answers admirably well, much better than I expected, it is a capital thing, though at first we did not pull exactly together.

14th   *Blank*

Whilst the army lay in winter cantonments, the Duke rode to Cadiz to meet and confer with the Spanish Central Cortez on the campaign ahead. The Spanish promised both supplies and men and conferred command of the Spanish army on Wellington, despite the open opposition of some of the Spanish generals.

15th   Lord Wellington has gone to Cadiz.

16th   *Blank*

The Duke of York was keen to remove a number of badly depleted battalions from the peninsular to recruit and sought to replace them with new battalions. Wellington was less keen, recognising that one veteran was worth at least two recruits and was three times more likely to remain fit for duty in the trying conditions of Spain. He therefore came up with the expedient of combining two of these battalions together as 'Provisional Battalions' incorporating all of the fit men of both battalions.

Those deemed unfit and any excess of officers and NCO's were shipped back to Britain to recruit. What now became officially the 1st Provisional Battalion had been unofficially (as regards Horse Guards) formed nearly a year earlier without the provision of a number[5], but the four battalions were officially recognised at the end of 1812. Some of these battalions fought as such throughout the remainder of the Peninsular War.

17th   There is pay issuing now to the army in guineas, there has been a proclamation issued by the Portuguese government that they are to be taken by the Portuguese at 23 pesetas and 2 vintems and an half. I perceive by the General Orders of some days back that the following regiments being weak have been formed into *Provisional Battalions*, viz 4 company's 2nd Battalion 31st & 4 company's 2nd Battalion 66th form the 1st Provisional Regiment. 4 company's Queens[6] & 4 company's 53rd, 2nd Provisional Battalion. 4 company's 2nd Battalion 24th 4 company's 2nd Battalion 58th, 3rd Provisional Battalion. 4 company's [2nd Battalion] 30th 4 company's 2nd Battalion 44th, 4th Provisional Battalion. The light battalions of the King's German Legion are removed from the light to the 1st Division.

      Memo. The staff of the remaining companies of the above regiments forming provisional battalions, with the men unfit for service [to] go home.

18th   I was informed by our commissary that they pay for beef 140 reas or ten pence half penny English money per pound for beef and 120 or nine pence for mutton. The 1st Brigade draws 3,027 rations, 2nd between 2 & 3,000.

19th – 20th *Blank*

21st   A general court martial has opened in the division, General Vandeleur president.

22nd   A mail from England.

23rd   *Blank*

24th   Lieutenant John Gardiner[7] joined this day from England.

25th   Today being Christmas day, we had cock fighting and various other sports. Percival[8] & Cox[9] joined today from England, very rainy day.

26th   General Ballesteros[10] has resigned his command in consequence of Lord Wellington being appointed Generalissimo of the Spanish armies.

27th   *Blank*

28th   It is said that if Ballesteros had obeyed Lord Wellington's orders, we should never have retired from Madrid & the operations against Burgos would not have been interrupted.

29th – 30th *Blank*

31st   Drank the old year out this night in great style.

January 1813

1st   General Alten and staff dined with us today. We had a mail from England today which brought glorious news from Russia[11], it is reported that the French are fortifying the line of the Douro.

2nd   I remark now that the people here are ploughing up their green corn.

3rd   Another mail, more glowing news. I walked to Fuentes de Onoro today and saw the position Lord Wellington occupied, when he was attacked here by the French about 2 years ago.[12] It is reported that the French have evacuated & dismantled Valencia.

4th   *Blank*

5th   It is reported that the enemy are concentrating at Salamanca, General Hill is at Coria, a thick fog today.

6th   The same report today concerning the concentrating at Salamanca, it is also reported that we are to march to Alverca, foggy day.

7th   It is reported today that there are only a few of the enemy at Salamanca and that those few are going away, clear day and frosty.

8th   Another mail, papers to the 22nd December, more glorious news from Russia, raining, fair at Almeida.

9th   *Blank*

10th   The 1st Battalion went out to the plain between this & Espeja & met there the 3rd Battalion collected on the plain, fine day.

11th   Rain

12th   White frost, fine

13th   Rain

14th   White frost. I rode today with Leach to Vilar Formoso, a dirty little Portuguese village on the bank of the Turon which river divides the two countries & came home through Fuentes d'Onoro.

15th   Frosty

16th – 17th *Blank*

18th   The Light Division have got up a theatre by subscription; the chapel at Gallegos is the theatre, the first performance is to be this evening and is to be the comedy of *She Stoops to Conquer*[13]. The hussars are invited to dine with us today. I went out shooting today did not dine at the mess, rainy day.

19th – 24th *Blank*

25th   A clear warm day, out shooting, had good sport, mail from England. I remarked that they begin to plough their fallow land about here now.

26th   Lord Wellington returned to head quarters yesterday, he came by Lisbon which place he entered on the 17th.

27th   Fine day.

28th   Ditto. By last papers it appears that Maitland has demanded a court martial.[14]

29th   Fine day & rather frosty.

30th   Very windy, hard frost last night.

31st   Same weather as yesterday, this is the only really cold weather we have had this winter, it has been without exception the mildest winter I ever knew.

February

1st   Cold, but not so cold as yesterday. Mail from England.

2nd   The cacadores march to Ituero today.

3rd   Mail from England, General Vandeleur moves his head quarters to Guinaldo today.

4th   The theatrical geniuses of the division perform *The Rivals*[15] this evening. The hussars are invited to dine with us. A warm day, the 2nd Battalion march to El Bodon today.

5th   A fine warm day. Conversing with a Spanish peasant who was ploughing today, he asked me if the Spanish troops kill all their working bullocks wherever they go, to feed on.
        There are various reports concerning the French, one day we hear that they are advancing, another that they are evacuating the country. Went to the play last night, it was very well performed indeed, the theatre scenery is excellent.

6th   The nights are now frosty & the days clear & warm.

7th   Papers arrived yesterday, glorious news from Russia, a cloudy mild day.

8th – 10th *Blank*

11th   Windy.

12th   Rainy. *The Rivals* is to be performed over again tonight & Lord Wellington will be there. The hussars & 2nd Battalion are invited.

13th   Went to the play last night, it went off uncommonly well, a fine day.

14th   Rainy.

15th   Fine, rather cloudy.

16th Drew a bill on England today for £27 10s. There is a scarcity of meat and they talk of issuing salt fish in lieu of meat.

17th *Blank*

18th The 1st Battalion are invited to dine with the 3rd today.

19th I dined with the 3rd Battalion at Espeja yesterday and returned home today, a fine day.

20th Fine.

21st Windy but warm.

22nd The Spaniards have levied a contribution on this place. A fresh supply of bullocks has arrived to our division, they are Portuguese bullocks and are much finer bullocks than we in general have. The usual weight of bullocks is 350lbs. the commissary has signed for a lot at 500lbs, one was killed today that weighed upwards of 800lbs.

23rd Rain.

24th Rain. The 40th Regiment & 6th Cacadores have been engaged with the enemy near Coria. Our battalion are invited to dine with the hussars today, I do not intend to go.

25th Rode to Freineda today, it is a very fine day. I saw Lord Wellington's stud, they are in fine order, he has 13 saddle horses, it is a dirty village. Came home through Fuentes d'Onoro, no troops there.

26th The 3rd Battalion dined with us today, fine day.

27th Ditto. We have made a racket court here against the church.

28th We are invited to dine with the 2nd Battalion at El Bodon today. Fine day. It is said that the 4th Division have come from their cantonment on the Douro to this side of the Coa.

March
1st Returned from El Bodon today, a fine day.

71

2nd   Fine, but not quite so hot. It is said that Soult & 10 men per company have gone to France[16]. The carnival which began on the 28th ended today, the women claim the command while it lasts.

3rd   Fine weather, rather windy.

4th   Fine weather & windy.

5th   Fine weather but very windy.

6th   Same weather.

7th   The *Raising of the Wind*[17] & *Fortunes Frolic*[18] were performed last night & very well done.

8th – 9th *Blank*

10th   The soldiers perform *The Brothers*[19] & *The Poor Soldier*[20] tonight.

11th   I was not at the soldier's play last night but understand it was very well done. Layton goes to England the day after tomorrow, I have bought a pony from him for which I gave a bill for £13 15s.

12th   The 43rd dine with us today.

13th   There is a Grand Fete today at Rodrigo for the installation of General Cole as Knight of the Bath.[21]

14th   Cox who had been sent on command to Celorico returned today & Johnston with him.

15th   Not quite so windy.

16th   Mild day.

17th   Mild day.

18th   Same weather.

19th   Cloudy warm day with a few drops of rain, I wish much it may rain to bring on the grass. It is said the French are advancing.

20th   Cloudy & looks like as if it would soon rain. The horse artillery and General Alten and staff dine with us today and the British officers of the 17th Portuguese Regiment who have come to this brigade instead of the 20th. Colonel Barnard went to Espeja yesterday to resume the command of the 3rd Battalion. General Kempt[22] was expected at Gallegos last night to take command of the 1st Brigade, Colonel Beckwith having been appointed on the staff in America. A mail arrived the night before last.

21st   Fine warm day, it appears from the English papers that Joseph Bonaparte[23] has gone from Valladolid to Madrid, Suchet[24] is in Valencia & Soult[25] in Toledo.

22nd It rained this morning until about 9 o'clock, the rest of the day cloudy and windy.

23rd Very windy, but not cloudy, saw the first swallow today & have seen this year.

24th   Fine clear day, rather windy.

25th   Fine warm day, bathed for the first time this year. [section in code]

26th   Windy day & rather cloudy.

27th   It appears by the Lisbon Gazette of 22nd of this month, that Sir J. Murray[26] has landed at Alicante to take command of the Anglo-Sicilian Army. By the same gazette there is a Portuguese lottery advertised. Spanish gazettes, copied in the above, state confidently that Soult has gone to France and taken some proportion of the army with him. English papers also say that Caffarelli[27] has gone, the Army of Portugal it appears, is commanded by Count d'Erlon[28] so that Count Souham[29] who came from France to take command of that army and who wrote such a flaming dispatch of the retreat of the British Army from Burgos must have taken his departure also. Today a cloudy day with high cold winds and sleet.

28th   Windy but not cold.

29th   Fine warm days, we were inspected by our new brigadier, General Kempt. The men were in very high order, the 6 companies had on parade 505 rank & file, besides sergeants & buglers.

30th Fine day.

31st Very warm. A packet arrived last night. Towards afternoon it rained a little.

April
1st Fine day.

2nd Windy & cloudy, sleet.

3rd Fine day, 2nd Battalion dined with us today. Packet from England. General Kempt also dined with us.

4th Windy day. As there is a talk of a part of the regiment being detached to Castillejo de dos Casas, I walked there today, I think we shall be very very comfortable.

5th Fine day.

6th The regiment is invited to dine with the 43rd today. I do not go.

7th Fine day. I sold my long bat & forage to Mckenzie[30] for £6.

8th We had a brigade field day this day on the plain between this & Espeja, the movements were done very badly indeed.

9th Fine day. I rode to Almeida today. The dinner hour is altered to four o'clock and we have an evening parade at 6.

10th It is at last settled that our company & Smith's go to Castillejos. Showery today.

11th Showery with sunshine.

12th Same weather.

13th Ditto ditto. I understand there is to be no detachment of companies from this place.

14th Rode to Freineda today. Saw a peasant in the village of Almeida today sewing lint.

15th The theatricals of the division performed at Gallegos this evening, *She Stoops to Conquer* and *The Apprentice*[31], Lord Wellington was there. Rained at intervals today.

16th Such officers as chose to send may get them full rations of corn about seven leagues from here, they go tomorrow.

17th No rain. It is in order for the two right companies to go to Castillejo de dos Casas on Monday after the field day which will be on that day. We began collecting green forage by a General Order yesterday.

      The horse artillery moved some days ago from Aldea del Obispo to make room for General Castanos[32] & staff.

18th We walked over today and divided the town of Castillejo. No rain.

19th After the brigade field day on Espeja plain our two companies marched & occupied Castillejo. We are to meet half way to parade. No rain.

20th I have a good quarter, Stewart[33] is doubled up with me, we have good forage here.

21st Met the four companies half way to parade this morning and had a march beyond Aldea del Obispo.

22nd The regimental mess breaks up today.

23rd Paraded half way this morning again. The Spaniards complain greatly of want of rain.

24th Paraded half way this morning for muster. Stewart mustered the regiment today, McKenzie has been appointed paymaster of the depot.

25th Met half way to parade and had a march to Aldea del Obispo. I rode to Almeida today & saw that the lint which I saw sown on the 14th has sprung up.

26th A windy day with sleet.

27th Very windy & rainy.

28th Same weather. I saw a peasant the other day at Almeida ploughing. I asked him the price of the field he was ploughing, he said he did not know but pointing to the next, said that was worth 35 dollars. I paced it and it was 26 paces long & 7 ditto broad. The peasantry about the frontiers here now [are] very active, they are ploughing all their land. There is a great deal of land ploughed up now that has not been cultivated since the first invasion of the country by the French.

29th Rainy today but not so cold.

30th Fine day with very little rain.

May
1st Very rainy.

2nd Same weather. Rode to Almeida, on my return met 3 wagons of the Waggon Train who were going to Almeida to be attached to our division.

3rd Showery and sunshine.

4th Fine day, no rain.

5th Mckenzie cashed me a bill for £25, I paid 6 shillings and 1 penny a dollar.

6th Fine day. There was a brigade field day ordered today on Espeja plain. We marched to the ground and were sent home again, General Kempt having fallen from his horse the other day.

7th Very rainy. Rode as far as Fort Concepcion on my way to Almeida, the rain coming on very heavy, took shelter in the fort until it was over and then returned home.

8th Went to Fort Concepcion today with my gun, there are in the main body of the work 52 embrasures. There is one gate with a draw bridge on the side of the work that looks toward Aldea del Obispo and in the centre of the 3 curtains are passages into the ditch from which there are many sally ports out into the country and in each angle of the curtain a passage up to the ramparts. In the ditch opposite each curtain is a work, all of which are so completely destroyed that it is impossible to ascertain their exact form, but they appear to have six embrasures each, the gateway leads through one of them. The circular outwork outside the ditch appears to have had 10 embrasures, one half of it is completely destroyed. The outer work of all is so completely destroyed that it is impossible to form an idea of what it was.

Today is a fair day at Almeida as is the 8th of every month. There are an immense number of hawks in Fort Concepcion, one of which I shot. Showery today.

9th   Went to Almeida today, rode round the outside of the works of the town, it has six bastions in front of each curtain. In the ditch is a work, one of them is what I have often thought would be useful, viz a double work or one within another. Showery.

10th There was a brigade field day this day on Espeja plain. Lord Wellington I understand reviews the Blues[34] tomorrow near Sabugal. A fine day without rain.

11th A fine hot day. Went out to day to try and shoot some quail which are very abundant here, could not get them to rise. I shot a half grown hare.

12th Rode today down to the bridge of the Coa where Craufurd's fight took place[35]. The ground is amazingly rocky and uneven. The bridge has three arches, one of which has been destroyed by the French and repaired with wood. Came home through Almeida, a fine day.

13th Went out quail shooting today, Killed a brace & missed a good many more. Showery.

The 52nd Regiment had moved from Guinaldo to [La] Albergueria [de Arganan] to make room for some Spanish troops but have marched back again. General Alten had the mounted officers of the division at points today.

14th Rainy day.

15th   Went to Vale da Mula to cut forage, a Portuguese sentry there said it was the Governor of Almeida's order that [it] be cut there. Showery day.

16th   Fine hot day.

Chapter 9

The Great Advance

The improvement in the weather and the beginning of the season for cutting forage indicated that it was time for the army to march. Despite the dreadful retreat that ended the 1812 campaign, hopes were extremely high in the allied ranks that the French could be expelled from Spain in the next campaign. The French losses in Russia and the subsequent depletion of the French armies in Spain gave the allies great confidence. The French planned to concentrate their forces along the river lines, forcing Wellington to sustain heavy losses crossing them. With this in mind, their initial operations were centred around Salamanca to defend the expansive River Tormes.

But Wellington had other ideas. Whilst Lord Hill's force, including the Light Division, accompanied in person by Wellington distracted the French from the main attack, by manoeuvring in their direction. The bulk of Wellington's army, led by Sir Thomas Graham, struck north east and succeeded in turning the flank of the French defensive positions and forcing them to abandon their prepared positions. Now that the plan was fully operational, Wellington joined Graham's force and Hill subsequently joined with his corps, reuniting the entire army. The French continued to retire until they arrived at the valley which holds the city of Vitoria where King Joseph finally ordered his forces to halt and form, to repulse the allied advance. The great battle everyone had expected had finally arrived.

17th   Lord Wellington reviewed the division this day on the Espeja plain, and was I understand very much pleased with them. The 1st Hussars were with us also, there are now 492 effective. The 4th Division it is said, moves tomorrow. We received pay this day up to January 24th.

18th The Spaniards say that General Castanos moves from Aldea del Obispo for Rodrigo tomorrow. The weather appears now to be settled. We have begun to cut barley for forage.

19th *Blank*

20th We are to commence marching tomorrow, we march I understand to Saelices el Chico. I am very glad we are going to move, for I am tired of this idle life.

21st We broke up from our cantonments, the 2nd Brigade broke up yesterday, and bivouacked last night near Carpio. The 1st Brigade marched this morning independently by regiments and forded the Agueda at Molinos des Flores[1]. We went the wrong road and passed near Saelices el Chico, bivouacked in a wood about 1 mile from the Agueda, the whole division together. Very good forage.

Colonel Barnard who has exchanged with Colonel Beckwith took command of the regiment today. I picked up my old servant Clements[2] on the road today and took him on the staff once more.

The country about the ground where we bivouacked is very beautiful. General Graham with all the divisions of the army except the 2nd & ours are moving on the other bank of the Douro; Lord Wellington is to be with these two divisions that move on Salamanca.

22nd Marched at day break to the [Castillejo de] Yeltes, when we arrived there we were told that 300 French cavalry who were in the village of St Martin del Rio [Martin de Yeltes?] about 2 miles on and were driving off cattle, the hussars (who with the 14th passed us today) went on, our battalion went on about 1 mile, halted here and then returned and bivouacked near the river. Very pretty country, we had no corn but very good grass.

23rd The division marched left in front at daybreak this morning, passed through St Martin del Rio, and Boadilla and bivouacked on the left bank of the Huebra, on the same ground on which we encamped on the night of the 17th November last, after the French had driven us across the river. We were about 2 miles from the village of San Munoz the Blues and Life Guards bivouack near us, their horses are in good condition.

There are attached to the division now 13 mules laden with

entrenching tools, several engineer artificers, an engineer officer, some sappers & miners.

I walked into the village of San Munoz today, it has been a good village but is terribly destroyed, the staff of the division are in there.

24th   Halted here all day, mustered by the paymaster, General Hill's Division are I understand about 3 miles to our right. Headquarters at Tamames. We are not far from Castillejo de Huebra [Cuarto del Pilar?], the place Leach & I dined at on the 22nd June last on our way up to Salamanca.

25th   Marched this morning about ¼ before 4 o'clock right in front, through Aldehuela [de la Boveda] (near Castro [Enriquez] the village Leach & I had slept at on the 23rd June last) to a wood about a mile beyond the village of Robliza [de Cojos] where we halted and bivouacked. Head quarters at Matilla [de los Canos del Rio].

As Hill's troops approached Salamanca, the French defenders retired north eastward towards Toro, Hill followed.

26th   Marched at the usual hour, left in front, through Calzada de Don Diego to the bank of the rivulet of Val de Munoz, near which we bivouacked. The French had picquets on the ground on which we halted of cavalry this morning, which retired into Salamanca (about a league off) on the appearance of our cavalry. The cavalry followed them down to the bridge which the French blockaded. About 3 hours after we halted on this ground we were ordered to fall in and march to a ford which we did and bivouacked on the left bank of the Tormes opposite the same ford which I crossed on the 24th June last. The cavalry crossed the river and the French left Salamanca, a Spaniard told me that the French had 4,000 men & that they have retired on the Toro road.

27th   Halted all day opposite the ford which is called the Vado (ford) de Canto [El Canto?]. I rode into Salamanca where I heard the following news, the French not 5,000, principally infantry, retired from the town when the cavalry crossed the river. The 1st [German] Hussars & 14th Light Dragoons with some light artillery followed them, when they came up with them the infantry formed squares. The guns came close up to them and did great execution, there were killed, wounded & taken prisoners about 300 men. I have since heard more.

I fell in with a Spanish woman who is better informed and gave me more information than I ever found or expected from a Spanish woman. She says that the general who commanded these men who were here yesterday was *Maucune*[3]. That the French officers talking of the British said that they were good soldiers & fought well, but that if they lost 20 thousand men they could not replace, with them it was different. They also said that if the British were not in the country 8,000 men could take possession of the whole of Spain. I asked her if she believed it, she said she did; the Spanish soldiers were brave, but their officers were worth nothing.

She said also that the French told her that they had orders from the Emperor to retire behind the Ebro without fighting if they could help it and there wait the result of the campaign with the Russians. They assured her also that they would be in Salamanca again in 3 months. She says also that Soult has not left Spain.

Another sensible remark she made was that in the British army there was but one commander, the Lord Wellington, with the French every general had his own army.

The French did not plunder the town when they left it, but levied 5,000 rations. The town is much improved since we left it in November last, it is cleaner, the markets & shops are better supplied.

Head quarters are here, I saw Lord Wellington in the cathedral in which there was a *Te Deum* performing, he had a grey frock coat on with his *sword & sash*.

I cannot conceive why General Maucune remained so long here, he lost between 3 & 400 men without gaining any object whatever, his men were all drunk, officers & all.

28th Marched at the usual hour left in front to the village of Aldeanueva de Figeuroa (about 4½ leagues from Salamanca on the Toro road) and bivouacked on the outside of that village. Crossed the Tormes by the ford in our front. Lord Wellington leaves this part of the army unaccompanied by his staff except Colonel Campbell and an aide de camp and rides in one day 14 leagues to join General Graham's army. Towards evening it began to rain very hard, the Portuguese having no tents, the 17th Portuguese Regiment was ordered into the village, but there being the small pox in it, our battalion were ordered to give up their tents to them and go into the town, which they did[4]. I preferred remaining in camp as did most of the officers.

29th   A fine day and not hot, halted all day. Went out shooting today, it is a beautiful sporting country in appearance, bagged a brace of partridge which was all I fired at. General Hill's Corps (for he now no longer commands the 2nd Division only, but there are some Portuguese brigades attached to that division which form a corps of which he has the command. General Stewart commands the 2nd Division) is about 2½ miles on our right.

It is said we do not move from here for a day or two yet. Lord Wellington's baggage & part of his staff are here.

30th   Fine day. Halted all day. There are some French on this side of the Douro at La Nava del Rey and their cavalry at Alaejos one league on this side of it.

I rode this evening to Parada de Rubiales, the village our division bivouacked near on the 29th June last. I saw a peasant in this place who left Parada la Nava del Rey on account of the French who came there on Thursday.

Canizal (the position we retired to on the 18th July last when driven from Castrejon) is only 1 league from here, saw Hill's encampment, his head quarters are at [La] Orbada, I understand that it was General Villatte[5] who commands the troops at Salamanca the other day and that his dispatch has been intercepted, he magnifies our numbers and the valour of his troops in usual French style.

We have a supporting battalion to the picquets every night.

31st   There came an order last night for the division to get under arms ¼ before 3 o'clock this morning, we accordingly formed contiguous close columns of battalions 100 yards in front of the village and at sunrise marched home. General Alten has today received intelligence that the enemy have retired across the Douro to Tordesillas. Rode to a hill in front, from which I saw Toro. We have scarcely any cavalry with us, Victor Alten's Brigade[6] are watching some ford on the Douro and the greater part of those attached to Hill are at Alba de Tormes, the Household Brigade are still at Salamanca as also a Portuguese Brigade of infantry belonging to Hill's Corps.

The order for turning out the division tomorrow morning was given this evening and afterwards countermanded.

June

1st   Our company went on picquet this morning at about ½ past 2 o'clock on the road to Fuentesauco. Rained hard at night and very cold. Head quarters baggage left this today.

2nd   The division marched this morning at 4 o'clock through Fuentesauco & [La] Boveda de Toro to a pine wood about 5½ leagues from Aldeanueva [de Figueroa] & about 2 from Toro, arrived there at about 12, halted for 2 hours and ½ and cooked, moved on then towards Toro, bivouacked opposite to it on the left bank of the river.

        Hill does not move today. The French, principally cavalry, retired from Toro this morning and destroyed the bridge. General Graham crossed the Esla yesterday with the loss of 12 men drowned. The 10th Hussars came up with the enemy's cavalry after they had left Toro, charged them and made 206 prisoners with a very trifling loss on their part[7]. Lord March[8](as we were coming into our bivouack) was riding to General Hill with orders. I do not think this road so highly cultivated as the road by which we went up to the Douro last year. But I have remarked in this country, wherever there is corn it is very fine and very few instances of *blight*.

3rd   The division moved right in front and got over the Douro with great difficulty; the enemy having completely destroyed two arches of the bridge, while the division was halted on the bank of the river after getting over I rode into the town and went into the castle when I saw the prisoners taken yesterday by the 10th. They were fine looking men and some few of them very much cut about the head. But their horses, at least those that I saw, more miserable than I could have imagined.

        After the brigade got over we moved to Tagarabuena about 1 mile from Toro. Walked into Toro after breakfast. There had been brought in since morning a picquet of 50 cavalry and 2 officers who were taken by Don Julian Sanchez, they had two guns. I went to the castle and saw them, there was one poor fellow run through his body with a pike, I saw the wound dressed, he bore it very patiently.

        Toro is a good town, but the dullest for its size I ever saw in Spain. Hill is moving here, we have parties from our division working to rejoin the bridge.

4th   The division marched this morning at the usual hour through Casasola [de Arion], Villabarba & La Mota de Toro [Mota de Marques], & another village (San Cebrian [de Mazote]) to a small oak wood near the Convent of Espina [La Santa Espina] which has once been a fine building about 7 leagues from Toro. Passed the 4th Division near Villabarba & the 3rd near [Castillo de] La Mota.

5th   Marched this morning at 5 o'clock to Castromonte where we halted for about half an hour, then moved on to La Mudarra, near which we bivouacked. It is about 1 & ½ leagues from our last night's encampment and 4 leagues from Valladolid. The Commissariat stores are not well up. It rained this evening, there are supporting battalions to the picquet every night.

6th   Fine day. Received orders to march to Ampudia 4 leagues & there wait for orders. Marched by the outside Villalba de los Alcores (into which I rode, it is an old Moorish walled town with a castle, it looks well outside, but is very poor inside. I did not see one very good looking house) and through a small village called Valoria [del Alcor], to Ampudia, near which we bivouacked. The country for the most part level & uncultivated though very good looking ground and rather woody near Ampudia to our left, it falls into an immense plain appreciably well cultivated and full of towns. Ampudia is such another Moorish town as Villalba, good looking at a distance, and very poor inside. The houses hereabouts are all built of mud and not whitewashed and look very shabby. There is a castle here also, through which I went, it has a very ancient appearance and is in most excellent repair considering all things.

    I saw a captain of the 4th Chasseurs, a Swiss, who deserted from the French 8 days ago and came in today. He says that Marshal Jourdan[9] commands in chief; Soult[10] he says, has gone to France for disobeying King Joseph in disgrace, and their orders are to go behind the Ebro.

    The 4th Division are here bivouacked on our left; head quarters of the army in the town. There are two encampments on our left, about a league & half, one near a village called Villerias [de Campos], which must be General Graham's column. The 3rd Division are not here, but at Valoria. The 6th & 7th Divisions with General V. Alten's Brigade are moving on a road on our right under the command of the Earl of Dalhousie.[11]

85

There are a great many old Moorish fortifications hereabouts, one, a castle about 2 miles from us to the left, situated on a hill called the Castle of Torremormojon, with a village below it of the same name. We are badly off for wood here, we are now on the main road to Palencia and 4 leagues from it. The leagues in this part of the country are not long. Very rainy night.

7th   Marched this morning at 5 o'clock near Autilla [del Pino] and another village to Palencia 3 & ½ leagues. The order of march was on this road by which we are advancing as follows.

D'Urban's Portuguese Brigade of cavalry, Ponsonby's Brigade, Hussar Brigade, Light Division, 4th Division, Reserve of Artillery, Household Brigade of Cavalry, 3rd Division. We marched through Palencia & encamped close to it. King Joseph reviewed the troops on the ground on which we encamped yesterday morning and set off immediately after the review, the last of them left this morning, at 7 o'clock. Palencia is a city & capital of a province of that name in the Kingdom of Leon; it is a very ancient looking place and has been a Moorish fortress, it has an old wall round it, entire in most places.

Even for a Spanish city its interior is not good, although superior to Toro, the approaches to it are very beautiful, it is situated on the left bank of the Carrion over which at the town are two bridges. About a mile from the town on the side by which we entered is a canal called Canal de Castilla with a lock where the road crosses it. It has a cathedral which I was in, it is very handsome and elegant but not magnificent. The inhabitants say there is a bishop's palace and 6 convents. It is the dirtiest Spanish city I ever was in. The inhabitants were very much astonished at our tents, they say they never saw them before and peeped with curiosity into every one.

It rained today and was cold and cloudy. I saw John[12] of General Graham's Staff in Palencia who said he was coming into the town. I understand all the British divisions of the army are hereabouts this night. The country through which we passed until we descended into the plain in which Palencia is situated is totally uncultivated and apparently very bad stony soil. Palencia is situated in a fertile and cultivated flat with heights on both sides. The people are civil and appeared glad to see us.

8th   Marched this morning at 5 o'clock through Fuentes de Valdepero (a village with a Moorish castle in high apparent preservation.

The French cavalry were here yesterday when ours arrived here). Monzon [de Campos] a village with a castle on a hill above it, Amusco another Moorish village. To Tamara [de Campos] another old fortress near which we bivouacked. A good looking village called Pina [de Campos] about 2 miles to our left. The country pretty well cultivated through which we passed. Rained very hard and incessantly all night.

9th   Moved at about 6 o'clock to a rather drier ground near Pina. The Portuguese regiments (who have no tents) into Pina. I saw some of the British Hussar Brigade at Tamara as we came by. Showery all day, fine night.

10th   Marched at 4 o'clock left in front as usual, through Fromista and Requena [de Campos] to Lantadilla, the division bivouacked outside of the town as also the 4th Division, but the weather threatening rain, our company and the 3rd Battalion were sent into quarters in the village in order to give up our tents to other companies. The public mules which used to carry camp kettles for the men, now carry three tents each per company. We passed the Canal de Castilla twice, once near Fromista near a lock and again after having passed Requena. The roads were very bad, the 6th & 7th Divisions are encamped near Tamara; General Hill was at Torquemada yesterday.

There was a report yesterday that we were to march upon Reinosa which is just at the source of the Ebro and by that means, turn the line of the river and we have been marching direct upon it ever since leaving Palencia, but we left that road to our left when we came to Requena today and are now moving on Burgos.

We have papers up to the 18th containing the official dispatch concerning Sir J. Murray's fight with Suchet. The inhabitants of this part of Spain are uglier, dirtier and worse dressed than on the frontiers or indeed any part of the country I have been in. They are [sic] exactly resemble the Portuguese, both in dress & appearance. The villages are also of the worst description I have seen in Spain. This place is on the right bank of the Pisuerga, over which is a bridge of 7 arches. The country through which we are marching is an extensive flat plain, full of dykes.

11th   Marched through Arenillas [de Riopisuerga] to Villasandino situated on the right bank of the Rio Odra, over which is a bridge of 10 arches. There are an immense quantity of pigeons here. I found a wild duck's nest in the middle of a barley field. We have been moving ever since leaving Palencia in a low open country, in general very well cultivated and full of drains.

12th Marched at the usual hour, left in front, crossed a ridge or sierra which terminates the plain in this direction. Just over the ridge is the village of Castrillo de Murcia and between this and another ridge, is a beautiful little valley. The Brigade of General V. Alten was waiting in this valley for us, moved across the valley and marched up a ravine in the opposite ridge in which we passed through the villages of Villandiego & Yudego. From some heights above Yudego I got the 1st view of Burgos, marched a little further and then halted for some hours, during which time the cavalry were skirmishing in front. Marched on at last through the village of Isar, in another valley to a plain (from which we had a better view of Burgos. It appears a very good looking place, the castle is on a very commanding situation on a hill, the town appears to be built round the base of the hill). Just as we came on the plain, a heavy cannonading commence[d] about a league in our front, remained here on the plain for about 3 hours, during which time the cannonading continued, the cause of which was a body of the enemies [sic] infantry who had been surprised by our cavalry, retiring in squares to cross a bridge between them and Burgos. A division of infantry were moving on to the front just as we arrived on the plain, but could not be brought up in time, so that the enemy got over the bridge. I understand that if our division had been marched on at once to the bridge that must all have been taken prisoners. It rained hard all this time. We moved in the evening back to the village of Hornillos del Camino and encamped outside of it; it is situated in the same valley as Isar.

After the debacle of the previous year, no one was looking forward to besieging Burgos castle again. But to everyone's surprise the French set off a huge mine underneath the walls, reducing much of the castle to rubble and raining huge chunks of masonry on the city below and the French troops as they marched away. For the British troops, there was no better sight.

13th We heard an explosion this morning at about 6 o'clock and as it has been reported among the peasantry that Burgos would be blown up, I hope it is done. Received orders to be ready to march at 8 but not to pack baggage or fall in till ordered. Marched at about 9 a mile in front of the village and halted. Lord Wellington came in from the front, Burgos is entirely destroyed by the explosion heard this morning. Marched through Isar & Villanueva de Argano to Tobar, about 4 leagues, the whole road through the above mentioned valley. I was told today by one of the German Hussars that the business of yesterday was on the part of the enemy. The[re] was a complete scene of confusion that Lord Wellington [who] was making a reconnaissance & stumbled on them unexpectedly & that he says himself if he had brought us down to the bridge they must all have been taken. Graham has been all this time moving direct on the Ebro.

14th Marched this morning (after having been delayed a long time by Ponsonby's Brigade of cavalry) right in front. Got out of the valley, at the commencement of the march into the most miserable a country I have seen in Spain, rocky, hilly and entirely uncultivated, passed the villages of Ruyales de Paramo, Huermeces & Quintanilla Sobresierra, to a wood near Quintanapalla, a very long march, the morning was bitter cold, and the day very hot.

15th Marched at the usual hour, left in front, through the same miserable barren country & crossed the Ebro at Puente Arenas near which we bivouacked. The bed of the river is very far below the level of the country through which we have been marching, consequently the pass down to the river is very steep, it is the most formidable (with the exception of Barba del Puerco) I ever saw. The valley through which the river runs, which opens to the view in descending the pass now was the most beautiful I ever saw. It is abundantly plentiful in fruit, corn, vegetables & everything & is such a contrast to the barren mountains & precipice which surround it, for there are most terrible heights on both banks of the river, that it is the most heavenly spot I ever saw. There is a great quantity of fresh butter selling hereabouts, every species of provision is very cheap here, our mess bough[t] 7 loaves of bread for 4 vintems & 3 Quartos each. An officer of the 2nd Battalion told me he bought 3 sheep & a 4 pound loaf of bread for 2 dollars.

16th Marched this morning at ½ past 3 o'clock right in front, left of battalion leading through Bisjueces & Aldea de Medina to the neighbourhood of Medina [de Pomar] where we encamped on the left bank of the River Nela. Crossed another river, the Trueba before coming to Medina by a bridge of old appearance with a gateway at each end. The pass up the heights on this bank of the river is most beautifully grand, it runs for some way along the bank of the river, the mountains through which it winds are thickly wooded and every hundred yards presents a fresh view of the most majestic nature. On ascending a fine little valley opened to view in which the 5th Division were encamped and finally on reaching the top a beautifully rich & extensive plain is seen, surrounded by mountains & plentifully wooded. In this valley is situated Medina, the fields in this valley are surrounded by hedges and ditches & it more resembles England than any part of Spain I ever saw. But the best ensemble of the scene that surpasses any part of England I know, is this valley being surrounded by beautiful mountains. There is near Medina a large convent called Santa Clara. There is a bridge of 6 arches over the Nela.

17th Marched left in front at 6 o'clock this morning through La Cerca to the neighbourhood of Rio de Losa & encamped in heights above it. The country through which we passed very mountainous and at the same time exceedingly beautiful, particularly the latter part, the mountains in this part of the country are all plentifully wooded and the vallies [sic] richly cultivated. Towards the latter end of the march there was a great deal of pine wood among the mountains and what I never observed in Spain before, fine beech trees. I also some [sic saw?] as fine English oaks as ever I saw in England.

Chapter 10

San Millan

As Wellington's troops marched inexorably towards Vitoria, the French troops hastily retired. Occasionally units of each side literally bumped into each other as their paths criss-crossed through the hills. One such incident centred around the village of San Millan. Here the lead brigade of Maucune's division was discovered resting and was instantly attacked very ferociously by Vandeleur's Brigade. As the French were reeling under the close pursuit of the 52nd Foot, the second brigade accidentally emerged from a narrow defile in rear of the 52nd but was quickly forced to retire by the 95th who were following up.

The 52nd now turned round and charged back whilst the 95th continued to press on their rear. Maucune's 2nd Brigade finding itself assailed from both front and rear, broke and fled into the surrounding hills. This tactic worked, indeed all but about 300 Frenchmen escaped capture and the 2nd Brigade reformed when the men met Reille's troops in a neighbouring valley.

18th   Received orders to march this morning at 4 o'clock with a squadron & an half of hussars in front of the 1st Battalion 95th Regiment which is to form the advanced guard. The 1st Battalion is to be, I hear, at Villanueva [de Valdegovia], one league in front of the rest of the division which is to be at San Millan [de Zadornil]. We are to take with us our mule & the tent mule for a company, the rest is to be left at San Millan. Marched accordingly through El Boveda and nearby Tobillas (the country hereabouts is still more beautiful than anything I have hitherto seen. I can scarcely conceive a landscape more heavenly than that in which Tobillas is situated. It puts me in mind, even the village itself, of pictures of Italian scenery).

On coming near San Millan we halted and soon after heard

shots firing, and soon after several hussars came in with some of the 3rd French Hussars prisoners, there were several wounded on both sides.[1] Soon after [we] understood that there were two regiments of cavalry & some infantry in San Millan, our battalion was ordered to go on, supported by the 3rd and attack them if these regiments proved to be part of a division of 2 brigades (Maucune our Salamanca & Burgos friend) & these regiments in the village were the head of the division, consequently the other brigades were (as their line of march joined ours at St Millan) in our rear. St Millan is in a valley or ravine through which a small river, the Omecillo, the road runs along the valley through Gurendes & Villanueva.

According to the orders we received part of the regiments moved down direct on the village in skirmishing order, while the rest moved along the hills at the foot of which winds the road, to turn the village and at the same time command their flank as the[y] retired along the road. This movement made them quit the village and they retired as fast as they could go through the above villages (& we after them still keeping [to] the heights as far as Villanueva where we were ordered to halt) leaving the other brigade to shift for themselves, which brigade we saw a league in our rear just as we formed up & all the rest of the division were on the road to cut off their retreat, they seeing this, fled away into the mountains on their right, leaving all their baggage which fell into our hands. General Pignolé who commanded the brigade we attacked & his aide de camp are killed, the number of killed, wounded & prisoners I do not know. We have not lost many, we have only one officer wounded & he is the only one in the division. Our battalion as I said above, formed up in rear of Villanueva & our company was sent on there as a picquet to look out. We saw the enemy formed up on a field by the road side at 2 miles in our front & while we were there we saw them attacked[2] & retire shortly after we moved on & then returned again to Villanueva where the division encamped. Rained a little.

19th Marched this morning left in front through Villanane, Villamaderne, Tuesta (from which we saw on our right Espejo a good looking village) & Salinas de Anana [or Anana Gesaltza] a good village where there are an impressive number of *salt pans*. (The houses in these villages are of a better appearance than any village houses I have seen in Spain, they are generally built 3 or 4 stories high). About 2 miles after passing through the last village we halted for some time, soon after moved on a little, the 4th Division were all this time engaged at a pass near, some of the cacadores of our division were sent up a mountain above it & killed a great number. Encamped on this ground, very rainy.

20th Halted here all day, our company was sent to the front on picquet. The place we are in now is a valley, we are encamped at one side, close at the foot of a ridge of very high mountains, the 2nd Battalion & 1st cacadores are on the top of the mountain & to the left of the rest of the division. I rode up to their encampment today, the view from it is most beautiful, the ascent of the mountain is steep on this side but on the other side it is quite perpendicular & between it & another ridge is a narrow valley with a small river running through it. In this valley are the 4th Division encamped and through this valley the enemy retreated yesterday when the 4th Division forced the pass. About a league & ½ in front I saw Vitoria & on this side of it the enemy encamped. The view from this is very extensive, the country hereabouts it, as all this side of the Ebro is beautiful & abundant.

Here, on the very eve of the Battle of Vitoria, the journal unfortunately ceases for some months and his actions in the great battle are completely lost[3]. The Battle of Vitoria occurred the very next day 21st June 1813 and the 95th played a significant part in it. The 1st Battalion led the column leaving the village of Puebla on its right and the division formed near the River Zadorra in the centre of Wellington's battle line. As soon as Lord Hill's troops advanced, thus opening the battle on the right wing of Wellington's army, the Light Division moved forward also. By moving along the river a little to its left the Bridge of Tres Puentes was discovered to be fully intact and unoccupied by any French force. The Light Division crossed the river here and surreptitiously formed up on the enemy bank. When the Third Division then sought to storm a bridge a little way to its left, the Light Division advanced rapidly to support this movement and successfully opened up the way for them by driving the French skirmishers back.

The division now came under heavy fire from French artillery placed on the heights of Arinez, but its rapid advance across the plain caused the French to retire with haste. Soon the French army was in complete rout and the division drove those in front of them past the city of Vitoria. But here it ran into the huge mass of wagons of the French train, coupled with an enormous variety of vehicles being employed to transport the treasure and other valuable goods stolen from across

Spain by the French army. Although the officers attempted to maintain discipline within the division, large numbers managed to fall out of the columns to plunder these abandoned wagons. Although efforts were made to prevent such acts by the provost, many soldiers made a fortune that night. Private Costello captured a large sack of gold coins and a mule to carry it, he had at least £500 in coin, much of which he deposited to the trust of his quartermaster. Others sought out foodstuffs and wines and others fine clothing, furniture or paintings; indeed the camp fires that night were a scene of great revelry, with the men selling every treasure imaginable for a pittance, at a fraction of their real value.

But James was not a witness to these revelries as he lay out on the plain having been struck by a musket ball presumably near the village of Arinez, which severely wounded him in his arm. The following day he would have been picked up by a wagon and transported to a hospital hastily set up in a converted church or convent. However, the wound was not serious enough to be considered necessary for an amputation, which probably means that the musket ball went through the muscle and missed the bone entirely.

Wellington's army was encamped along the Spanish fringes of the Pyrenees whilst the last two remaining vestiges of French troops in Spain were dealt with. The garrison of Pamplona was blockaded by the Spanish, whilst San Sebastian was subjected to a formal siege under General Sir Thomas Graham.

Most of the army believed that the French were now finished in Spain, however Marshal Soult had other ideas. Having hastily refitted his army, Soult launched an attack through the main valleys of the Pyrenees with the joint aim of defeating Wellington's isolated forces and relieving the garrison of Pamplona. His attack commencing on 25th July did initially catch Wellington's troops unprepared and despite a vigorous defence of their positions at Roncesvalles and Maya, they were pushed back by overwhelming numbers. This retreat continued until Wellington was able to pull his army together to stop the French advance at Sorauren where battle was joined on 28th and again on the 30th July, Soult's assaults were heavily defeated before the French retired in great haste.

The Light Division's part in these operations was limited. Having been based at Zubieta, the division performed a long forced march but only reached Sorauren on the 31st where it halted, being told to march back! After an incredible forced march back into the Pyrenees, the division did catch up with the French retreat and a thousand or so prisoners were taken, but the men were too exhausted to continue to follow the French and the rest escaped.

We do not know how long James' recuperation lasted before he was fit enough to rejoin his battalion in the Pyrenees. However it is certain that he was back with the battalion within a month, as he was present at Sorauren[4] and he also travelled to San Sebastian in late August to view the siege operations then underway to capture this strong fortress, and was present to witness its fall by storm on 31st August 1813.

Wellington's army was no longer threatened by the fortresses in their rear (Pamplona being now close to starvation and its surrender inevitable), now looked to enter France itself.

Chapter 11

Into France

Wellington's army crossed the Bidassoa River near the sea, which formed the French border at this point, whilst the Light Division passed near Vera on the upper Bidassoa and drove the French from a number of redoubts in the mountains including the capture of the Great Rhune. Here James' letters and diary resume abruptly as the advance over the Bidassoa was about to be launched.

To Miss Gairdner
Camp near Vera, 6 October 1813

My dear Laura,
I received your letter the other day for which many thanks. I am happy to hear that you have at last fixed upon an abode in Wales. I look forward to the pleasure of paying you a visit with much delight but when that will be is beyond the possibility of my calculation, my aunt said at the bottom of your letter that she would write in a few days, which letter I have been anxiously waiting for, there are however three packets from England here tomorrow for we have none later than the fifteenth and as it ought not to be longer than seven days passage to this part of the country we calculate on receiving a packet once a week, we shall I suppose have two or three in a lump one of these fine days. Your letter is I perceive dated from Ilfracombe, what brought you there? And why did you not stay at Clifton until the Welsh habitation was vacant and then make one march of it direct? We have been stationary in this position ever since the 2nd of August, and are all most heartily tired of it, for the forage is all eaten up and our animals are nearly starving, I took one trip to San Sebastian for three or four days and was lucky enough to be there when it was carried by storm and saw the whole business which was

very gallantly contested on both sides. There are as is usual in camps fifty very different reports every day concerning the probable movements of the army.

The prevailing report for the last month has been that we were to advance immediately into France, yet here we are still. The report today is that we shall attack in three days but I cannot conceive why we could not have done that just as well three weeks ago as three days hence or why if we are to advance, we have waited so long, for we have more men hereabouts (including Spaniards) than the enemy have. However time will show what is to be done. I sincerely wish we may attack them, or they attack us, anything by way of a change for I am heartily sick of seeing the same mountains and the same river day after day; for we cannot leave the camp with comfort for a long time for fear of anything being done whilst we are away. Besides the country is so mountainous hereabouts that as our horses have very little to eat we cannot attempt to ride them. James Walker, as you know, was wounded in one of the actions that took place in consequence of Soult's attempt to relieve Pamplona, he is at Vitoria, I had a letter from him two days ago, he has been very ill of a fever which he brought on himself in consequence of catching cold after he was wounded, but is now doing very well. Murray is quite well and is very fond of the army, my wound has healed up at last and the stiffness of the elbow is a little relaxed, I am in great hopes now that time will bring it entirely about and that it will be as well as ever. I was very sorry to see in the newspaper the death of Mrs Mallet, it must have caused very great affliction among the Gibbon family. Are the Gairdners still at Clifton and what are they about? How do the little Gairdner's get on, young what's his name, the eldest boy must be a good sized chap by this time, I must say Laura I think you are a very idle lazy set, you and the old lady and Miss Jane, (since she does not choose to acknowledge the other name), you write a letter of half a dozen lines once a year and think you have done wonders. I know that I am a very bad correspondent, but I have two excuses, which you have not, in the first place I am always almost on the move and in the next place there is nothing that happens here that is at all interesting to you, that you will not see in the papers long before my letters come to hand. Now any and everything that happens on the other side of the Bay of Biscay is interesting to a pack of poor devils shut up in the Pyrenees with nothing to vary the sameness of the day but military occurrences, and military conversation. As to the other two culprits they never make any attempt, I cannot believe that efforts and perseverance of our worthy friend Mr Pepys can have been so entirely thrown away that they cannot write a letter and if I am to judge by yours a very good one. As for Gordon you may tell him that if he does not commence at a very seasonable time I will give him a good licking the very first time we meet.

How does the music come on? You ought to be a capital performer and the other young ladies ought to be making good progress. My fluting has died away for want of practise. I lost my flute last campaign with the rest of my baggage, and have not played since, not having been able to get another. We have an excellent band in our battalion, I do not think there is a better in the service, they have a very good collection of Spanish music. When we come to England I will get you copies of the best of what they have. English music, especially what is new, is a rarity here, it is only from the bands of regiments lately come out that we hear it. I think after all I have heard no music equal in real harmony, no music which appeals so directly, so forcibly to heart, as the original simple Scottish airs. The Spanish music is however very pretty though there is no great variety in it, the patriotic and national songs are very good and very pleasing when sung by two females, for the Spaniards, as well as Portuguese and Germans have a natural taste for music which is not in the English, if two, four or any number of persons to beguile whatever work they may be about strike up a song, they divide themselves into first, second and even third and sing a treble, tenor and bass, as correctly as if it were composed for them. It is very beautiful to hear a whole troop of German dragoons on a night march, strike up with one accord, and instead of roaring away on one discordant key (as many Englishmen would do were they inclined to be musical) sing a regular first, second, and third to their national martial airs.

His letter was interrupted by the advance over the Bidassoa and resumes:

France 14 October 1813

What we have long wished for has at last taken place; on the morning of the 7th ultimo, our division with the Spaniards under Generals Giron and Longa[1] attacked the Pass of Vera, while the 1st and 5th Divisions of British, and the Galician army crossed the Bidassoa at its mouth and entered France on the enemy's right. The mountains we attacked over which is the Pass of Vera were the only part of the Pyrenees the enemy had still possession of. It is very strong and they had added to its natural strength by field works, but as we were superior in number we turned them out of their position with little loss. The principal sufferers were the Portuguese cacadores and our 2nd Battalion which has had three officers killed and five wounded. Two of those killed were very unfortunate, they were Lieutenants Campbell and Hill[2], fine young men, but a few [days] arrived from England, and this was the very first time they ever were in action. We are now encamped in France, on a height commanding a fine view of St Jean de Luz (and about 3 miles from that place) also a view of the sea and of the interior of France as far as the eye can search. It is a beautiful abundant country, and is a very agreeable change from the place we left in Spain for we have abundance of forage here of all kinds. I yesterday saw a beautiful sight. We observed a French brig come out of the River Adour and coast along towards St Jean de Luz. As soon as she was perceived by our cruisers she was chased. One of them came up with and brought her to action, as the wind blew off shore she could not get away, and after a short time returning the fire of the vessel that attacked her, her crew got into boats and after setting fire to her, left her, after burning a short time she blew up with a beautiful explosion, precisely at the same time the Spaniards on our right having pushed on too far in advance towards the French village of Sare were attacked, thus there was a land and sea fight at the same time. We have been on this ground now a week but expect every day to move on and drive the enemy beyond the Adour. We have papers up to the 28th yet I have received no letters these four last mails. Shocking idle people! Remember me to all my friends. Tell my aunt I expect soon to hear from her and believe me dear Laura, yours affectionately James P Gairdner.

15th October Major Watts has just sent me a *ham* from Passages a sea port about 4 leagues from this which is the only intimation (and that not a disagreeable one you may suppose) I have had of his arrival in this country.

JPG Nothing new.

The Journal now abruptly resumes:

Journal of November 1813 - July 1814[3]

November

19th Our post was relieved this morning by the right wing of the 43rd, we marched to our quarters[4] which are very good, our company and ourselves are in the same house but we are very well off.

There was an explosion heard last night or rather this morning at about 3 o'clock which is supposed to have been an attempt of the enemy to blow up the causeway of the house occupied today by the 3rd Division. The same rainy weather as usual. I was told by a woman in Bassussarry last night that her husband had just returned to the village and that he had been taken by Marshal [Blank – Soult?] (who was reconnoitring which caused all this skirmishing) as a guide.

20th   This is the first fine day we have had since the 12th. I was on forage duty.

21st   I went on command this morning with the bat men to Renteria [Errenteria] for corn for the regiment, went through St Jean de Luz (a very nice place, completely French, there are excellent inns, coffee houses and shops and some beautiful houses in it, the harbour appears to be very bad). Head quarters & 2 batteries of Guards are in St Jean de Luz. Urrugne, Irun & Oiartzun to Renteria where I arrived just before dark, Renteria is full of sick, I could not get a billet in the town, but got one a quarter of a league off, which was of no use to me, I was obliged [to] lay in a field with the bat men. The line of works that the enemy had from the sea (in front of St Jean de Luz) to the foot of La Rhune appears to be very strong and the works very well constructed.

22nd Got the corn after a great deal of trouble at about 10 o'clock today, set off at about 12, crossed the Bidassoa and halted for the night in a deserted house on this side of it.

23rd Returned to the cantonments of the regiment by the same road viz through Urrugne, St Jean de Luz &c. I found when I arrived at the cantonments that our division had this morning been engaged in driving back the enemy's picquets in order to take up a more secure line for our own. We have by this means thrown forward our left, the picquets are now in front of Bassussarry and the reserve of the picquets in it. There is a lake on our left in front of the 2nd Brigade picquets. In consequence of this move ours and the 3rd Battalion have been obliged to give up our good quarters and occupy some villainous houses in the neighbourhood of the Chateau d'Arcangues. The 43rd by going further than they ought to have done had a lieutenant killed & a captain taken prisoner.[5]

100

24th   I walked up to the picquets today, there is from one of the picquet houses a very good view of Bayonne, which is between two & three miles off. The town does not appear to be fortified except by field works at which the enemy are labouring very hard, there is a citadel on the other side of the river, regularly fortified with large barracks inside.

There has been a packet from England since I went away on command containing most glorious news from Germany.[6]

25th   *Blank*

26th   I had a letter today from an officer of the heavy dragoons, they are on the Ebro. Drew a bill for £50 today at 6 per dollar. We are fortifying the Chateau Bassussarry & the church where the 3rd Battalion was.

27th   Our battalion relieved the outpost of Bassussarry this morning, there is a better line of picquets than before but we are ridiculously close to each other. Our company on inlying picquet today. Showery.

28th   We relieved the right hand outlying picquet this morning. We have a vidette at this picquet which is alternately a man of the 18th Hussars & one of the German hussars. The French have a vidette within about 40 yards who is also a German and when our vidette is a German they generally converse together. Some officers came down to the picquet today & saluted us very politely. Rainy day, very bad night. We have made abattis[7] in front of our picquets.

29th   Relieved by the right wing of the 43rd Regiment this morning. Rainy.

30th November-2nd December. *Blank*

3rd   Went to Arbonne today on a board of survey.[8]

4th   Very ill last night.

5th   Not quite well yet.

6th   Fine day, went to St Jean de Luz, saw Colonel Barnard who was wounded very badly on the 10th & who is now nearly recovered.

101

There were some pontoons passed through our cantonments last night, it is said that our right is to cross the Nive & move on as soon as the weather will permit.

7th   Our battalion relieved the brigade outpost at Bassussarry this morning. A packet has arrived with glorious news from the north.

8th   Our company on outlying picquet today. The right of the army consisting of General Hill's Corps & Marshal Beresford's (the 3rd & 6th Divisions) are to cross the Nive & move on tomorrow, the picquets of the 3rd Division which were on our right were relieved this evening by the 7th Division, we are not to be relieved until the evening.

Chapter 12

The Battle of the Nive

Wellington's army was inconveniently placed with his force penned between the sea on its left and the River Nive on their right and with the fortified city of Bayonne in its front. To break out of this strait-jacket, Wellington pushed a large portion of his army across the Nive, where it could advance around Bayonne, whilst his remaining troops continued to hold positions around Arcangues. Wellington's problem however was that Soult was able to easily pass his army through Bayonne and could bring superior numbers against either wing of Wellington's army. This critical situation was compounded when the pontoon bridges over the Nive were broken during heavy rains leaving the two wings isolated and unable to support each other.

The Light Brigade suffered from the first of the heavy attacks launched by the French on the left wing at Arcangues.

9th About day break the firing commenced on the right, but we did not hear much the whole day in that direction, soon after the firing of musketry commenced on the left by Sir John Hope's Corps which continued very heavy the whole day & which was sometimes accompanied by artillery, which I believe belonged to the enemy. We could both see & hear that Sir J. Hope's people were giving ground. Towards evening our left picquets attacked those of the enemy which ran in without firing a shot to their entrenched camp. The picket opposite our company which was the right picquet, retired on seeing this & we advanced & took possession of the house that they left, on which they commenced firing on us. We established our picquets on this line but during the night they were drawn in to the old place. We were relieved before dark by the right wing of the 43rd & we returned to our cantonments. General Hill I hear met with scarcely any opposition and is now on the Adour. The 4th Division were brought up to support ours in case of any attack. Showery day.

10th About two hours after day break the enemy in great force attacked and drove in our picquets & those of General Hope's corps on whom they made a desperate attack, with us then was a terrible confusion, and though the picquets had observed the enemy's force collecting in their front for some time, yet when the[y] did attack, they took some of them completely by surprise. When our company arrived at the Chateau d'Arcangues we were ordered to halt there for that the division was to maintain that position, the rest of the battalion came in by companies as the[y] could, but our company was sent out from the chateau to reoccupy the ridge in front of it in order to support the 3rd Battalion who were actually *retiring from the ridge when we received to order to occupy it to support them.* This was mentioned to the commandant who however had not sense to comprehend that it was not only useless but dangerous to send one company up to occupy a ridge on which we were not able to communicate right & left.

However we were ordered to go, leaving a subdivision at the house below the chateau; Hopwood & myself went up with the advanced subdivision and felt our way to the top of the ridge with a few men, the enemy had not yet occupied it but were close to it and immediately after we arrived there, one ball went through the heads of both Hopwood & Sergeant Brotherwood (thus died uselessly two as brave soldiers as ever stepped [out], I have since heard our commandant attempt to maintain that it was not his intention we should occupy this place, that however I will always assert whenever I hear the subject mentioned, to be false. Both Hopwood & myself were too well aware of the useless danger we were going to meet, to run into it without an order, I said and always shall say that Hopwood lost his life through the ignorance of the commanding officer and if Colonel Barnard had commanded the regiment this day poor Hopwood, Brotherwood and the other sufferers of the company this day could have been spared). I went up to Hopwood as soon as I saw him fall, took him by the hand and called him by his name, he half opened his eyes which were closed but never spoke, his brains were knocked out of the wound. This melancholy event left me in command of the company, as I was under the eyes of the commanding officer and so situated that it was in his power by sound of bugle to order me to retire when he thought proper, I (though I knew that every moment I remained there hazarded the loss of the whole subdivision which I had there, for we could not see ten yards before us, and as we were advanced considerably out of the line of skirmishers, the enemy were on our right & left in our rear, I confess I never expected to return with a sound skin) determined not to quit this place until I was either driven from it or ordered from it, the former of which happened very soon for the enemy seeing we were unsupported and out of our place, sent some men who came through the hedge on our left & fired into us, we ran into the road & retired to the house the other subdivision was at and I certainly never ran quicker in my life, a help of that kind gives a man a wonderful agility. We kept the house, beyond which we ought never to have advanced & were relieved at dark by another company. This house is established as a picquet house & the line drawn from it right & left is a very good one, when relieved we returned to the chateau. General Sir J Hope[1] has been attacked this morning in a very desperate manner with very superior forces, which he has repulsed, he is himself slightly wounded & has lost many men. The tirallaide lasted on all sides until dark.

The 4th Division moved up to support us immediately, for they were but a short distance in the rear, the 3rd which had crossed the water came up on the right of the 4th at about midday. Sir L. Cole[2] had orders to defend this position until the last. We had an officer taken prisoner today & about 18 men[3]. Rainy day.

Captain John Kincaid records[4] that 'An officer of ours, Mr Hopewood, and one of our serjeants, had been killed in the field opposite, within twenty yards of where the enemy's skirmishers now were. We were very anxious to get possession of their bodies, but had not force enough to effect it. Several French soldiers came through the hedge, at different times, with the intention, as we thought, of plundering, but our men shot every one who attempted to go near them, until towards evening, when a French officer approached, waving a white handkerchief and pointing to some of his men who were following him with shovels. Seeing that his intention was to bury them, we instantly ceased firing, nor did we renew it again that night.'

Following the Battle of Leipzig when the allies beat Napoleon's army severely, the German states began transferring their allegiance to the allies, seeing this as their opportunity to throw off the French yoke.

There were however a number of German regiments serving with the French army and these now sought opportunities to secretly pass over to the allies.

On the night of 10 December three German battalions marched from the French lines into those of the British. Wellington had received prior knowledge of their intention to pass over to the allies and he had promised that they would not be made prisoners of war, but would be immediately transported to Germany to help in the overthrow of Napoleon there. Two Nassau battalions of the 2nd Nassau Regiment and the Frankfurt Battalion passed over this night. The Baden Battalion was to have been a part of this, but failed because its commander, who was the only one in on the secret, had been wounded that very day during the fighting. Marshal Soult reacted the following day by disarming the Baden Battalion and word was passed to Marshal Suchet in Catalonia forcing him to disarm the 1st Nassau Regiment, and all Wurzburg and Westphalian troops with his army, causing him a loss of 2,400 men.

11th   The brigade of Nassau (the same which was opposite to our division when we first came on the heights of Vera) deserted last night to Sir J. Hope, they had been engaged very sharply during the day and at night came over, Staff and all. The deserters from the enemy are very great now, the deserters say that he [Soult] has seven divisions on this side of Bayonne, that the army all together consists of nine divisions, making altogether about 55,000 men, whereof about 3,000 are cavalry. General Kempt, our brigadier, wanted to take the ridge opposite the chateau which is the enemy's line of picquets (the same poor Hopwood was killed on) and establish our picquets there, he called some of us and showed his plan of attack which was to have been made by ours & the 3rd Battalion 95th. General Alten did not approve of the attack and I believe every man & officer in the regiment was of the same opinion (for my own part recollecting the ground beyond it I felt convinced that though we might take, we could never keep it) luckily it was not done. There was a good deal of firing on the left which I understand was occasioned by the enemy trying to retake some ground Hope took from them. Foy is with a division still at St Jean de Pied de Port. I relieved Lee's[5] Company on picquet this evening. Rainy.

12th   The enemy's picquet in my front commenced working last night at about 8 o'clock and continued at it all night. When day broke this morning I discovered four embrasures open in a work, they about an hour after stopped the embrasures with bushes & continued working all day, which I believe is all for show. However it created an alarm in the chateau & everything was disposed to receive an immediate attack, the enemy did at one time show a great force opposite the division.

There was a great deal of firing at one time on the left in which I hear the Guards suffered very severely & brought it all on themselves by firing on a battalion that was relieving some post. I was relieved this evening on picquet by Cox[6]. Fine day.

13th The enemy retired last night and took up their old line of picquets that they occupied previous to their attack on the 10th. Our picquets felt their way on and occupied their old line. As soon as it was daylight I went up and found poor Hopwoods' body, which the enemy had scarcely covered over & buried it. Poor fellow!

Soon after day light [I] heard heavy firing in the direction of where General Hill is, which continued almost all day.

Lord Wellington rode by in that direction at about 10 o'clock and ordered the 4th Division to move up. I understand and a deserter also said that Soult has brought his provisions to his army by boats down the Adour and that he has no other sufficient conveyance for them, so that General Hill's movement upon the Adour by depriving him of this resource puts him to a very great inconvenience and I suppose all his manoeuvres now have in view this end viz to force General Hill from the line of the Adour. His attack on our left on the 10th was probably made under the idea that that point had been weakened in order to strengthen General Hill's attack the preceding day on the right and last night he concentrated his principal force to attack General Hill this morning but he was I understand repulsed with very great loss. There is a report that he had 18 companies of grenadiers ready to storm the church and chateau of Arcangues, the battery they constructed opposite our picquet is a complete humbug.

I was sent with the company to occupy our old cantonment but was afterwards ordered back to the chateau. The picquets are taken by brigades now not battalions, because [of] that when our battalion is on picquet the post is weaker than at any other time, the chateau being unoccupied. Fine day.

14th Lord Wellington came to the chateau today from the direction of General Hill and seemed in very light spirits, I heard him say to

General Kempt that the enemy had been four times repulsed with immense loss, General Hill had only his own corps up. They (the enemy) were I understand all drunk when they attacked. All quiet today. The number of deserters that come in is very great. Rainy.

15th The company on outlying picquet today at the old place. Everything is as before, the enemy appear very much afraid of being attacked, they saw some guns move to our right & they fell in their outposts & manned their work. One of the enemy's sentries opposite my picquet deserted from his post today about 3 o'clock to the picquet on my right. While I was at my dinner a man came up & told me that the officer of the French picquet wanted to speak to me, I accordingly went down & passed the abattis. Two officers of the 55th [French] Regiment came to meet me, we shook hands very cordially & when I asked them if they wanted anything, they produced a keg of brandy & saw they only came to drink my health & chat a little, which after doing we parted, they were very civil. Rainy day.

16th Relieved this morning by the company of the 17th [Portuguese Line] and went & occupied the reserve post. Rainy.

17th Relieved this morning, our old cantonment is given up to the Portuguese working party, there is a battery making in the garden of the chateau & another at the church. Fine day. General Hill's head quarters are at *Vieux Mouguerre*

18th Rainy night, fine day, I went in to the French picquet today to take a letter for the officer of ours [Church] who was taken on the 10th.

19th Very bad weather.

20th Ditto. We are all to dine together on Christmas day.

21st Ditto.

22nd Went on a working party with the company to the neighbourhood of Arbonne just in rear of Pue[7] to make roads. These roads are making under the superintendence of the Staff Corps & are to extend from the main road in rear of the position we are fortifying, to the road from Bayonne to Roncesvalles. I was in the battery today at the church of Arcangues, there are nine guns in it, 5 of which are French ship guns & 4 are long English brass 6 pounders, it is very strong. The wood below it, which is of young trees, very thickly planted, is cut down about 3 feet from the ground and the trees laid along, which makes a most impenetrable abattis. The battery at the chateau is not yet finished, it is I believe to mount (en barbette[8]) two 24 pound carronades & 1 x 5½ inch howitzer.

The desertions from the enemy still continue to be very great, 3 came in to *our* picquets last night & 3 the night before, and not only foreigners but Frenchmen are among the number.

23rd   Rainy.

24th   First fine day since the 18th. An officer (an Englishman) of the Portuguese artillery went by our house today & said that it was positively certain that we go on tomorrow morning when a signal gun will be fired. Nobody else knows anything of it, which is very strange, but it is said positively that Soult has retired from the line of the Adour, leaving here only the men he intends to occupy Bayonne. In this case it is most it is most probable we shall soon move.

A German who was taken today in coming to talk to our advanced sentry at which he was very much vexed, told me that there were 3 divisions on this side of the river. It is very strange that after all that happened it is not yet clearly understood among the foreigners of the French army do not generally know whether to believe that their country is against France or not. When you ask them if Bonaparte has been obliged to cross the Rhine, they say they have heard it, but do not know whether to believe it or not. Several pontoons passed by our house to the right today.

25th   Our company relieved the outpost today, fine day, hard frost last night.

Edward Costello records that a man of his company was guilty this night of fraternising with the enemy too much. They did however manage somehow to retrieve the situation without the knowledge of the officer commanding the picket, our James: 'On Christmas night, our company was on picket near a dwelling called Garrett's house. We clubbed half a dollar each, and sent Grindley, our comrade, into the French picket-house to purchase brandy, but when he stayed longer than was usual, we became alarmed and sent two other men in quest of him. From the nearest French sentry, they learned that Grindley was lying drunk in their picket-house. Fearful that the circumstances should come to the knowledge of Lieutenant Gardiner, the officer of our picket, they went to bring him back with them Grindley was very drunk, and just as they were emerging with him from the French lines, who should ride down to the front post but Sir James Kempt, who commanded our division at that time, Grindley was instantly ordered to be confined; he was very fortunate to escape with only a slight punishment".[9]

26th   On outlying picquet today, same weather. The enemy are eternally drilling now so that they must have received some part of the new conscription.

27th   Relieved this morning.

28th   The Church of Arcangues is now one of the strongest works I ever saw, it is absolutely un-attackable.

29th   *Blank*

30th   Rode to St Jean de Luz today, heard on the road that the enemy had withdrawn their picquets which were opposite our division into the entrenched camp. While we were in St Jean de Luz there came a report there from General Alten that the enemy were forming up columns opposite to him & that he apprehended an attack, this report as usual lost nothing by the distance it came, the Guards were ordered to fall in & everybody had it that the division was attacked, which made us all bolt off, however we had not got 3 miles on the road when we heard that it was all a false alarm and that the columns they showed were to protect any attack that might be made on them in consequence of their withdrawing their picquets; which by the bye is a very curious circumstance & I can imagine no reason for it, except that by contracting their line of outposts they may prevent the frequent desertions they have lately had.

The turn of the year spent in winter quarters allowed James the time to review what had been a stunningly successful year for Wellington.

31st   The enemy were very much offended yesterday when our picquets occupied the ground they gave up and said they retired in order to have some space of neutral ground between us, however they did not fire and General Alten has agreed with them, that our picquets are to occupy the ground they gave up during the day and retire to the old ground again at night. We had a dance this night at the chateau to bring in the New Year.

Thus have we seen an end of the year *1813* and of a more glorious, active and eventful era the annals of history do not furnish a second. Our own Peninsular campaign has been eminently successful, the 21st of May saw the allied armies on the banks of the Agueda and the 9th of December on that of the Adour after having been victorious in three general actions and become masters of two regular fortresses, the one by siege & the other by blockade not to mention the Castle of Burgos which the enemy abandoned, and which last year resisted the efforts of that same army at the approach of which it this year fell without an effort.

This campaign though attended with unexampled success has not been marked by one single instance of those unexpected throws of fortune which disarrange the best concerted measures and which turn the scale of success instantaneously from one side to another. We have had no instance of disaffection among our enemies (except indeed the desertion of the Nassau Brigade on the 10th ultimo, a circumstance in itself too trifling to have at all influenced the success of operations in general and which did not take place until the event of the campaign was determined), no unexpected losses by weather or other unforeseen accidents. All has been general-ship and manoeuvring, every advantage has been looked forward to and calculated upon and in the history of war there never has I believe been a campaign which affords a finer lesson for a soldier, in which so much has been effected by the genius of the commander and so little has been owing to luck or chance.

At the same time however that the measures of Lord Wellington were projected with sagacity and executed with vigour, those of the French commanders (until Marshal Soult took the command) appear to have been palsied by irresolution & inaction.

The campaign commenced on the 21st of May. A part of the army (the 2nd & Light Divisions) moved on the old (and what the enemy expected would be the only) route, viz on Salamanca while the greater part under General Graham crossing the Douro in Portugal, thereby turning that line of defence, moved on the Esla. And in contemplating this manoeuvre must we not pay the tribute of admiration to the foresight of Lord Wellington, was not the very cantonment of the troops destined to move on this point a preliminary and necessary step, in all our former winters we have had the right of our army extended a considerable way towards the south of Spain, this winter it extended no further than Coria & thereabouts while the left was cantoned on the Douro, and what the enemy imagined to be taken up only as a convenient cantonment was in fact occupying a post which enabled Lord Wellington as soon as he commenced the campaign to turn one of the enemy's strongest lines of defence, on which they most probably calculated to keep the British army in check until they had collected and arranged their troops to dispute seriously passage of the Ebro.

The 2nd and our division marched on Salamanca, we found General Maucune there with a division who for what cause I know not stayed there, with his own division only and with none other within two days march of him, long enough to lose upwards of 300 men in prisoners besides killed, without gaining one single object. As soon as the left of the army had crossed the Esla which was effected without loss. The right moved from Salamanca on Toro where we crossed the Douro. From Toro, we made a very rapid march on Burgos, while General Graham directed his march on the source of the Ebro. When we arrived at Burgos, we saw another instance of that want of vigour and information which did not use to be a characteristic of the French army. A division of French troops was encamped with a river in its rear, over which was only one bridge to retire by, the castle of Burgos which it was natural for the enemy to suppose would soon become an object of attack and which it was their intention to fortify, was in no state of forwardness. The consequence was that this division only escaped annihilation from Lord Wellington not being able to gain (owing to the rapidity of his march) exact information of their situation and force. And the castle of Burgos which in the year 1812 made so fine a defence was in the year 1813 blown up & abandoned.

As soon as this event was ascertained, we changed our direction and advanced by forced marches towards the source of the Ebro and crossed, I believe, one of the strongest rivers, as a military line of defence in Europe, without firing a shot and without even the enemy having the slightest knowledge of it, so little did the French expect, so little had they taken measures to prevent this manoeuvre, that several divisions of their army were still in winter quarters and even when they knew we had crossed, so ignorant were they in what force and in what direction we were marching, that our division while on the march to surprise a French division lying quietly cantoned at a village called Espejo, fell in with, near San Millan, our old friend Maucune on his march (most probably for Vitoria the place of rendezvous) and after rough handling one brigade compelled the other to disperse into the mountains with the loss of all its baggage. The 2nd, 4th & Light Divisions marched direct on Vitoria where a part of the French army was in position and the rest marching on that point only knowing that Lord Wellington's army had crossed the Ebro, but in what force & in what direction they were marching, they were ignorant. This eminently favourable and commanding situation in which Lord Wellington now stood, resulted solely from that amazing rapidity of movement which brought his whole army in the midst of that of the enemy before they scarcely knew that he had commenced the campaign.

The King of Prussia says that 'He who at the commencement of the campaign is the most alert to assemble his troops and march forward to attack a town or post, will oblige his enemy to be regulated by his movements and to remain on the defensive.' This is an advantage that a British army owing to the immense sums of ready money expended on it, possesses beyond any other army in Europe. Lord Wellington has always been and principally for this reason, remarkable for being able at all times to assemble his army and take the field at the shortest notice. It was by availing himself of this, that he arrived at Burgos before it was in a state of defence (for I have heard that palisades and every requisite material for strengthening that fortress were there collected, but the work was not even begun) it was by availing himself of this that he crossed the Ebro without loss and without the knowledge of the enemy (for I have heard that when the French generals were told that the British had crossed the Ebro at Puente de Arenas and thereabouts, they said it was impossible it could not be anything more than a band of guerrillas, that it was not a point practicable for a regular army) and it was by availing himself of this, that he arrived before their position at Vitoria with three divisions of his army, while they were so completely ignorant of what was going on that they knew nothing of any part of the allied army, but what was in their front. While Lord Wellington was moving three other divisions to arrive by other roads at a particular point at a precise and critical moment and was moving two others to cross the River Zadorra in their rear and render their defeat and the loss of their artillery and baggage inevitable.

The Battle of Vitoria is, I believe, an action which effects more credit & honour on the commander that gained it than any other action in the history of war. The event was such as a like combination of able manoeuvres promised, the enemy retreats on Pamplona into which of all his artillery and baggage he brought only *one howitzer*. It was this rapidity of movement which enabled Lord Wellington to invest Pamplona before it could be provisioned which finally gave him the possession of that celebrated fortress without the slaughter of a siege.

The campaign was prosecuted with a vigour worthy its glorious commencement and at the same time with a prudence & caution, not intoxicated with success. San Sebastian was besieged, and Pamplona closely blockaded, but at this time Marshal Soult arrived to take command of the French army commissioned by the Emperor Napoleon as his lieutenant to re-establish the affairs in Spain; from this time the palsied and irresolute measures of the French were changed into those that were vigorous and offensive though not attended with success. In the end of July he collected his army, forced the pass of Maya and made a desperate attempt to raise the blockade of Pamplona, Lord Wellington threw back his right, covering Pamplona with five divisions, leaving our division as a disposable force, but not giving up San Sebastian which had repulsed one attempt to storm. Soult made repeated and desperate attacks on Lord Wellington's position with (as he (Lord W) says) hopes of success even beyond the relief of Pamplona. His attacks were all repulsed and he was finally compelled to retreat precipitately to all the positions prior to his advance after having suffered immense loss.

The siege of San Sebastian was continued and finally the place was carried by storm on the very same day that Soult made an ineffectual attempt to relieve it. Pamplona in the meantime held out and the allied army made no movement of consequence into the interior of France, waiting only for the fall of that place which was known to be much distressed for provisions. At length Pamplona surrendered on the 1st November, on the 10th which was as soon after as the weather would permit, the allied armies made an attack on the enemy's entrenched position on the lower Nivelle and the enemy withdrew under cover of Bayonne and to the right bank of the Nive. On the 9th of December the right of the army under General Hill crossed the Nive and established itself on the Adour.

The next day, the 10th, Marshal Soult with the hope of compelling the right to retire from the Adour (and by the British troops occupying a bank of that river, his principal means of transport for the right of his army which was by boats down that river, was stopped) and supposing also that our left had been much weakened in order to enable our right to move on, collected 50,000 men and made a desperate attack on our left which was not however attended than with a partial and temporary success, he drove in the picquets of our division & of the 1st and 5th and followed us to the position on which we were to stand. He looked at us there for three days and retiring from our front on the night of the 12th, marched his troops to the right during the night and on the morning of the 13th made an equally desperate and more unsuccessful attack on General Hill. Finding his efforts on all points unsuccessful he retired to his old positions and General Hill is still on the Adour. Soult has since that been quiet, but his situation on the bank of such a river as the Adour and with a fortress & the sea on his right, put it in his power to manoeuvre with very little danger as he was able to weaken his right flank to strengthen his left without fear of a counter attack being made on that point; and he can also at any time collect a force and make an attack from that point.

January 1814

1st   *Blank*

2nd   On the centre inlying picquet.

3rd   On the centre outlying picquet I had some conversation today with two French officers, on the picquet opposite to me to whom I gave two books containing all the bulletins (from different allied generals and from Lord Cathcart[10] & Sir C Stewart[11]) of the last campaign.

There have been signals passed from the right, that the enemy are moving in that direction.

4th   Was informed at daybreak that the division was to march to the right & that the picquets were to wait until relieved by some other division & then follow our own division. The enemy in our front did everything this morning as usual, they manned their entrenched camp and remained under arms until about 9 o'clock when they dismissed & went into the town, their conscripts were drilling just as usual. When they saw such a great number of our troops moving to the right they turned out about 400 men & piled arms in column to the left of the road. I hear that Soult yesterday attacked the 3rd Division relieved by the 85th and marched and joined the division at Ahetze. Our division marched this morning at daybreak and relieved the picquets of the 4th Division who had closed to their right. The 5th Division, Lord Aylmer's[12] Brigade, who closed to their right also relieved in the first place our picquets at Bassussarry and afterwards the picquets formerly of the 4th Division that our division retired this morning. Soon after we joined the division at Arrauntz, we were cantoned at Herauritz. It is said that the enemy has retired from the point they were threatening on our right.

5th   Marched at about 10 o'clock, crossed the Nive at Ustaritz by a pontoon bridge & encamped on the right bank of it, on the ground occupied last night by the 4th Division who have marched to the right. If we move at all it is to be to Hasparren to support the 3rd Division, about 2½ leagues from this. The country about here is very beautiful, the Nive is a fine clear river, rather rapid but not deep. The enemy retired last night but have again shown a force on the right. They have it is said crossed the Joyeuse with two divisions and occupied [La] Bastide [Clairence], Lord Wellington intends to attack them, which he would have done yesterday, but they were moving a force on their extreme right.

6th   Marched about a league & a half to a ground occupied last night by the 4th Division (which is on the Grande route from Bayonne to St Jean de Pied de Port, where the enemy have a garrison of 500 men) who have gone with the 3rd & 7th Division to attack the enemy on this side of the Joyeuse. Fine day.

7th   Rainy. Packed up & accoutred at day break. We received an order about 9 o'clock that we were to stay here 3 hours. We are I hear to take up the cantonments lately occupied by the 4th Division. As soon as these divisions (the 3rd, 4th & 7th) made their appearance, the enemy gave up Bastide & recrossed the Joyeuse. Marched towards evening & got to our cantonments (in Arraute [Charritte]) at dark. Terrible night. The 2nd Brigade whose cantonments (the same we occupied previous to the change made on the 23rd November) are a long way off, encamped this night.

8th   We have very fair quarters, we (our company) are close on the river.

9th   The tide affects this river very much, there are both sea & fresh water fish caught in it.

10th – 11th *Blank*

12th   There was a report today the 6,000 men of the enemy had come out of Bayonne today & then gone back again.

13th   *Blank*

14th   On picquet today, our brigade only gives three companies for picquet now & they are relieved daily. The 6th Division's picquets are on our right & the 5th (our old Bassussarry picquets) on our left. There was a working party from our brigade *damming* up a canal in front of our picquets today, a French picquet opposite fired several shots at them which however did no damage, nor did it make them discontinue; two officers with cocked hats came up to the picquet & it was ordered to discontinue firing. Rainy.

15th   Relieved this morning, rainy day. We have another month's pay just issued, which brings us up to the 24th July.[13]

16th   Very rainy.

17th   Bad day.

18th – 19th Bad day.

20th   Fair.

21st   *Blank*

22nd   On picquet, fair day. The enemy have retired from their entrenched camp & from Anglet, which is now neutral ground, fine day.

23rd   Frosty cold day. It is said that Prince Schwarzenberg[14] has entered France at Besancon & that he has possession of Lyons.

24th   Ditto, snowy. It is said that Soult has detached 3 divisions to join Bonaparte.

25th   Ditto.

The battalions of the 95th were reassigned following the return of Colonel Wade, and the 1st Brigade then marched with Wellington's army in pursuit of Marshal Soult towards Toulouse.

26th   In consequence of Colonel Wade coming out again, our battalion changes into the 2nd Brigade & the 2nd Battalion comes here. This gives the command of the 2nd Brigade to Colonel Barnard. Marched today & occupied the quarters of the 2nd Battalion at Sare a little to the right of our last cantonments at that place on the 19th November. The first has gone off. Rainy.

27th   Terrible day.

28th– 31st Ditto.

February
1st   Set out on command for corn today, went to Renteria where I was lucky enough to get cover for myself & party. A terrible bad day.

2nd   Attempted in vain to get my corn today, went to Passages, Lord Wellington was there.

3rd   Got my corn today at Passages on board of ship after a great deal of trouble & was obliged to hire boats at my own expense to bring it up to Renteria.

4th   Set off today to return to the regiment. Slept at Urugne but none of the party came so far.

News of the allied advance into France now gave hope that the war was finally drawing to a close, but there was to be much hard marching and fighting before it did finally end.

5th   Returned to the regiment. As I passed through St Jean de Luz, I

Above: A portrait of Captain J.P. Gairdner by Christa Hook.

Above: St Jean de Luz by Batty.

Below: The Bastille Elephant.

Above: The Battle of the Pyrenees.

Below: Battle of Toulouse by William Heath.

Above: French prisoners at Salamanca.

Below: River Bidassoa by Batty.

Above: The Church of Arcangues.

Below: La Rhune by Batty.

Left: Rifleman officer's jacket.

Above left: James Gairdner's nemesis, Alexander Cameron of the 95th.

Right: An Officer of the 95th, Paris 1815.

Below: A depiction of the Battle of Nivelle, 10 November 1813.

Above: A copy of a portrait of James Penman Gairdner in later life.

Left: The James Penman Gairdner obelisk.

Below: Wooden House, Kelso.

heard that another packet had arrived this morning. The Duke d'Angouleme, nephew in law of Louis XVIII is at St Jean de Luz, the allies have entered France in great force in different points. Prince Schwarzenberg's head quarters were by his last account at St Dizie, Bonaparte's at Epernay. There has been some skirmishing at Vitry. Besides this army there is a Russian army under Barclay de Tolly[15], Blucher has crossed the Rhine in three columns, viz. at Coblentz, Mannheim & Cassel. Besides all these armies it is said that 60,000 men will enter by Piedmont to communicate with Lord Wellington. Wittgenstein[16] has crossed at Fort Louis[17]. Besides these are the Wurtemburgers, Bavarians, Saxons &c.

Bernadotte[18] has not yet done with the Danes, he insists on their ceding Norway in lieu of Swedish Pomerania and they are to furnish 15,000 men to assist in the reduction of Hamburg. Bulow[19] with a Prussian army is in Holland acting in concert with General Graham, they have had an action with the French at Breda. It appears that the French under General of Division Decaen[20] lately from Catalonia fought very well. Affairs are in this glorious fortune, Lord Wellington is very anxious to move on and nothing has prevented it but the badness of the weather. Pontoons were moving up today, also a Congreve Rocket Brigade[21], I passed them on the road. This is the first fine day we have had since the 26th. The inhabitants say that this is the rainiest season they ever recollect.

6th   Fine day.

7th   Rainy.

8th   The Congreve rockets are gone to General Hill.

9th – 10th *Blank*

11th   I understand that all the small boats in Passages & St Jean de Luz are embargoed and that materials are collecting for the construction of a bridge over the Adour below the town.

12th   There is a report of a battle having been fought between the allies & Bonaparte. General Hill has moved to the right, the 7th Division has taken up his ground. Fine weather.

13th   Rainy last night, cloudy day. My patron was sowing wheat today. They strew the wheat on the ground and hough the earth over it.

We had a church parade today. I heard some firing in the direction of St Jean de Pied de Port.

14th   Lord Wellington went to the right today with his light luggage. Gloomy weather but no rain.

15th   *Blank*

16th   Received an order at 4 o'clock this morning to march at day break, marched through Arrauntz, Herauritz and Ustaritz where we crossed the Nive and marched through a very barren country about 16 English miles. Lord Wellington is at Saint Palais.

17th   Marched at about 9 o'clock to Labastide on the Joyeuse near which we encamped. The enemy who have always kept Labastide retired from it on the first appearance of Marshal Beresford's columns and are now on the other bank of the Gave d'Oleron where Soult himself is with 10 divisions. Labastide is a nice village, the people all completely French[22] which language they all talk, even to each other. The peasants about here also all talk French, their mother tongue is the Gascon an infinitely more comprehensible lingo than the Basque, it has a good deal of French in it. The inhabitants of this country are not only civil but remarkably good natured and affable, they are very clean and the younger part of them both male & female very handsome. They live apparently to a great age. The inhabitants are very civil indeed and seem very glad that the English are advancing. How ridiculous now appear to us those doubts and fears we had held out to us of the peasantry rising in arms and the impolicy of entering France. We never have been better treated in Spain or Portugal & the further we advance we find them more glad to see us. The weather is very cold, three of our companies are in houses, I am not one of the lucky ones. The 4th Division are at Bidache on the Gave.

18th   There was a good deal of firing last night. The 2nd Division had some fighting the day before yesterday before the enemy got over the river. General Pringle[23] is wounded. Rode to [Quartier de] Pessarou a village about 2½ miles in front. Very cold.

New clothing arrived for the various regiments at the port of St Jean de Luz and the 1st Battalion 95th was ordered to march back to the coast to be issued with their new uniforms, all of the wagons being needed for transporting more urgent supplies for the army. Because of this the battalion missed the Battle of Orthez.

19th Snowy day. Walked to Pessarou to market. The whole division put under cover this evening received the order this evening to proceed to St Jean de Luz for clothing.

20th Marched to Ustaritz this day where we got good quarters. Snowed & was very cold.

21st Marched to Sare to the quarters we occupied on the 19th November. On the march we met the 5th Division marching to the right to cross the Nive, they got the order suddenly last night. The Spaniards are moving up to their old ground. Marshal Beresford whose head quarters were at Ustaritz moved this morning to Labastide.

22nd To St Jean de Luz where we occupied the cantonments of the Guards; there is a great talk here of Sir J. Hope, commencing the operation of crossing the Adour below the town tomorrow. There was a ball at the mayor's house this evening to which I went, but it was very dull work. Got a very good dinner in the French style at Le Cerf hotel. I left all my baggage at Sare, Don Carlos's division is in the old cantonments of the 1st & 5th Divisions.

Sir John Hope managed to get a battalion of the Guards across the River Adour below Bayonne and then dug in whilst attempts were made to construct a pontoon bridge to allow further units to cross and to establish a secure bridgehead.

23rd Halted all day. There is a great deal of firing in the direction of Bayonne. There is a bridge to be made below the town by the 1st Division, but there is a French frigate in the river which is what the batteries are now attempting to destroy. Frere's Spanish Division marched through here this morning.

About 700 Guards crossed the Adour in rafts this evening at 5 o'clock without opposition. The boats to make the bridge could not get in this evening on account of the great surf & the foul wind. The enemy succeeded in towing the frigate under the works. The rockets that were fired at her did not go near her.

James does not mention it, but according to Leach, the new clothing for the battalion was finally issued on 23rd February and the following day the battalion commenced its march to rejoin the army.

24th   Marched to the quarters we were in on the 21st ultimo. The Guards were attacked last night by about 1,400 of the garrison of Bayonne who came on with skirmishers in their front, but some Congreve rockets being let at them, they went off bodily. The Guards had only 3 or 4 men wounded. There are more troops crossing; the 16th Dragoons & a brigade of light artillery are over. The wind is fair for the boats to get in, and it is said that the bridge will be finished tonight. There are to be some gunboats above the bridge between it & the boom. We heard a good deal of musketry popping (most likely the Spanish & French picquets) and now and then a cannon shot.

     I was on duty today to bring up stragglers of which there were a great number as almost every man in the regiment started beastly drunk.

25th   Marched to Ustaritz. The boats got in yesterday evening, it is said that the frigate was nearly destroyed. Fine day, no frost.

26th   Through Hasparren to La Bastide de Clairence. The division left this on Monday for St Martin two leagues off. The Gave d'Oleron it is said was crossed yesterday. The inhabitants on this side of the Pyrenees are the handsomest race of people I ever saw. Rained a little; on baggage guard.

27th   Through Oregue, Beguios, Luxe [-Sumberraute] to Garris, a nice town where head quarters were same day and not at Saint Palais, a long march with hilly country & bad roads. We heard a good deal of cannonading. The inhabitants say it is in the direction of Orthez which is on the other side of the Gave de Pau where the enemy have a strong position and redoubt. The Gave d'Oleron was crossed with little loss on the 25th at Sauveterre. Near this village are the heights that the 39th Regiment[24] were engaged on.

     Excellent quarters. The people of the country seem more enthusiastic in favour of the Bourbons & more sick of the war & more glad to see us the further we advance, they do not however attempt outwardly to show it by greeting the troops with huzzas &c.

28th To Saint Palais about two English miles. The 79th Regiment[25] was here & ordered not to leave this place until relieved by some regiment marching up from the rear. Each regiment is also to want to be relieved, we accordingly were obliged to relieve the 79th & know not how long we may be detained.

At least the river was crossed yesterday at Orthez where head quarters were last night & are repeated tonight at Pau. Got excellent quarters, the people hereabouts know how to live. Saint Palais is a good town situated on the Bidouze, there was a very good cattle market today.

March

1st About 60 French prisoners & two officers were marched in here last night by a party of the 74th[26], they were taken at Orthez, an officer and party of our regiment are sent on with them.

The people here talk of some proclamation to be made at Pau. There is a college near this. Rather a dull place as almost all the genteel people particularly the females have gone away.

2nd Rainy

3rd Ditto. On a working party beyond Garris to get a pontoon out of the mud. My old landlord at Garris told me that the French had left Bayonne & retired into the citadel, that when the British entered they turned the guns of the citadel on the town & the British to save it evacuated it.

I went over the ground on which the 2nd Division were engaged on the 16th ultimo. There is a beautiful view from these heights, the country hereabouts is very well cultivated, it is hilly but not mountainous and is very well wooded, there are a great many vineyards, when the country is in full leaf it must be heavenly. The wine here is very good, it has a curious tartness in it, even the oldest of it which is very pleasant, some of the white wine is *exactly* still champagne.

The bridge of Sauveterre [de Bearn] is carried away by the rains. The heavy German brigade of cavalry are here & at Garris. Had a dance tonight in the justice hall.

4th On guard. An order has come from head quarters for us to join the army & the commissariat is to move off with us. By all accounts there has been a severe battle at Orthez[27]. It is said that Bonaparte himself ordered that position to be defended. Rain.

5th   Rain. The peasants here wear smock frocks like the English & look remarkably clean. Their bullocks too are all clothed.

6th   No rain, cold. The bridge is to be finished today, several more prisoners have come in. the cavalry have moved today. We move tomorrow. Had a dance.

7th   To Sauveterre, 2 leagues, an excellent town larger than Saint Palais, it has the remains of an old castle. There is here a very handsome bridge of three arches, one of which the French have completely destroyed. It is on the Gave d'Oleron. The country about here is beautiful. The enemy have not I hear retired on Bordeaux but on Toulouse. Ponsonby's Brigade[28] of cavalry are coming up and several Spaniards. Snowed the first part of the day.

8th   To Orthez four leagues (the French country league is very long, the post league is more than an English league) an excellent [town] larger considerably than Sauveterre, the market was amazingly crowded, and very well & cheaply supplied. Fowls were selling for 3 francs a pair, turkeys 3 francs each & everything in proportion. It is full of wounded and we got bad quarters. The people are not very civil, I met here with the first instance of incivility I have met with in France. The houses about the bridge over the Gave de Pau bear many marks of musket balls and a few of round shot. It is true that Lord Wellington was wounded here the other day[29]. There is the remains of an old castle here. The roads here are all main roads.

     The peasants turned out & fired on our foraging party today, they wounded several horses, mine among the rest.

     The action here was very severe, the enemy it is said, fought very well, the 3rd, 4th & 7th Divisions were principally engaged, ours was very little engaged. Our loss is estimated at about 2,200, that of the enemy at 12,000. Snowed in the morning.

9th   Through Sallespisse & Sault de Navailles to Hagetmau, a very good large village. I was on forage duty and went from it to Montsoue about 5 miles off, people very civil.

     General Beresford with the 4th & 7th Divisions has marched to Bordeaux. Beautiful well cultivated country, snowed.

10th   Through Saint Sever (which head quarters have just left for Aire [sur-l'Adour]) and by Saint Maurice [sur Adour] to Grenade [sur l'Adour]. We crossed the Adour by a wooden bridge at Saint Sever, the ground on [the] left bank of the river is very commanding, that on the right quite flat, consequently Marshal Soult could not dispute the passage of the river. Our division which was near here move to the front this morning. The heavy German cavalry in Grenade [sur l'Adour]. Snowed very cold.

11th Through Cazeres [sur l'Adour], close by Aire and through Barcelonne [du-Gers] & joined the division which is cantoned right & left of the road. One battalion went into a small village called Gee [-Riviere]. The country we have been in since crossing the Adour is perfectly flat and very well cultivated.

Aire is on the other bank of the Adour, the[re] is no bridge there. The enemy are about 3 leagues off. A little after passing Aire we passed a division post which divided the department of Landes which we were leaving from that of Gers which we were entering.

12th Our General Court Martial assembled again today at General Kempt's quarters. Showery.

1st Brigade moved to Sarron. They speak worse French here than at Saint Palais & thereabouts and are an ugly dirty set.

13th Showery. We move tomorrow. It is said that General Hope is besieging the citadel of Bayonne.

14th When the regiment moved, our company made up to 80 R[ank] & F[ile] being first for picquet, went to the bridge of Corneillan with orders to cross it and watch. Corneillan is on a tongue on the left bank of the River Adour and Saint Mont another village each about 1 mile from the bridge, the 2nd Division marched from these villages this morning at 4 o'clock. Their baggage we met with having crossed the river & was marching on Barcelonne. Our situation was thus very perplexing, we began to doubt whether we were on the proper bank of the river, when the Quarter Master General came bouncing in the piquets of the 1st Brigade & he told us that we were wrong, that we had our backs to the enemy, he took us away with him and we joined the division which was beside the main road a little way in rear of Saint Germe. Their orders are to defend Barcelonne to the last. The reason of all this is because Soult is manoeuvring on our right on the other bank of the river. The 3rd & 6th Division have crossed & moved in that direction, the country people talk of an affair on the right yesterday. 12,000 Spaniards are to be up this evening. Beresford's two divisions have arrived without opposition at Bordeaux where they have been rapturously received, it is said that they have declared openly for the Bourbons.[30] Being first for fatigue I was sent to keep stragglers out of our quarters at Gee, to which the regiment returned in the evening with orders to accoutre and pile arms at daybreak and be in readiness to move. Cold day and rather rainy.

15th   Fell in and piled arms at daybreak, there are a great number of Spaniards of Freire's Division[31] straggling about here. Cold day & rainy.

16th   Cold but not so much so as yesterday. Walked up to Saint Mont, fine view from it, saw the enemy's country & picquets. Saw the Chateau de Viella[32] where Pierre Soult's head quarters are. The cavalry picquets of the enemy in front of Tarsac were driven in at one o'clock, there was about a squadron of them who were not at first disposed to go away. Our 2nd Battalion were there to support them.

17th   Fine warm day walked to Tarsac, we move tomorrow.

18th   The division marched through Saint Germe, Lacaussade, Tasque (here we forded the L'Arros the enemy having destroyed the bridge, though of no use as the ford was passable for everything, we left the main road for Toulouse here & took that for Tarbes on which the enemy have retired. They left this, this morning.) to Plaisance. Part of the division [went] into town and part, among which was our company, crossed the L'Arros which flows here & went into houses there. The houses we went into had been formerly an inn, it has been lately occupied by a French picquet who have completely destroyed it, they compelled the inhabitants to leave it, the poor old man told me with tears, that he was ruined.

    The 4th Division are following us on the same road. The 2nd, 3rd & 6th are moving on the other side of the river today.

    The bridge here is destroyed as indeed they destroy every bridge, even the most trifling. We are fed routinely on what the country furnishes, which is paid for by ready money by the commissaries.

19th Through Ladeveze [Riviere] (while passing through it heard cavalry skirmishing) to Auriebat on a high ridge of hills from which there is a most beautiful view. Looking to the south is a perfectly level valley through which flows the Adour (at about 5 miles distant is Maubourguet), to the north is also a fine valley, the hills beyond it covered with vines, all the hilly ground grows nothing but vines. We halted here & encamped. There was a murder committed on a peasant last night in the neighbourhood of our quarters. I went out for forage & while going I heard a heavy cannonade; we received our orders to march & I was recalled. Marched along the ridge of Auriebat through Sauveterre, Monfaucon, Barbachen to some farm houses beyond Haget. While on the march we saw fighting which began about the village of Lafitole & continued on the road through Vic [en Bigorre] & beyond it. The civility we met here was very great, the people are however much frightened. I met as I came out of Haget a French soldier walking along fully armed and accoutred, as handsome a Frenchman as ever I saw, he told me when I enquired, that he was a native of Haget & had deserted. Hot day.

The French had prepared a very strong position on the heights above Tarbes with several tiers of redoubts. All three battalions of the 95th were committed to the attack. Despite being heavily outnumbered, the Rifles forced the French to retire, but at some cost.

20th Marched through Rabastens [de Bigorre] (very good looking town –Ponsonby's heavy cavalry there) along to main road to Tarbes where we heard the enemy were in position. On the left of the road was a ridge of heights, to the right of it the country was quite flat. The cavalry moved in our front until they discovered a part of the ridge occupied by the enemy's infantry, this was about 2 miles from Tarbes. They then halted until our division came up, our 2nd Battalion & the left wing of the 1st was ordered to dislodge them from a woody height a short way in rear of which on another height, they had a very strong column. They gave up this height without opposition, but immediately after made a very determined attempt to retake it. They drove in our people that were up there but the remainder of the 1st & the 3rd Battalions 95th arrived just at this time & the rest of the division close at our heels, we drove them back again with great loss. They made no further attempt, however our 3 battalions lost in this short time 9 officers killed and wounded. I never saw on any occasion so many men killed by skirmishers as the many lost on this occasion. Had there been a troop of cavalry with us, they would have made 2 or 3 hundred prisoners. We halted here for some time, during which time we saw the 6th Division move along a ridge to our left, the enemy retiring before them and under their cannonade, the force in our front also went off. We followed them & entered. On the other ridge to our left, General Hill's Corps at this time engaged with their left.

A strong column of Spaniards moved up between us & the 7th Division. The enemy all retired to another ridge where they showed a great force, the ridge appeared very strong, the 6th Division now moved on the extreme right of it & got on it before dark. We were moved down under the foot of it, to be ready to attack it as soon as the 6th Division should be sufficiently advanced, however night coming on put a stop to our movements & we halted here all night. They showed evident dispositions of retiring before dark, however just about dark they brought their guns to bear upon us & cannonaded until it was quite dark. They had scarcely any lights. This is rather a difficult country he brought us into. Tarbes appears to be an excellent town.

21st The enemy retired last night, marched through Tournay to Lannemezan, the country from Tournay to Lannemezan terribly wild & uncultivated, good cavalry country. The houses in these towns very decent & full. Rain.

22nd Through Monlong to Gaussan 3 leagues, at Monlong we descended from the heights into the plain country. This is the road to Toulouse but not the shortest, the greatest part of the enemy's army have retired by the Saint Gaudens road which is the most direct from Tarbes. Very crowded quarters, rain.

23rd Marched by Castelnau [Magnoac], through Thermes [Magnoac], Boulogne [sur-Gesse] to Peguilhan. Fertile country well inhabited. General Hill is on the Saint Gaudens road, the 3rd, 4th & 6th are on this. Head quarters Boulogne.

24th Marched by Anan & through L'Isle en Dodon to Martisserre. General Hill took some prisoners yesterday at Saint Gaudens. Baggage guard & headquarters at L'Isle en Dodon.

25th By Lombez (where we came into the main road) & Samatan to Seysses-Saves off the main road to the left. This is about 5 leagues from Toulouse. The vegetation about Lombez is pretty forwards. Rain.

26th Through Sainte Foy [de-Peyrolieres], St Lys, Fonsorbes to Plaisance [du-Touch] in which place we doubled up with the cavalry by particular order on account of the badness of the weather. We had not been in the village above an hour when I saw the people running about in every direction, carrying away their children & sheep, crying out that the French were coming. I went up to the main street & saw several of the 15th Hussars, both men & horses coming in wounded. I heard afterwards that the hussars established their advanced post at Tournefueille, about 2 miles from here, a village on the Touch, a small stream that the reserve of the post were in front of the village & had taken off their saddles & accoutrements. The enemy came on with about 400 infantry & some cavalry, the advanced troop of hussars in front of the village was obliged to remain skirmishing with *infantry* until the reserve got saddled & accoutred & retired. The enemy took possession of the post & established a picquet there. This slovenly trick is just like raw English cavalry.

27th The division marched at 8 o'clock to Tournefueille, the enemy were driven over the river & their right brigade cantoned in Tournefueille, we returned to Plaisance.

28th The division marched at daybreak through Cugnaux, halted a long time on the outside of it. The orders were for the Light Division to cross the Garonne at Portet [sur Garonne] and General Hill's Corps was to cross at Muret. General Hill's bridge was completely bungled & they had not pontoons enough, Lord Wellington is very angry indeed; the operations being thus suspended, the division was cantoned [at] Cugnaux, the company (which since Cox was wound[ed] on the 20th[33] I command) was sent on picquet first, to a large house on the main road to Toulouse, near the village of St Simon from which the enemy retired this morning at 8 o'clock. In the evening the picquets were advanced to a gentle rise in front of St Simon, which commands a good view of Toulouse and is about three miles from it. Fine day – there do not appear to be any men on the heights opposite Portet and Muret.

29th   The picquets were altered today, I was moved a little more to my left. Terribly windy last night, rained today.

It is astonishing, the quantity in the houses here every one of which is deserted. The people complain much of the conduct of the French soldiers. Not relieved until late, joined this division which has been cantoned today in St Simon.

30th   Rained. Our battalion is the supporting battalion, marched at daybreak to support the picquets & then marched back to our quarters with orders to remain accoutred. Fine evening.

Wellington had General Hill's corps pass the river south of Toulouse, but found that the approaches to the city from this direction were too low lying and marshy.

31st   On a General Court Martial at day break, beautiful day. General Hill has crossed the river, the enemy are at this moment detaching troops towards him. I walked down to the picquets, I saw one column above Toulouse on the road leading from it and one on the heights over the river. Toulouse is a beautiful looking city. The picquets are about two miles from it. The houses appear to be mostly of brick. We expect to move today. The most heavenly day we have had this season.

April
1st   The same delightful weather; the vegetation in this valley is very forward. The gentlemen's *Maison de Plaisance*[34] of which there are great numbers hereabouts and all of which are deserted are very beautiful and contain every comfort. *It is really a heavenly country.* Lord Wellington thought from the movements of the enemy last night, that they intended an attack on this point & sent an order to General Alten to be prepared, in consequence of which we marched to the front at daylight & returned to our quarters about 2 hours after, all very quiet. Saw the 1st swallow this season today.

2nd   General Hill has been obliged to re-cross the Garonne in consequence of the roads in his front being so destroyed as to be impassable for artillery, he met with no opposition in crossing, nor did he fire a shot while there. A very bad look out.

Wellington now switched his plans to cross the river to the north of Toulouse.

3rd   Some pontoons went by last night. There is to be a bridge laid tonight at Grenade about 4 leagues below Toulouse. We expect to move.

4th   Received the order this morning at one o'clock, to fall in immediately, march to the alarm post; the division as soon as relieved by the 2nd Division to march on the road to Grenade. The 2nd Division relieved us at about ½ past 3 o'clock & we marched along the road to Grenade until we came opposite to a small village called Gagnac [sur Garonne] about half way between Toulouse & Grenade on the opposite bank [of] the river, when we halted by the road side. The enemy had a cavalry picquet at Gagnac who shortly after went away. Some time after this I saw our cavalry & infantry over the river advancing on the main road towards Toulouse. The enemy had about a troop of cavalry watching the road but I saw no infantry. Very rainy. The division encamped but afterwards part went into houses, I was one of the fortunate ones.

5th   Received an order at 3 o'clock to be up at the camp ¼ before 4 o'clock, marched up accordingly. Rained terribly, at about 8 o'clock went back to our quarters & the other three companies came in & doubled up with the three already covered. There are a great number of Spaniards cantoned hereabouts.

6th   Rainy.

7th   Received an order to turn out at day break & if we heard 3 guns from General Hill to march immediately to the alarm post. Fine day.

8th   Had a church parade. We were turned out of our quarters by the Spaniards; the [pontoon] bridge at Grenade was laid down again today & the Spaniards crossed. We went back to our quarters.

9th   I went out partridge shooting today, the number of partridges here is very great. The division marched at 12 o'clock to a bridge which was making about half way between Grenade & Toulouse. It was to have been made at day break, it was however scarcely begun when we arrived there. Lord Wellington was very angry & blew up the officer[35]. We marched back to our quarters.

The last battle of the war occurred on Sunday 10th April, when Wellington launched an attack on the French positions on the heights overlooking Toulouse. Unbeknownst to the combatants Napoleon had abdicated but the news had yet to arrive leading to a heavy loss on both sides. The 95th were involved in a diversionary attack whilst the main thrust went in against the French-held heights.

10th   Easter Sunday. Marched at about 3 o'clock in the morning & crossed at the above mentioned bridge, marched on the road to Toulouse. The plan of operations was this – the 3rd Division (which was on our right with its right on the river) & our division to make strong demonstrations against the city of Toulouse, the Spaniards, who moved up to our left, to attack the heights in their front. After that the 4th & 6th Divisions, who had moved in the night, had got sufficiently advanced to cooperate in the attack. The position the enemy occupied was very strong, it was not turnable, its right & left being on the canal & the town in its rear as a second line. The ascent to it was a perfect glacis, it was equally strong on all points and the enemy had fortified some houses & a chapel on [the] summit of the ridge & thrown up some closed redoubts. We sent some skirmishers down towards the canal to make a noise, by some mistake the Spaniards attacked before the 4th & 6th Divisions were come up and though they behaved very gallantly were twice repulsed with immense loss, a part of them that retired over the plain to where we were & who were followed by some skirmishers of the enemy, were so panic struck that there was no rallying them. Ours & the 52nd Regiments formed line & run on, the enemy retired. It was not until some time after this that the 4th & 6th Divisions came up, the attack was again renewed & the position at last carried with immense loss, the 6th Division suffered amazingly. The enemy withdrew into the town except from two closed redoubts where the Spaniards attacked. These were cannonaded by a brigade of Portuguese guns which were uncommonly well served, they were commanded by Colonel Arentschildt[36] who laid every gun himself. I went into the forts after the enemy retired, which was very soon & saw 6 dead mules inside besides a great number outside the most advanced. Thus at last the whole position was carried, the enemy retired into the town, keeping strong picquets on the road to Perpignan, the only one that now lay open to him. We lay all near the position this night, no baggage.

11th   The enemy are still in situ. I rode over the position, nothing can be stronger by nature.

James was certainly one of the first allowed into Toulouse and he later saw the Duke enter in triumph.

12th   The enemy are all off. They retired their rearguard at about 3 o'clock. I was ordered, being first for command to go to the rear with the wounded of the division, luckily for me their destination was changed to Toulouse, so that I got over my command without the least trouble; I left the division & went after to the bridge on the canal, nobody was allowed into the place. General Picton was there and there was an inhabitant who had come out with the white cockade & scarf.

I soon after got into Toulouse and went up to the Place de Commerce where there was an immense crowd assembled, most of the[m] with the white cockade; the white flag was flying over the bust of Napoleon on the top of the Capitoleum which is a beautiful building outside[37]. The Garde Bourgeois[38] were on duty at all the gates & saluted every British officer that entered. The people were anxiously expecting Lord Wellington who soon after came in & was very well received.

General Hill's corps crossed the bridge and marched through the city to the front, the 4th & 6th Divisions also marched on. Towards evening our division was cantoned in the suburbs beyond the canal.

Came in to the city in the evening to dine at the Hotel d'Angleterre and heard to my great astonishment that Bonaparte had been obliged to abdicate the throne and that Louis XVIII had been proclaimed in Paris, that news had just arrived[39]. Went to the theatre after dinner and the same intelligence was read on the stage and some articles from the new constitution, amidst the applauses of the audience. Bonaparte has signed his abdication and is to receive a certain annuity, I heard 6 million livres & is to reside in some island in the Mediterranean[40].

The theatre is neat, well attended, the performers and scenery very good, they have the same abominable custom of putting the prompter among the lamps as in Spain & Portugal.

Toulouse is an excellent city abundantly supplied with everything, but it is by no means so handsome as Madrid, which I still think is the handsomest city I ever saw. The city itself has gates at every entrance as at Madrid, but they are very different, those of Madrid are beautiful and form the principal ornaments of the city, those of Toulouse are dirty wooden things. Toulouse is surrounded everywhere by suburbs which are as well built as the city itself. The bridge over the Garonne is very neat, it is of stone & consists of arches. The celebrated canal of Languedoc which commences here has several bridges over it.

The cathedral is very plain, it has some painted glass which is however nothing extraordinary. The organ is very large but not showy at all. The streets are narrow, crooked and like a French town, paved entirely with round stones having no flagged pavement for foot passengers.

13th   Changed our quarters today to this side of the canal, better houses. Went to the theatre. Beautiful weather.

14th   Colonel Coghlan of the 61st was buried today[41], his funeral was attended by all the officers of the Light Division & by Lord Wellington & all the Staff. The service was first read in the Protestant chapel which is a very plain but neat building.

Lord Wellington gives a ball tonight, the paper with which the walls of rooms is papered uncommonly beautiful, superior to anything I ever saw in England.

15th   Lord Wellington & Marshal Soult are in correspondence concerning the cessation of hostilities, but it seems they cannot agree.

The people here say that Soult after having lost his position wished to hold Toulouse to the last, but was opposed by Count d'Armagnac[42] who is a native of this place & Clausel[43]. General Taupin was killed[44] & General d'Harispe wounded[45], d'Harispe has remained here.

Marshal Soult adamantly refused to accept a ceasefire until he received formal notification of the end of hostilities. Wellington therefore sent his forces in pursuit of the French army, his troops however were clearly not keen.

16th   Marshal Soult refuses to act pacifically until he gets an official dispatch from Paris which it seems he has not yet got, so that we shall march to the front tomorrow, we are very sorry for it.

17th   March at 5 o'clock, followed by the 3rd Division through Castanet [Tolosan], Donneville & Baziege, beyond which we encamped. Just as we got to our camp ground which was beside the main road, we saw a carriage and four horses attended by one English

& 3 French dragoons going as hard as they could towards Toulouse. This was Count Gazan[46] and another officer going from Soult to Lord Wellington.

18th Very high wind. Took a ride through Montesquieu & Villenouvelle, in the evening we went into houses near [Blank], as we were marching to our quarters we met Count Gazan coming back again. Soult has agreed to an armistice.

Marshal Soult finally agreed to an armistice and this seemingly interminable war eventually came to a close. Wellington's army returned to Toulouse and then moved to the west, the 95th being cantoned at Castelsarrasin for some six weeks.

19th Halted all day.

20th Marched through Toulouse to Lanarget, a nice village about 4 miles from Toulouse.

With the ending of the fighting, it seems that things began to unravel with great rapidity for the French. Only a few days later they were encountering not only large numbers of French troops returning to their homes, but also numbers of released prisoners of war.

21st Through Saint Jory & Castelnau [d'Estretefonds] to Pompignan, met several diligences on the road today. Met some of the Imperial Guard who came from Paris which they left on the 9th. We met an immense number of French soldiers most of them with the white cockade, who have left their regiments and are going home. Met also some Spaniards who have been prisoners going to Spain. Billeted on an inn, we made a party & got a dinner, very fair one, an excellent inn.

22nd Through Grisolles, Dieupentale, Monbequi, Finhan, St Martin [Belcasse], to Castelsarrasin, which is I hear to be our cantonment until the peace is concluded. It is a very nice little city, the people remarkably civil. We have excellent quarters, the 52nd are here besides ourselves. We are 3 leagues from Montauban where there is a French garrison under General Loverdo[47], a worthy colleague of Soult's, he refused to take the white cockade until compelled to do it by the inhabitants and we are 10 leagues from Toulouse. There are regular diligences from here to Toulouse which go in

8 hours. The females here are much better looking than in Toulouse.

23rd Had our band on the promenade this evening by the request of the inhabitants. There is to be a grand fete here in 8 days, that being the day of the patron saint of this place. We have established a regimental mess at one of the inns.

24th A Te Deum was sung in the church on account of the restoration of the Bourbons at which the British officers were present by the request of the inhabitants.

There has been a conspiracy to carry off or kill Lord Wellington. General St Hilaire[48] who was left behind when Soult retired and remained concealed for some time in Toulouse, his principal coadjutor was a noted advocate; how he was discovered I have not heard, but he is now in prison.

25th A French division came into Moissac about a league from this to canton. Some of our officers were there when they came in, they were very sulky and on seeing some of the inhabitants who had a black cockade within the white in compliment to the English, they tore it out. There are several people heard in the evenings when drunk in the inns to cry *Vive l'Empereur.*

26th Some officers of the 82nd[49] were at Moissac today & were turned out by General Rey[50] the commanding officer. Some of our officers were at Montauban where they were very well received. Our mess dissolved today.

27th I rode to Moissac, there is a sentry there to prevent any British officer from going in. Rode down the bank of the Tarn to its junction with the Garonne, the banks of these two rivers are uncommonly beautiful, the opposite bank of the Tarn is high and rugged, this bank is flat & highly fertile & cultivated. Moissac is on the other side of the river, there has been a bridge there some years ago but there is only a ferry now.

28th I rode to Montauban today, waited on General Count Reille the senior officer[51], to request his permission to see the place which he granted very politely, he is a handsome fine looking man. He was walking in his garden with two other generals, they all wore the white cockade. Montauban is a very nice place, it is situated on the right bank of the Tarn over which is a bridge. It is [a] much better built and nicer city than Toulouse & about half the size of it. The French had begun to cut up the streets & fortify the entrances to it.

29th *Blank*

30th There is a great fair here today.

May
1st This being the day of the patron saint of Castelsarrasin there were great rejoicings here, processions, te deum &c.
   Rode to Montech where the 43rd are cantoned & returned, a beautiful ride along the bank of the Garonne, it is a heavenly country. At night we had the long promised ball given by the inhabitants, it was very well attended & went off admirably well.

2nd Rode to Moissac, we are now permitted to enter, it is rather larger than Castelsarrasin but not so well built.

3rd To Montauban, the Duke d'Angouleme is to pass through there on the 6th.

4th – 5th *Blank*

6th To Montauban, the streets were hung with garlands & inscriptions & lamps hung for illuminations in honour of the arrival of the prince which took place at about dark. Before he entered the town he reviewed some troops, at his entrance the illustrations commenced which were very good. He went to the cathedral, in the evening there was a ball to which I went & had a distinct view of him & also of Marshals Soult & Suchet who accompanied him.

7th The Duke d'Angouleme & the two marshals reviewed the garrisons of Montauban, Moissac &c this morning, after having seen this we returned to Castelsarrasin. I have often heard much of French discipline, but I observed in the ranks this day the same improper familiarity between the officers & men that there is in the Spanish & Portuguese armies, as for the French officers, they [are] anything but gentlemen. The soldiers were very fine looking men & well dressed. The duke after the review went off for

Bordeaux. Soult & Suchet are two as vulgar looking fellows as I ever set eyes on.

There was a French garrison at Castelsarrasin which caused some friction with Wellington's troops, the French officers being particularly surly regarding the recent defeat. But the local populace happily welcomed the British soldiers and engaged with them in every imaginable social activity.

8th   We the officers of the garrison gave a ball this night.

9th   The number of lame people here is wonderful & it prevails more particularly among the lower order of people.

It would seem that many lost their hearts to the beauties of Castelsarrasin and James was apparently close to losing his.

10th   Took a ride out into the country with a party of ladies. The society of this place is delightful, the females are exceedingly pleasant & agreeable, they have the complete French manner in which I have seen nothing loose or improper, nothing that I should be sorry to see in my own wife or sister & they have a great deal of vivacity & badinage which the British females want & which renders them more insipid. There are several good families here & it is sufficient to be a British officer to be received by each of them as one of its members. I never spent so delightful a time since I have been a soldier. Though not yet absolutely in love, I dread the thought of leaving this place even to go to England.

With the end of the war in Europe, many regiments now found themselves being shipped to North America to fight the Americans who were attempting to capture Canada.

11th   Several regiments are going to America but none of our division are among the number.

12th   *Blank*

13th   Rain

14th   The picnic which we were to have had tomorrow is put off until the 17th. Rain.

15th   *Blank*

16th   The soldiers acted a play this evening.

17th   We had a picnic in a large meadow on the bank of the Garonne near Saint Porquier, with horse racing & dancing, we passed a most delightful day.

18th – 21st *Blank*

22nd   Rain

23rd   Rain

24th   Rain. The inhabitants gave us a picnic in an old abbey (now a dwelling house) called Belle Perche[52] on the other side of the Garonne. Delightful day. We danced also at night at Castelsarrasin.

25th   Rain.

The difficult relations with the French garrisons got steadily worse.

26th   The officers of the French garrison at Montauban have behaved in a very blackguard way to some of our officers, telling them that they were tired of seeing the English, turned them out of the place & desired never to see them again. The inhabitants took [their] part with our officers against the French officers. There is an order from General Alten forbidding British officers to enter towns occupied by the French.

27th – 28th *Blank*

29th   Te deum sung today in honour of the restoration of the Bourbons.

News arrived that the army was to march for the coast. This appears to have been received with great regret by the troops, certainly James makes it clear that he would leave Castelsarrasin with greater regret than anywhere else he had ever been.

30th   We have this day received the order to march the day after tomorrow. I never felt such regret at the thought of quitting a place in my life. I quitted England and my family with delight when I set off to join the army in the peninsula but the thought of leaving Castelsarrasin perhaps never to see it more, gives me greater pain that [*sic*] I could have thought possible.

31st   We were to have had a picnic today but in consequence of our departure tomorrow it was changed to a ball, it was a melancholy one.

June
1st   The regiment marched to Montech at 7 o'clock, I followed at about 3, promising to return in a day or two as we do not go far from this for the first 3 or four days. The departure of the British troops from here is universally & sincerely regretted.

2nd   Marched to Bourret where we crossed the Garonne at a ferry. Bourret is a small but pretty little village where the 94th[53] were quartered while we were at Castelsarrasin. I rode back to Castelsarrasin.

3rd   The 52nd Regiment marched this morning to Lafitte. I remained here all day, the gentlemen of the town gave a dinner to all the British officers, here there were 16 lingerers sat down to it. Storm this evening.

4th   Remained at Castelsarrasin.

James was forced to prise himself away from Castelsarrasin at last and catch up with his battalion on the march. Finally he admits the cause of his regret; a young beauty had stolen his heart.

5th   I tore myself away from Castelsarrasin at last & I can say that I never left any place with such real regret in my life. I am convinced that which is expressed by the inhabitants is sincere. I never spent so delightful a period as that I have spent in this place. I have formed attachments, one in particular that I shall never either regret or forget & I am convinced I have left one person behind me here who I am sure will not forget me & whom if ever I forget may I never be blessed with beauty's smile again.
    Had a melancholy ride to Tournecoupe (through Lafitte) where I overtook the regiment. Tournecoupe is a paltry little village but beautifully situated on a commanding height which overlooks a

delightful valley through which runs a stream. It has the ruins of a castle. Country well cultivated & in some places hilly.

6th   To Lectoure a very nice town situated in the same manner as Lectoure [did he mean to say Tournecoupe?] on a commanding situation (all the towns and villages in this part of the country are thus situated & all bear the appearance of having been formerly fortresses). This town is said to be of celebrity in the time of Julius Caesar. It commands a beautiful view of the country all round it, which is open & richly cultivated, there is on one side a fine forest. Beautiful well cultivated country.

[Unfortunately a page is missing covering 7-12th June]

13th   To a village off the main road & about 4 leagues from Bordeaux called Portets, an exceedingly pretty village and a great number of very nice country seats belonging to gentlemen in Bordeaux.

14th   Through Bordeaux & encamped about an English mile beyond it, in a field where the Duke of Wellington reviewed our regiment & the 52nd after the march; this was the most oppressively hot day I have felt this year.

15th   To a large moor about 2 leagues from Bordeaux where the greater part of the army are encamped.

16th   Rode to camp & returned to Bordeaux.

17th   Visited the palace[54], a simple neat building & the cathedral which is also very simple & neat. I admire its interior much, though I believe it is not generally liked. The exterior is as with almost all cathedrals, blocked up with rambling houses.[55]

18th   Rode out to camp.

As the army patiently waited at Bordeaux for shipping either to America or homeward, a number of officers, James included, requested leave of absence to sail home independently.

19th   Applied for leave to England.

20th   Got leave for 2 months. Went to camp for my baggage.

141

21st   Returned.

22nd Visited the asylum for deaf and dumb.

23rd Set off for Pauillac 10 leagues down the river, the rendezvous for transports. Went as far as Ambes where we slept not being able to go any further until the night tide.

24th   To Pauillac, there are a great many officers here waiting for passages.

25th – 26th *Blank*

27th   Embarked on board the *Concord* brig of Shields[56] bound for the Baltic, she is to land us in the Channel. Lay at anchor all night.

28th   Got as far with the tide as Verdon roads,[57] anchored.

29th   Got as far by the morning tide as Verdon roads where we anchored until a breeze springing up, we got under weigh & got out to sea.

Probably a combination of sheer mental exhaustion and a boring monotonous passage led to a two week gap in James' diary, which he then finished with a short overview of his time in the Peninsula.

July
9th   After all the fatigues & dangers of three campaigns during an absence of 2 years & 8 months, I landed this day at Portsmouth.

Chapter 13

Napoleon Returns

James rejoined his battalion at Dover barracks in the late autumn of 1814, where it was in garrison, having sailed back from France in the previous July. Some time in the late spring of 1815 James received a short letter from his father which betrays the time delays in their correspondence, referring to his injury at the Battle of Vitoria and hoping for his full recovery; but more importantly, emphatically insisting that James, having been born in America, could not under any circumstances fight with the British army against the Americans. It is an excellent illustration of the confused loyalties of many between the old and the new. The irony was that the letter did not arrive before the war with America ended and if the battalion had indeed been sent to America in the summer of 1814 it arrived too late to stop James fighting there.

To Lieutenant J P Gairdner

Shady Grove 6 November 1814[1]

My dear James,
A very short time ago I received your favour of 23 March 1813, at [the] same time got accounts of your being wounded at the Battle of Vitoria, but getting better. I trust that I will soon have the pleasure of hearing from you. I find none of my letters have lately got to hand, the present will probably share the same fate, it is principally, as the war is likely to continue with this country, to say that you must on no account come here as a foe, it is your native country, you cannot fight against it. If the regiment is ordered out, you must resign if you cannot exchange into another that is not likely to be sent out. I was in great hopes that peace would have been concluded at Ghent and that I

should soon have had the pleasure of seeing you here, for when the peace is general you could surely get leave of absence for a year at least. In hopes of hearing from you soon, I remain my dear boy, your most affectionate father, James Gairdner.

Luckily James was not required to break this particular taboo, before something of much greater portent caused him to move in a new and completely unexpected direction. The Emperor Napoleon had arrived back in France and retaken his throne from King Louis XVIII.

This news sent shock waves throughout Europe and it was not very long before the troops were ordered for Belgium to reinforce Wellington's allied army.

April 1815

25th Embarked at Dover at 6 o'clock in the evening, got under weigh[2] at about eleven and landed at Ostend this morning at about 6 o'clock [27th].

27th From thence we marched about a mile and there embarked in barges for Ghent. Went as far as Bruges, where we arrived at about 8 o'clock, stayed there all night and slept in the barges. The country from Ostend here is very flat and principally swampy, pasture low, the peasants appear to be very poor and dirty and ill clad.

28th Went on this morning at four o'clock and reached Ghent by six in the evening; got good billets. The country between Bruges and this place is one uninterrupted flat but exceedingly well cultivated and rich. It is however very swampy in some places, I did not see any good country house. The country is also well wooded.

29th We are to stay here some days. We waited on the King of France this evening.[3]

30th Ghent is exactly what I have always fancied a Flemish city to be, large irregularly built and clumsy, the houses for the most part very old but not ruinous. All the markets are abundantly supplied and very cheap. There are several churches here, I went to the cathedral this morning, there are some very fine pieces of sculpture in the chancel, the building itself is not handsome either within or without, even if it was it could not be seen as it is completely and closely surrounded by houses[4], there are several pictures but I am no judge of them, none however struck me as being particularly fine. There are large working parties fortifying the city.

I went to the theatre this evening, there is but one open now, it is for the French comic opera and farce. I found the performance much better than I expected, there is a Mr Huet[5] who has a good voice, his wife also sings pretty well and acts in the second class of comedy admirably. Huet is a good actor in that way; the orchestra is good and the music in general pretty, the leader of the orchestra did not in general play any instrument himself but directed not only the orchestra but the singers with a stick he held in his right hand and by the motions of his left. There are no brilliant performances in the orchestra, but no bad ones.

The house is in an oblong shape, there are three lines of boxes besides the upper ones, the pit is divided into the parterre and pagonel, the latter which is nearest the orchestra is genteel. It is like the theatres in France with one chandelier, besides the stage lamps, it is however sufficiently lighted.

May

1st   Marshal Marmont is at Alost organising the deserters, parties of whom arrive here daily, the Duc de Beri[6] is here.

2nd   *Blank*

James sent a letter to his father from Ghent which he finally finished on 2nd May, but he had started it some ten days previously at Dover.

To James Gairdner Esq, Shady Grove, Near Augusta, Georgia

Dover, 23rd April 1815[7]

My dear father,
This cursed war has knocked all my plans in the head; I thought a month ago that by this time I should have been on my way to see you, but this scoundrel Bonaparte to the astonishment of the world has as it were by magic revealed himself without spilling a drop of blood on that throne which it cost Europe just twelve months ago so much blood and treasure to pull him down from. Our regiment has received orders to embark for Flanders and we sail from this place the day after tomorrow. The campaign will doubtless be an active one but it ought

not to be a long one; it is very fortunate that the peace is made with America.

I saw Mr Moodie when I was in London a few days ago, he I suppose will go out immediately[8]. I am very sorry that affairs have so turned out that I cannot accompany him. We are all very busy in making preparations for our departure, as soon as we get on the other side of the water I will finish this and tell you all the news. My aunt and her family have been very unfortunate in the season of the year they chose for their removal so far north, they have all been ill since they went there[9]. I hope that this business will soon be over and that I shall be able to accomplish my visit by the next autumn.

Ghent, 29th April 1815
We have at last arrived here, we embarked at Dover the 25th, arrived at Ostend the 27th, and from thence we came up to this place in boats by the canal, we arrived here last night. We shall stay here two or three days and from hence proceed to join the army, which is cantoned along the frontier of France. Hostilities have not yet commenced, but will I should think soon. The King of France Louis XVIII is here, with the principal part of those who are attached to his cause, there are deserters from France coming in here from time to time, a party came in today. The King of Holland[10] is at Brussels as also Lord Wellington. The people of this country *say* that they wish well to the cause, but of their sincerity I am not yet able to judge, they are generally accused of preferring the French to the Dutch. They are of course sorry for the war and annoyed at the prospect of having their country made a thoroughfare for troops. They hate both Russians and Prussians and seem only [to] like the English so far as that they consider them somewhat better than the others. When you say that England is at a great expense, they say that at present she must lay out a great deal of money, but that she will end by being the gainer, in fact they seem to dislike their own situation and to distrust every nation. The country as far as we have seen it is an uninterrupted flat, but extremely well cultivated and plentiful. Living is cheap here, except where large bodies of troops are or have been stationed, but the country in being flat has no beauty or variety and must I think in winter be very unhealthy as it is very swampy. This is a lame irregularly built, clumsy looking city, exactly what I [had] fancied a Flemish city to be, the inhabitants appear to [live comfort]tably and are very civil and obliging. They say that they [feel] that with the exception of the army the whole nation is for the king, but that with the exception of Louis and the Duchess d'Angouleme, not one of the

146

Bourbon family are beloved.

30th April

We waited on the King of France yesterday afternoon, he appeared pleased with the attention, but he is very unwieldy and infirm, and it seems to be a great effort to him to move about. He is really to be pitied at his time of life and in his state of health, to have such a set to deal with, he is too good a man to be a king of France, they are a set that require to be ruled with a rod of iron, Bonaparte has so demoralised the nation that until the present generation are killed off, they will not be worth anything, but will be like a hornet's nest in the middle of Europe. It is a most extraordinary age this we live in, the preparations for war are going on here with wonderful activity and the French papers wish to persuade the nation, that all the world are delighted with the return of Bonaparte to the throne.

2nd May 1815

We have stayed here much longer than we expected and there is still no talk of our leaving this. We may very likely stay a week or ten days longer. The post goes off tonight, therefore I must close this, I will write to you frequently and as the communication is open now I shall hope to hear from you often.

Believe me my dearest father, your dutiful & affectionate son J P Gairdner.

3rd   Went this morning to the church of Saint Michael[11] and stayed there during the whole service, I was very much pleased with the orchestra and the service which was not at all like church music in general, but much lighter and more tasty. The orchestra consisted of six violins, one bass violin, one serpent, 2 French horns & I think two clarinets. The leader who was the principal singer governed the whole with the motions of the staff as at the theatre, he had a good voice, and his singing is pleasing. There were about half a dozen other singers among whom was one boy with a good voice. There is besides an organ rather small, which took a part in the service now and then. There were one or two good paintings, one of the crucifixion by Van Dyck[12] and one which pleased me much of the finding of the cross, a fete of which this day is the celebration, it is by Mr Paelinck[13] of this place, an historical and portrait painter who is now painting the royal family of Holland[14].

4th   Went to the theatre tonight, Madamoiselle Le Clerc from the Theatre Feydeau of Paris[15] made her 1st appearance tonight, she sings well but is not so good an actress I think as Madame, the music of the farce, *Le Tableau Parlant*[16] is very pretty. Madame Catalani is to be here on Monday.

5th   There is in this place on the tower of the prison a set of canalus, a kind of music for which this country is celebrated and I believe there only.

6th   *Blank*

7th   Lord Wellington who came from Brussels last night reviewed our regiment this morning, he went away again today.

8th   Madame Catalani[17] had a concert this evening in the Salle de la Sodalite[18]. I went there and was delighted, her singing is really astonishing. The song *Son Regina Del Cor* fine, with variations which was heavenly, *Della Trous* and *Via Senza fion il pinto* a duo with Madame Pucitta and the song and chorus of *Viva Enrico* and finished with *God Save the King*, which was enthusiastically received. A Mr Georges played two concertos on the violin very finely. The room was very well filled though the people here thought nine francs an immense sum to pay.

      My landlord introduced me today to a reading room which belongs to the Societe Litterate of their place, so that I can now go there when I choose. The people of this place pride themselves much on their cotton manufactories, it seems that until within the last ten years they did not know how to spin cotton but that an inhabitant of Ghent smuggled a set of apparatus from England (for which had he been caught he would have been hung) and taught the art here, which was much encouraged by Bonaparte, the man might have been rich but was very extravagant. They also make a vast quantity of linen, the country too grows more grain than the inhabitants can consume. This place is very badly lighted indeed.

9th   I have not seen a pretty woman since I left England.

10th   Marched this morning at 8 o'clock to Alost[19] 5 leagues, when we came there [we] were obliged to turn off to the village called Welle[20], in consequence of Alost being full of French emigrants.

Welle is a straggling village, a commune, the people are poor, the farm houses not very clean, but even here all the necessaries of life are plentiful and cheap. There is a great quantity of hops grown here, the country from Ghent [to] here is perfectly flat & cultivated, the road very good and nearly a straight line, it is shaded on both sides with trees, principally beech. The ground about this village is in some places very swampy, there is a good deal of grass and clover grown hereabouts, and there [are] a great many cows &c in the meadows, but I have seen very few sheep since I have been in the country. Very few of the peasants hereabouts talk French. There is a great deal of rye grown in this country for what reason I cannot tell as the soil seems rich enough for anything.

James encountered men being balloted for the militia of the new Netherlands army at the rate of 1 in 12 of the men of eligible age.

11th Halted all day, the inhabitants of this commune drew for the militia today, there are 134 men of the age to serve in the commune where of 11 fall. That is at the rate of 1/12, those who fall to serve do not seem at all to mind it but get drunk on their bounty & sing. I rode into Alost this evening, it is a small but clean town. Marmont resides there[21].

12th Marched at 3 o'clock this morning to Brussels 5 leagues, passed through the small town of Asche[22] half way. The road the same as from Ghent, paved in the middle, these roads they call the paves, the cross roads are merely cut, not made and must be very bad in winter. The country about Brussels is more uneven rather, but is still a very low country, and is not what can be called hilly.

13th Brussels is a very large city, larger than Ghent & more populous, this contains about 90,000, Ghent about 60,000 souls. The streets generally speaking are built in the same irregular un-uniform way as at Ghent, the Place Royale however is a very beautiful square and the coup d'oleil is the church[23] which forms the centre of one of the sides as you ascend is very good, there is near it the park, a very nice promenade lead out in different walks, very well shaded. The King and Prince of Orange, Lord Wellington & the British Ambassador live in the neighbourhood of the park. There [are] a great number of English people here and they are the prettiest women here, they live principally in a row of houses looking on the park; I saw the Hanoverian regiments relieve the Guards today, they are dressed completely like British soldiers except that the officers wear a yellow sash.

The band was very good, much softer than our English bands are, when they played God Save the King at the presenting of arms, all the officers who were standing by put their hands to their caps until the tune was finished. While listening to the band a inhabitant of this place accosted me and we took a turn together in the park, he complained much of the king being surrounded by ministers in the French interest, he raged that the minister of justice is the only man among them that has the good of his country at heart, that the king is a good well meaning man but weak, that the prince is liked and that those of the Belgians who are not inclined to France are delighted at Lord Wellington being here, and place their hopes in him, he says he distrusts all Frenchmen and does not like the émigrés and those who desert to Louis, being so near the frontier. Whilst talking to me in the way, he always stopped if anyone was passing. I believe from what little I have seen and heard, that the Belgians would sooner be united to France than to our nation and I think it very natural. There are a great number of beggars here, not only in the city but in the vicinity.

The draft horses in this country are very good and sell for about 25 or 30 Napoleons. They also use for the draft of small burthens such as bales, parcels, barrels etc, dogs and goats & I have seen them draw very heavy weights sometimes. The inhabitants are obliged by law to feed the soldiers billeted on them as well their own countrymen as foreigners (excepting of course British soldiers) for which government allows 6 sols a day per man. A part of the inhabitants of this city, even the poorest, talk French even among themselves, another part talk Flemish and can talk French. There is plenty of coal in this country which is more conveniently used than wood; they burn it in stoves, it comes from the country about Thons.[24]

Two of the officers of our Second Battalion came in here today, they came in a cabriolet the price of which was 24 francs for about 36 miles English. They are quartered about 3 or four miles from the frontier, the French are about the same distance on their side, the frontier is watched by patroles [sic] of cavalry, the French shot a German the other day for going the short way over the frontier.

14th   I went today into the cathedral during the morning service, the music was very pretty, it was principally the great organ which appeared as surely the softest of its size I ever heard, there were no good singers. The interior of the buildings is handsome & some of the painted glass very fine, there is a chapel to the left looking to the altar which is beautiful, the windows are fine and the carved wood of the shafts that divide them rich & light. There was a great deal of confession going on, which I can never look at without laughing. There was a school of charity children at the service.

I was also in that church in the Place Royale, it is a modern building both inside and outside. The Maison de Ville is a fine building, there is a spire in the centre of very great height and very beautiful architecture. The poorer sort of women here wear a scarf of black silk exactly like the Spanish mantilla, it has a good effect.

I went to the Allee Verte a promenade outside the gates much frequented on Sunday, there was a very good turnout of carriages, the best I ever saw out of England.

I never was so struck with the beauty of the Place Royale as this evening by moonlight, buildings certainly look better by that light. The place is not well lighted, the lamps are few but good. The water is better here than at Ghent, there are many fountains here but no handsome ones. What a much better idea all foreigners have of singing, than Englishmen. The English are caricatured here in one shop I think very illiberally.

15th There are several Prussian officers here, they are the best dressed and most gentlemanly looking of any foreign officers I see.

16th *Blank*

17th A sergeant's guard of our regiment had a row last night with the mob of this town who attacked them in the execution of their duty & our guard shot one of the rioters.

I went to the museum today, there is a collection of pictures there on much the same plan as our Somerset House exhibition in England[25]. I admired some of the pictures very much, but some people found fault with them, there is also a collection of ancient pictures by Rubens & others which for the wit of me I cannot admire, there are some old carvings in wood, very curious.

3rd Lord Wellington reviewed our division today in the Allee Verte, our regiment is in General Kempt's Brigade with the 28th, 32nd,

151

& 79th. General Pack has the 42nd, 44th, 92nd & 1st, besides which is a Hanoverian brigade.

James was now so busy that he failed to write in his journal for ten days, but he did write one letter home during this period, although it took him the entire period to complete it. He wrote to Laura on the latest political news and to make strong demands for a more regular correspondence from his family at home.

Many British soldiers writing home at this period made clear their suspicions of the Belgians, believing that they would happily receive Napoleon again. James also wrote disparagingly about the Belgians, but he did not see them in the same respect, he simply didn't like them.

However when he completed the letter over two weeks later he had decided that he liked Brussels.

> Brussels 27 May 1815
> Dear Laura,
> I wrote a letter to my aunt from Ghent about a fortnight ago which I hope was received[26]. I write this to tell you that you must exert your energies a little oftener than is your usual custom, I expect to hear frequently from you now. We stayed at Ghent about a fortnight and then marched here where we have been about the same time and there is no talk of our moving; preparations for war are going on, on all sides. Everything is active here, there is a strange mixture of different uniforms and nations all moving like a stream towards devoted France, all the deserters of whom there are many, and all the accounts from France describe the discontent against Bonaparte's government to be increasing daily. I think the reinstatement of the Bourbons or at any rate the destruction of Bonaparte will not be a matter of much difficulty. We have been lucky in marching through the best part of the country and in making so long a stay in the two principal cities of the Netherlands: the country is abundant beyond anything I ever saw. It is a fine country for campaigning in and may be a very good one for those to live in whose ideas of comfort extend no farther than good eating and drinking, but for my own part I would rather live amidst the wild uncultivated nature of Romantic Spain with all its inconveniences than in dull flat lethargic Belgium with all its abundance. Oh there is an inspiring something in a wild country and its boundless prospect which lifts me as it were above myself, and I cannot help feeling something of the contrary sensation in a country like this where I can seldom see a hundred yards before me. If climate and the appearances nature assumes have an influence

in the formation of national character, and that they have I think it reasonable to suppose from the temporary effect they have on the mind of everyone, I wonder how this country can produce any people but such as are flat, dull and stupid as itself. The people of Belgium having been from the earliest times dependent on one foreign sovereign or other have no national character; they appear to me from what little I have seen, to unite many of the imperfections of the English and French without their perfections, they have all the unmeaning compliment and insincerity of the French without their gay easy familiarity of manner, and a great deal of the English distance and reserve without their sincerity. There are however among the better sort of people in every country exceptions to the general character. I have met with some who have been very civil, and as no traveller can expect to find friendships wherever he goes he ought to be satisfied if he generally meets with civility.

Brussels 13 June 1815

I must beg your pardon my dear Laura for having so long left this unfinished, but one thing or another has interrupted me day after day. In fact I have no good excuse so the less I say about it the better. This is a pleasant place, I did not at first like it as well as Ghent here, but upon better acquaintance it's much gayer, there are a great many English families here. By the bye my old friend Miss Whyte is here, I called on her as soon as I knew she was here and am delighted with her, she is a very pleasant woman indeed; young Jacobs[27] is quartered at a town about twenty miles off. This is a gay place, there is a park here, a very handsome promenade on which the beauty and fashion of the place display their attractions every evening, which attractions however are by no means formidable.

You accuse me of picking up a flame wherever I go. It is not the case here I assure, nor do I think it likely to be so, for with the exception of one or two English ladies (and they perhaps are only so in comparison with the very ordinary faces by which they are surrounded) I have not seen one handsome woman since I left England. The English women are certainly the handsomest, and when you know them intimately the most delightful women in the world, but it requires longer time to know them than foreigners. However they are still women, and as we grow wiser every day as we grow older I must not forget that 'there are three things a wise man will not trust'[28]. I believe you know the rest.

However the wisest are apt sometimes to forget their doctrine especially when attacked by the rhetoric of a pair of bright eyes. All that I can hope is (if such should be my case) to be an exception from the general rule and escape being punished for my credulity. Poor Mallet is a sad victim to his, I wonder how Jane can have the assurance to quote that passage when she is a living instance of the truth of it. By the bye there is a little girl here I should think about James' age the daughter of a Colonel Edwards who has a very large family and has come here to educate them[29], she is as like Jane as is possible and I intend to take the first opportunity of telling her so. There is no more talk of our marching than the first day we arrived, but I should think this state of inaction cannot last long. We have been told that we were only waiting for the arrival of the Russians, they have begun to arrive on the Rhine and will all be up by the end of this month, then I suppose it will begin. I will write regularly and shall expect to hear from you all. Remember me to my aunt, to Emily,[30] Mallet, Gordon and little Mary and believe me my dear Laura, your affectionate brother, James P Gairdner.

Suddenly, things changed dramatically, with rumours that the fighting had begun.

June

15th   There is something going on in front today, we have this evening received an order to be ready to march; The Prussians have it is said been attacked, it is also said that Bonaparte has joined the army.

Chapter 14

The Waterloo Campaign

Late on 15th June the alarm was sounded and the troops formed up in the Place Royale before marching at dawn. Initially the troops marched for the village of Waterloo where they would rest before marching on for Nivelles, the original rendezvous for the army. But at Waterloo, they received orders from the Duke of Wellington to march on to the crossroads at Quatre Bras, where the Netherlands troops were in action with the French advance guard.

When they arrived at the crossroads, the 95th was pushed out to the far left of the position and ordered to take and hold the tiny hamlet of Thyle. They were beaten in a race to the village by a French column, but they then took possession of a nearby copse and being reinforced by a battalion of Brunswickers, traded shots with the French for much of the day. A heavy French column forced the rifles to vacate the wood and to take a position on a small rise near the Namur road, which they held throughout, eventually gaining Thyle village as Wellington's troops advanced at the end of the battle.

This tactical withdrawal from the wood is confirmed by Private Costello, who states that whilst in the woods:

'I soon perceived the enemy's light troops in extended order, and in great force, coming down to oppose us. This caused a corresponding movement on our part, and we were ordered to take ground to our left. We passed close to a pond of water, with the main road separating us from the enemy. While executing this, the French commenced a very brisk fire on us, until we gained possession of a few houses on a rising ground on the main road, which two companies of our rifles instantly occupied.'[1]

James, however, was not to be involved in the final advance. He was wounded in the foot during the fighting retreat to the small hill and had to retire to the rear.

16th   Received an order last night at about half past 11 to assemble immediately in the Place Royale in consequence of the difficulty of assembling the division, it did not march until near four o'clock this morning, an officer of each regiment being left to bring up the stragglers. I was left to bring up those of our regiment. We got off at about 8 o'clock. The Corps of the Duke of Brunswick marched through at about 7 o'clock. We marched on the road to Charleroi through the forest of Soignes, through the village of Waterloo (where the forest ends) and through Genappe. When we arrived at the latter place we heard skirmishing, hurried on and joined the regiment. The division was at this time engaged in front of the village of Genappe[2] on both sides of the chaussee, the country there is an open low country intersected with woods and previous to the arrival of our division there was only a small Belgian force to watch this point. It is on the extreme right of the Prussians, the French were in great force and were advancing with great confidence, commanded by Bonaparte in person.[3] Our regiment when I joined were occupying some hedges and remaining quiet, they had already gained some ground of [sic] the French. Shortly after I joined, the Brunswickers came up and we all advanced, the Brunswickers behaved I thought very well. We took a wood from the enemy which they might have defended better; when we arrived at the extremity of which we saw them in massy columns and as we were without support we of course lay down to watch them, indeed I wonder much at their giving up this wood so easily and as we were only about 400 skirmishers without support I felt very uneasy. While thus situated the Adjutant came with an order for us to retire and occupy some houses on a ridge in our rear. There was no order for the Brunswickers to retire, however they came away with us, the consequence was that the French crowded into the wood when they saw us leave it and followed up. We were obliged to halt on a base ridge above it and there make a stand. I there received a wound in the foot and went to the rear & I afterwards heard that three attempts were made to retake the wood that night, but the French kept it after all. Our regiment suffered much this day as did the whole division, particularly the highland regiments which were several times charged by French cavalry. The wounded remained all this night in houses just behind the position. A very serious attack was made this day on the Prussians.

Being wounded, James needed to find some means of transport to Brussels and incredibly, he and his fellow wounded officers were able to hire a cart to move them there. This was fortunate, as soon after, Wellington heard of the defeat of the Prussians and ordered the army to retire on a position just south of Waterloo. Any wounded unable to be evacuated would be left to the mercy of the French.

17th   This morning we hired a cart and went into Brussels being unable to walk; there are a great number of wounded, the whole army is moving to the left. Went to my old billet, the people are very civil. Lord Wellington has retired to a position in front of Waterloo, it is a better cavalry country than in front of Genappe, there being no wood there.

James was not at the Battle of Waterloo but was forced to remain in the rear at Brussels, where he was constantly alarmed by false rumours of defeat, until late that night, when they finally heard of the great victory. His note for this day smacks of being written later when quite accurate casualty returns were available.

His comrades of the 1st Battalion had fought the battle in an exposed advance position in the very centre of Wellington's line, with three companies in a sandpit opposite La Haye Sainte on the other side of the Brussels chaussee and the rest of the battalion lining the ridge line above. They were under constant fire and at the end of the day they had lost twenty-one officers and men killed and 135 wounded.[4]

18th   The bloodiest, hardest contested and most decisive victory was gained this day on the position of Waterloo. I was at Brussels all day in which there were many reports and alarms spread. I felt very uneasy as I was unable to walk well & had no horse to ride. It was universally believed at one time that the French would be in Brussels in the evening and I believe that the people generally speaking were glad of it, however though they looked on the British army as conquered (and certainly the disorder and confusion into which the baggage and stragglers relayed through the place warranted such conclusions) yet I saw no disposition to insult.

It appears from this laid before the committee of the Waterloo fund that the British troops in line this day average 40,000. Belgique, Brunswick &c under Lord W[ellington] 50,000.
British, killed & wounded 9,999, Belgique 4,500,
Prussians killed & wounded in four days fighting 22,000.

Despite his wound, James bought a horse the following morning and rode out to rejoin the battalion, which involved him crossing the recent battlefield, which he found very shocking.

19th Bought a horse this morning and set off & joined the regiment. They were cooking just in front of the position & I never saw anything to equal the carnage on this field of battle, I have seen many sights of the kind but this out-beggars everything. The division marched at about 10 o'clock to Nivelles, to Monstreux[5] near which we encamped.

By all accounts the French army are completely disorganised, the Prussians got into their rear (an oversight on the part of Bonaparte which is to me incomprehensible) indeed it seems that he imagined that in the action of the 15th [16th] he had disabled the Prussians from acting any further, but what right he had to suppose I know not; even if he had given them a signal overthrow, still as he had not annihilated them, there was a possibility of those that remained annoying him if not pursued or watched. They however got in his rear, obliged his army to disband itself in order to get away, leaving its artillery equipages, in fact everything on the road, his troops never had so much at stake, and never fought so well before and so confident was Bonaparte of sleeping that night at Brussels that he said it publicly and proclamations were found in his baggage dated from the Chateau de Laeken[6], in which he alluded to his brother Jerome[7] as Governor General of the Low Countries.

So determined were his various attacks that nothing but determined bravery of British troops could have refused them, the Belgian troops in general behaved ill, some left the field in good order, marching coolly to the rear as regiments.

I am convinced that Bonaparte had very extensive correspondence and good understanding on this country and that had he been successful the army would have joined him in a mass and the new governor Jerome[8] would have had little difficulty in establishing French authority over a country, the lower order of which are mostly attached by habits and interest to France. Indeed it is impossible fully to appreciate the entire consequences of the gaining that battle by Bonaparte. The circumstance is worth mentioning because it shows the versatility of French character. Many of Bonaparte's officers who were killed, on being searched by the soldiers for plunder were found with white cockades on their breasts.

A French lady, the wife of an officer who is with him, speaking of Bonaparte believed his being a dead man, which has also been my opinion, she said of him *'Qu'il avait l'esprit vraiment comme un diable mais pas le courage du Coeur, il a peur de mourir, il n'est jamais abattu quelle grand que soient ses revers mais il n'ose pas affronter la mort.'* [He really has the spirit of a devil, but not the courage of the heart, he is afraid of dying, he is never downcast no matter how heavy should his setbacks be, but he does not dare to face death.] It has been said by some that when the Prussians first appeared he embarked upon one more desperate attempt & that he assembled such of his Guard as were near & charged at their head.

The army marched rapidly on Paris but despite his wound his new horse allowed James to keep up with the regiment.

20th   Through Feluy, a beautiful village and country, Marche [-lez-Ecaussinnes], Mignault to [Le] Roeulx, got into crowded quarters, the country through which we marched is very finely cultivated indeed.

21st   Through Mons, across the frontier into France and encamped at Malplaquet, the scene of Marlborough's glorious victory[9]. Mons is very badly fortified and the ground is bad but I believe it can be inundated in all the weak points. All accounts agree in representing the French soldiers as deserting to their homes in great numbers without arms.

22nd To Bavay, cantoned there, Bavay is a small town and has formerly been fortified, but now almost entirely deserted by the inhabitants, the only ones that have remained there are those that are very poor, they are much frightened.

I have often been much astonished at the information of the lower orders of Frenchmen on subjects of history. I was today talking with a poor man of this place on the state of affairs and asked how the nation allowed the army to dictate to them and set who they pleased on the throne, he seemed to understand perfectly how and why the French army were the strongest body in the nation and when I said that it was not so in England, he knew that well and cited the history of England in a way that astonished me.

23rd Our battalion marched to Gommegnies as a post of observation on the roads between [blank – Le Quesnoy and Bavay] we heard the cannonading at [Le] Quesnoy this evening.

24th Through Englefontaine to Poix [du Nord] rode on for quarters. The country is very fine, it is richer I think than the Belgian frontier, it is certainly much prettier as there is more wood which causes variety, there is another circumstance which gives a varied appearance to the face of the country, which is that every farm grows a little of everything, consequently even where the country is flat, you do not see a wide unbroken expanse of corn with nothing to relieve the eye. However I speak here only of the country, the villages and hamlets have an appearance of extreme poverty, the houses are built of wood and straw thatched, indeed the peasantry here (and there are no superior sort to them) appear to live almost in a state of nature, having as I said on their farms almost everything they consume, thus they have very little intercourse with the world and money an article almost unknown among them There is no class of people above that mere farmers inhabiting the country parts through which we passed, no appearance of a gentleman ventures out. Thus I can easily conceive that such a peasantry, poor, unarmed and ignorant of what is going on beyond their own immediate sphere cannot however numerous have any political weight. However provisions are abundant and of course cheap when left alone are I dare say happy enough in their own way.

25th To Maretz, tedious march, bad day, went on again for quarters, encamped.

26th Through Beaurevoir to Bellenglise, near which we encamped, there is one tolerably good house in Bellenglise, the first I have seen in the country, the rest of the village is as miserable as the others we have passed. There is near this place on the banks of which we were encamped, a canal made by Bonaparte, it was begun 15 years ago and has been navigable 7 years. It was worked by prisoners of war, it is thus that Bonaparte has made himself popular. By means of this canal there is inland navigation from Paris to Antwerp[10]. Near this place is a tunnel, I think 500 toises[11]. Being in want of sugar I rode to St Quentin about 6 miles from our camp, it is a pretty good town, [it] has been a fortress and is celebrated as the scene of the celebrated victory gained by the

Duc de Savoie commanding the armies of Phillip's against the Constable Montmorence in 1557[12] in honour of which Phillip built the Palace of Escurial, the Bonaparte government had begun to repair the fortifications.

27th Through Vermand, pretty situation, Caulaincourt where there is a chateau belonging to the Duke de Vicenza.[13] Through to Ham, there is a French garrison in the castle of Ham which have surrendered on some odd terms which I do not understand[14]. Peronne was taken by storm last night[15]. There are no very good houses in Ham; but I think that some of the villages begin to look a little better built than those further back.

28th To Roye, a large irregularly built old town like all the rest of the towns we have passed has been formerly a fortress. We passed one or two large chateau, or gentlemen's country seats, some of which have woods, enclosed land and walks, evidently for convenience of shade.

29th Through Tillolloy, Orvillers [Sorel], Cuvilly to Gournay [sur-Aronde]. Just after passing through Cuvilly we descended a hill which commanded an extensive view over a flat country but the country is not so well cultivated as that we have passed and very thinly inhabited, the soil is chalky and the quantity of fallow land very great; we got on a chaussee today for the first time since leaving Mons. The villages here are stone built but that does not proceed from the people being richer but from the article itself being abundant.

30th Through Estrees-St-Denis, Pont Sainte Maxence, where we crossed l'Oise by a bridge which was destroyed last year, the country on the other bank of the river is well cultivated and pretty, the south bank very commanding rocky and very heavily wooded. I went on for [our camp] ground but not hearing the name of the place where we were to halt I went on to Senlis, a city and the first good looking place I have seen this side of Paris. It is an ancient looking place, the people had their homes shut up and appeared quietly waiting to see how things were to end and which side they were to shout for. There was a report when I was there that Paris had surrendered [and] the Prussian advanced guard had an affair at Soissons.

After waiting some time I went back to Fleurines where the

division was encamped, the country between Senlis & the river one continued forest.

As the army stood in front of Paris awaiting the outcome of political negotiations following Napoleon's abdication[16], James found the time to record his views on the present state of France.

July

1st   Through Senlis, Louvres (where there is a very haut fonce [very dark] chateau[17] and is a good looking little village) to Vaudherland which was occupied by cavalry, we then turned off the road to the right and encamped near Goussainville, got the first sight of Paris today. As we approach Paris the country becomes better cultivated, the towns & villages are better built and country seats more frequent but the villages are for the most part deserted and consequently plundered. Bonaparte after his defeat returned to Paris where all was dismay, it was known that the army was annihilated, that the allies were advancing, the chamber of representatives intimated to Bonaparte the necessity of his abdication as the allied powers had declared him to be an insuperable obstacle to the peace of France, he abdicated in favour of Napoleon II but they took [no] notice of this article and the emperor became M. Bonaparte, still however popular, still the favourite of the Parisian populace.

The Chamber of Representatives continued their stormy debates to read them is really ridiculous and more resemble the squabbles of a meeting of tradesmen than the deliberations of the representatives of a great nation, [on] only one thing were they unanimous, aversion to the Bourbons. This body however cannot be looked upon as the real representation of the people, it was composed of Bonapartists & Jacobins, of all men of revolutionary & republican principles, of the various different shades with which France abounds[18]. All of them enemies to what they call the old regime, none of the friends of the House of Bourbon and of peace had seats there. The object of this body in their deliberations was to stop the allies if possible with the pretence that Bonaparte having abdicated the cause of the war was at an end.

The cry was merely changed from Vive l'Empereur to that of Vive la nation, their object was the same still to remain the disturbers of the peace of Europe, a nation of soldiers, a privileged banditti. But it is to be hoped that the allies will not

162

leave them the power to annoy with the will for the will they have; and always will have, 'The unconquerable will, the study of revenge, immortal hate'. Let no false idea of magnanimity prevent us from crushing the serpent that has stung us twice, for it is natural to suppose that the serpent will change its nature and be alive to gratitude as that the present demoralised race of Frenchmen born in war, educated to look on plunder, rapine & bloodshed as the truly honourable employments, the only road to wealth and consideration.

The allied armies advanced without regard to the overtures and declarations of the legislative body or their threats to declare the war national. The War Minister however, Davout[19], has shown great diligence and urging in assembling another army which with the National Guards of Paris amount it is said to 80 thousand men which now occupy Montmartre and Paris. There are negotiations going on, the army however is almost all closed up now and I have no doubt but that they will come in to the terms of the allies.

2nd Through Gonesse to Arnouville, encamped. Blucher has crossed the river at St Germain and is threatening the south side of Paris. We heard cannonading today. The French hold St Denis as a kind of advanced post of Montmartre, they are both very strong, Montmartre appears particularly so.

With Paris threatened from the south, the French defensive position became untenable and the Convention of St Cloud was signed on 3 July by which the French army was to retire south of the Loire. Effectively the war was at an end.

3rd Blucher was sharply engaged yesterday and this morning Lord Wellington rode by our camp, shortly after we heard that a convention had been signed for the evacuation of Paris.

4th By the convention signed yesterday by Lord W[ellington] & Blucher on the one hand and by Davout for the other. The French army are to evacuate St Denis today, Montmartre tomorrow and Paris the next day and are to retire behind the Loire in 8 days.

No mention is made of the king, it being supposed by the allies that he has never ceased to reign. The French on the other hand, still talk of La Nation and wear the national cockade. I went into St Denis, it is exceedingly strong, the French troops of the line were giving it up to the National Guard when I went in, I found myself where I had no business, among the French soldiers and I was told by the people that I had better go away as many of the soldiers were drunk and all of them very sulky. All the troops wore the tricoloured cockade, even the National Guards and all those of the inhabitants that wore a cockade wore that one.

5th   Closed up a little & rode to St Denis, headquarters, there a few white cockades hoisted, no national ones.

6th   To Montmartre which has now a British and Belgian garrison, it is impregnable I think, there are only about 20 pieces of cannon there, but they are of very large size[20]. The tricoloured flag is still flying and the cockade worn by the National Guard. There was a great row in Paris last night, the Imperial Guards declared that they were betrayed, and swore they would burn the city. They were prevented by the National Guard. The provisional government still talk of La Nation. I rode to the gates which are guarded by the National Guard.

7th   Marched to La Vertu on the Seine, quartered [here]. The chateau hereabouts are very pretty and the grounds well laid out for summer comfort. Rode to the gates of Paris, could not get in, headquarters are there. This villainous French army fired upon the commissioner appointed by Lord Wellington to see the convention performed and notwithstanding no one has been punished.

Chapter 15

Paris in Peace Time

King Louis XVIII entered Paris on 8 July to resume his reign. James was actually within the city when the king arrived and his observations on the reactions of the Parisian crowds are both astute and very interesting.

Over the coming weeks, he visited all of the great sites of Paris and he has left his very interesting assessment of them and also his views of the rapidly changing and fluctuating political situation.

8th Went to Paris, everybody is allowed to enter now, indeed there is one brigade encamped in the Champs Elysees[1]; I will not attempt to describe Paris. I had not formed any very great idea of the beauty of the city, but only of its public monuments, which are really magnificent.

 When I went in, in the morning, the tricoloured flag was flying on all public buildings except the Palace of the Tuilleries and almost everyone had the tricoloured cockade. It was known that the king was to make his entry in the course of the day; by degrees the tricoloured cockade began to disappear & a few white ones were hoisted, at last the flags on the public buildings were replaced by the white flag & the white cockade became general. The king made his entry amidst great shouting in the afternoon. The people are however very sulky.

 The appearance of Paris as I entered was upon the whole rather preposing [sic]. The people were from the uncertainty and novelty of their, of course, unsettled [circumstances]. All business was suspended and they were all on the wing, dressed out for promenade to see and hear what was going on. Add to which it was known that the king was to enter and at the quarter at which he would enter was the same as we went in by, viz one of the northern barriers, the crowd was principally moving that way. The first coup d'oeil was for that reason striking.

The disposition as I said observable in the crowd was that of sulky ill concealed resentment, but consistently with the national character, they became as it were intoxicated at their first shouts of Vive le Roi, they heard and joined in them and you might have seen the same men who in the morning of that day would have argued warmly yet sensibly in their aversion to the Bourbons and have declaimed about the right of the nation to choose their own government, you might see the same men in the evening cutting such capers as would make you believe them mad with joy. 'Vive la Bagatelle' [Long live nonsense] is truly the French motto, as long as there is something novel, a procession or fete, anything that will collect a crowd, whether it be the review of the victorious armies of their enemies, or the celebration of the victories of their own, whatever may be the standard feeling, the immediate effect is nearly the same, anything that is done with bustle excites a shout or huzza & temporary oblivion of all their set maxims and opinions. 'Tout est bon pourre qui on l'amuse' [Everything is good as long as it amuses]. Whatever may be the theory of the Parisians that is precisely their practise. Is this the national character of Frenchmen? Is not this littleness rather the effect of the revolution and of the subsequent Bonaparte system which strove to discourage all serious enquiry and which in a manner forced the public to look at events through the angling glass[2], very distorting vision of the Moniteur[3]. Which public in place of what is in England political discussion that is a rational comparison of the advantages gained to the country at large with the sacrifices made to obtain those advantages, is content to take the word of government (and that too of a government subject, like an oracle they can neither contradict nor answer) for actual advantages and future prospects the French character was always frivolous and futile, but I do not think it was always so little, so contemptibly time serving.

The French revolution overturned all established order, the first burst of liberty was like a phrenzy [sic] a nation more liable than most others to let its passions get the better of its reason, was worked up to a fever of enthusiasm which deceased even reason itself. Amidst the shock of contending parties and amidst the fears & suspicions which were blindly circulated by the designing intrigues of these different parties, crimes became so common, opinions and systems so monstrous were openly upheld and

166

succeeded each other, that the nation became demoralised. The character of nations, like those of individuals is formed by circumstances and may be changed by circumstances. A succession of publick [*sic*] and sudden changes each bringing with it a temporary ascendancy, a studied system of delusion on the part of government, an artful continuation of regulations whose end and object was to render the spirit of the nation warlike, have completely changed the character of the French nation and have converted a frivolous fickle but at the same time generous, gallant, honourable people, into a nation whose object is universal conquest, to impose slavery on other nations without enjoying liberty themselves, with whom the faith of engagements is [an] object of ridicule and who shamelessly and openly avow that monstrous Machiavellian principle often before practised but never before acknowledged, 'No matter how criminal so ever the means be, so the end is obtained.'

I remarked that they were particularly civil to the English and what surprised me, recognised them at first sight. I had a greatcoat on to hide some half dozen fractures in my trousers, at any rate our dress is not characteristically English, but at every step we heard (there were two of us) 'Voila des Anglais' [Here are the English] and having dismounted and put up my horse at an inn to walk about, in trying to get back along the boulevard at about the time the king was to enter, I got wedged into a crowd of dirty rascals and at last was tired of heaving my way through them, was stewing in despair staring at them and they at me, when someone said 'Il est Russe' [He is Russian], 'Non', said I 'Comment donc Anglais' [how so English]. 'Oui' and room was made for me immediately.

9th Our regiment marched this morning to the Bourse[4] de Belleville and relieved a wing of the 43rd Regiment. There are troops and artillery at all the gates, whose orders are very strict and their mode of proceeding laid down in case of a row very summary. We took up our quarters in one of three public houses frequented on Sundays by the lower order of Parisians where they dance. Want of foresight is a striking feature in the character of the lower order of Parisians, they literally look no further than the Sunday before them. All the saving from their weekly earnings are spent on this day, they consider themselves in the jollity of these places for the toils of the past week and are content to commence the ensuing one as poor as the last.

10th   Still on duty. The Emperors of Austria & Russia and the King of Prussia entered Paris yesterday evening.

I rode into Paris today, the streets are very bad, irregularly built, dirty, narrow and with the exception of the boulevard there is no place for foot passengers. The carriages of every description drive strait on and get out of the way for no one, so that a stranger on foot is always in danger of being run over & is sure of being bespattered with dirt. I rode this evening up to the fortified heights of Belleville, they are not naturally so strong as Montmartre but artificially more so. There are a great number of very heavy guns there, most of which are overturned and spiked. The country about there is very fine, there are several very good houses there, all of which are deserted. From it is a view of Vincennes in which is a French garrison which has not yet surrendered[5].

11th   Relieved this morning. The division has moved to Clichy where it is encamped, the Brunswick troops who have no tents are in the village of Clichy which is about a mile from the barriere.

Went to Paris, spent the day in the Louvre, it is more magnificent than I had conception of, I cannot attempt to describe it. The thing I was very happy to see is that the Prussians are claiming those things that were taken from them.

Bonaparte is very popular in Paris, his conquests were useful only to the capital and that too only in a way which would not have blinded other people. Were a king of England to seek to render a war popular by promising to adorn the city of London with pictures, statues, triumphal arches and public buildings executed and furnished at the expense of conquered nations, I do not think that the city of London would be as generous enough to accept of advantages purchased by the sacrifices of the whole nation, at any rate I am sure that the nation would have too much spirit to be dictated to by the city of London.

The state of these two capitals differs materially in this, that in France the population of Paris is one, that [the rest] of another and they are quite distinct. The former comprises almost all the upper classes, all the members of government, all persons of large fortune & therefore of great influence there, pay only occasional visits to their estates & even then, if they go to stay above a day or two, carry theirs truly with them.

The influential part of the inhabitants of London, those who from their intellectual refinements, their wealth & their professional inclinations give the principal tone to public opinion pass a considerable portion of his year in the country, in which they meet a very large proportion of the population no wise inferior to themselves in education, acquire merit & even wealth, whose habitual residence is in the country and whose opinions and feelings go a great way to the formation of public opinion. Consequently in England we never could see the metropolis dictating to the provinces as was the case in France during the Revolution.

But such advantages as I have enumerated above were quite sufficient to gain Parisians who look no further than the gratification of the moment and with whom to gratify vanity and give some cause for spirit & holiday is to make happy. Another cause why Bonaparte was popular is because he is necessary to the gratification of their ruling passion, national vanity.

He is wrong who supposes that desire of conquest existed only in the breast of Bonaparte and that the nation were his unwilling tools. I am convinced that the ruling desire of (if not the greater part of Frenchmen) at any rate of almost all Parisians is that all Frenchmen looked forward with pride to the expected period when France should be mistress of the world, this was not merely the darling object of the military but of the nation and they hope moreover to achieve this without any great sacrifices on their own part. The system that Bonaparte professed and bragged of was to make war support war, to make war with the blood of foreign nations. His avowed plan as his war against Russia in 1812 was to raise the Poles by exciting the hope of restoring their integrity as a kingdom, 'Russie a choquer toute la Pologne' [Russia has offended the whole of Poland] was his own expression. To arm the Poles and with them to conquer Russia while the French army occupied Poland, was the plan he avowed. Thus it is not to be wondered at that a nation greedy of conquest should be attached to a man universally & I think justly believed to be endowed with transcendent abilities and who promised to gratify their ruling passion which was also his own, with such little personal sacrifice on their part.

12th To the Louvre again, it is really magnificent.

13th I saw the King of Prussia in the Louvre today, he was very plainly dressed and is a fine looking fellow.

I went to the King's levee today in the Palace of the Tuilleries, saw Marshals Oudinot[6] and Serrurier[7] there. The Hall of Entrance onto the king's rooms is called the Hall of the Marshals from being hung with pictures of the Marshals of France. The levee was almost entirely military.

The avis [notice] at the commencement of the book of description of the statues states '*La majeure partie des statues exposees dans la galerie des antiques est le fruit des conquetes faites en Italie, conform est au traite de Tolentino elles out ete choisis au Capitole et au Vatican par les citoyenne Barthelemy, Bertholet, Moitte, Thouin et Minet, nommes commissaries par le government Francais a la recherché des objets de science et des arts' 'Tout les travaux qui out ete faits dans les salles qui composent la galerie des antiques du musee sort pour leur donner une nouvelle disposition soit pour leur decoration &c ont elle executes sans les defigurer et sous la conduite de est Raymond member de l'Institut de France.'* [Most of the statues displayed in the antique gallery are the result of the conquests made in Italy, and compliant to the treaty of Tolentino they were taken from the Capitol and the Vatican and chosen by citizens Barthelemy, Bertholet, Moitte, Thouin and Minet, appointed commissaries by the French government as the desired objects of science and the arts'. All the work that was laid out in the halls that make up the museum of the ancient gallery are designed to give them a new provision either for their decoration &c and have it executed without disfiguring them under the leadership of Raymond a member of the Institute de France]

14th   Went to the Luxembourg palace now called the palace of the house of peers. The gallery of Reubens there is very fine, however I want taste to admire Reubens. There are two pictures there by their favourite living painter David, the drawing is very fine but I do not like the style of colouring, it is too glaring, too glazed. The gallery of Vernet is exquisitely beautiful, on the whole I like his pictures and those of Hue[8] (whose style I cannot distinguish from Vernet's, except that the costume is more modern) better than anything I have seen in Paris.

The palace is a handsome building. By the bye, there is a statue by Pajou, a French artist, as Psyche Abandoned[9], which I prefer to any statue I ever saw, not even excepting the famous Venus de Medicis[10]. There is also one by Delaistre of Psyche & Love[11], Diana entering the bath[12] & Venus coming out of the bath by Allegrain[13] and La Baigneuse by Julien[14] all French artists & which are very fine. I went this evening to the Opera L'Academie de la Musique Francaise.[15] Had great difficulty in getting on in consequence to the king being there.

I do not admire French opera or mime, consequently was not at all amused. The opera was *Iphigenie*.[16] The ballet *La Dansomanie*[17] which was pretty, they have no very brilliant dancers. The comedy is however very humorous & is on the whole very good. The orchestra is very strong & excellent, the leader does not play but directs the band with the motions of a staff as at Ghent. The house is not handsome & is lighted by one chandelier. I was on the whole rather disappointed, their manner of changing the scenes by trap doors is excellent.

15th   Went today to the Jardin des Plantes or Museum of Natural History, the museum is spacious & the specimens appear in good preservation. The Anatomical Museum is very curious, there is among others the skeleton of the man who murdered the French General Kleber in Egypt.[18]

The live beasts are kept in the open air in enclosed places in the garden. The elephant is the largest I ever saw, after that I went to the Royal plate glass manufactory which is no very great curiosity and from thence to the Gobelins or Tapestry manufactory which is exceedingly curious. The tapestry is most beautiful, the paintings they [use?] to draw from are very fine, one in particular by Le Sueur[19] a French painter on the theme of *The Condemnation of the sons of Brutus*, I think much finer than David's picture on that subject. There is a fine tapestry piece of the death of General Desaix from a picture by Regnault. There are some fine paintings by Vincent[20], Gerard[21] & Regnault[22]. A middle sized tapestry piece is worth about 800 francs.

Independent of the many masterpieces of art which the artists of the country have an opportunity of studying in their own capital, they have another advantage, every two years there is in the gallery of the Louvre an exposition of those works of living painters and those who gain the praises of the institute are sent to Rome for three years at the expense of the institute to study. There is nothing of this kind in England, the inhabitants of Ghent showed an instance of public spirit of the same kind to their countrymen in public.

16th   Rode into Paris after dinner, the number of people walking in the public places is immense, it is I think much more crowded than London. The people are also exceedingly well dressed, particularly the women. I heard the Emperor of Austria's band play before his house, which it does every evening, which is very fine.

17th Rode to the Hospital of Invalides, Ecole Militaire, Champ de Mars, to the church of St. Sulpice,[23] there are some fine picture there. The cupola of the altar piece painted in fresco by Lemoyne[24] is very beautiful and the way in which the lighting throws on it from above, adds greatly to the effect.

I then went to the Pantheon, which I do not think any great curiosity and to Notre Dame, in which also I was much disappointed.

18th To the catacombs, very curious, the origin of this place was in a quarry, the stone which is exactly like what we call in England, Bath stone, as used for building. At last in 1786 the galleries formed by the taking away of these stones received their present destination.

I then went to the Luxembourg into the chamber where the peers hold their sittings, the rooms adjacent have very large pictures of Bonaparte's battles by David, but they are [now] covered with baize.

19th To the museum of French monuments. During the troubles and anxiety of the French Revolution, it became the rage to destroy not only all titular distinctions and hereditary powers of the living but also all the monuments of deceased merits and nobility. Mr Lemoin undertook to save them from the hands of these modern vandals and deposited in this museum all such as he could collect.

20th Went to the Royal ci-devant Imperial Library which is a large and apparently very fine collection launched like all the public establishments of the capital by the robberies of Bonaparte. It is open indiscriminately to everybody for the purposes of study.

There is another advantage of public instruction, that the French together have over us, and they take their advantage of it, which they often remarked how much better they are informing upon historical facts than the generality of English people. That may be attributed partly to the facility of access to establishments of this kind and also to the cheapness of books in this country.

Previous to this I have remarked, is that they are very fond of reading British papers.

Walk[ed] along the promenades and the public gardens and we came out at a road of almost several hundred yards a table bearing besides masses of this ephemeral literature and almost every person whoever as well at home reading them after which they discuss the news of the day. But a French pictorial is not like an English one, confined merely to political news and advertisements, critiques of every description are to be found there and even essays on all literary subjects. This kind of reading though its result that is very much solid knowledge, yet it gives a plausibility and an air of general information to their command.

Report is the rage of the French, they see talking or as they call it converse, as one of their first most lifelong merits.

Another consequence of the fondness of the French for journal reading is the facility which it affords to a despotic government, which restricts the press at its pleasure to give what tome it pleases to the public mind in anything with an advantage which Bonaparte was perfectly aware of '*je regne avec des gazettes*' [I reign by the newspapers] in his expression, M de Pradt p111.[25]

21st   The French army which retired from this place to the Loire & capitulating, is very much directed to the royal authority and the conduct is very economical, he maintains a kind [of] negotiation with the king and his proclamations to his army are such as excite great doubts with respect to the sincerity of his professions of submission. The convention itself is very much forward. It is said that Lord Castlereagh[26] has expressed his decided disapprobation of it and says that Lord Wellington is the greatest man in the world in the field of battle but a mere baby in the cabinet.

The Prussians are greatly displeased at his forbearance & disappointed in his character as for gaining battles say they who would not gain battles with such an army as he commanded.

I cannot understand the state of France now, it is a complete chaos. I do not think that the people know well what they wish, they have just undergone a violent convulsion and now begin to settle after it. Their feelings are I believe divided between wounded pride at having been conquered & fear of what will be the consequence knowing themselves, in the power of an enemy whom they have imagined and think it most likely that these fears are kept alive on purpose by some design. It is now doubtful how things will end, the opinion of some is that as soon as the allies go away, the Bourbons will be dethroned, not that there is any idea of Bonaparte, nor would he if he were to return tomorrow to renew the struggle, find a friend except in the lowest ranks of the army. But the very circumstance of the Bourbons having been twice put on the throne by foreigners is a great attack to their popularity, now sits on his throne merely because they were conquered, he is then a memento of this defeat, a perpetual source of irritation to a wound inflicted on their hardest point of their vanity. It will depend much on his own conduct whether he succeeds in conciliating the nation or not. I know he is the most likely man of those placed in these circumstances to head it.

There are a greater number of people without employ in Paris than in London. I mean of those kind of people in easy circumstances, people living on a moderate annuity who sit down in Paris to pass their lives. Here one may remark one of the most striking differences between the French and English characters. The English are much more domestic than the French. The English family circle, the home is one of the most perfect pictures of happiness according to the English idea of it that can be drawn. To it we look for content, a word for (which [is] no less singular than true).

Of the Bourbons, the French have none which renders the idea, it is the seal, the kingdom as it were of our happiness. All the joys and pleasure we meet with in our proceedings and parties of pleasure, elsewhere are fugitive strangers. Like ourselves, it is at home that we expect it as a matter of course. Whether these domestic habits are the cause or effect of the reserve of the English I will not pretend to say. But on this point they differ from the French, who less accustomed to look for happiness at home are the more accustomed to go abroad. Hence the absolute necessity with them, to live in a large town, hence their fondness for promenade, for appearances in public, hence their badauderie [gaping].

In France to live in the country is an idea too horrible to be dwelt on. 'Cest au ménage au person' [It is the person of the household] nobody can say he is in the world if his life is not passed in Paris. Thus everybody who calls himself a gentleman has his habitual abode in Paris or some city. There is nothing in France resembling a country gentleman. This is a great obstacle to national enterprise in the way of agricultural and manufacturing improvement. Again as Paris bears a greater pre-eminence over the other cities of France than London does over those of England. It swarms more with others of the description above mentioned.

22nd   The conventions are much blamed here and the English Lord Castlereagh, the army of the Loire it appears are very awkwardly disposed. Davout who commands it talks of submission in a most dictatorial style; Davout they say is to be sent to that army which will be disbanded and new organised.

I believe there is a great deal of villainy among the administration of Paris.

23rd   Rode to St Cloud, the banks of the Loire there are very fine. I was disappointed in the palace of St Cloud. There are a few very pretty pictures there, particularly Jean Broc's *The Death of Desaix*[27] and the *Education of Achilles* by Regnault[28] and two landscapes by de Valenciennes[29] & Bidauld.[30]

24th   Lord Wellington's army were reviewed today by the Allied sovereigns, it was very hot on duty.

25th   Rode today to Versailles. The town is very picturesque, the palace the most magnificent I ever saw, it is exactly to be the abode of a great king such as Louis XIV. The fountains which only play on particular occasions are reported the finest in Europe. The great palace has been allowed to go to ruin since the revolution, it is now refitting. The two smaller palaces, the Large & Small Trianon are the most beautiful little places I ever saw. There are some fine pictures there by Guerin,[31] Denis,[32] Vernet, Montgaland, Haguette[33] & Berjon[34] &c.

26th   Rode to Fontainbleau, about 45 miles south of Paris. I was much disappointed in both the palace & the country through which I passed. I passed through several villages near Paris, all of them very miserable and it was with difficulty I could get a breakfast on the road. The palace is a comfortable looking old castle situated in a large forest, the country is wild and rocky.

There are some Austrian troops quartered in the town.

27th   Returned home.

28th   We get our pay now regularly as it is due a few days after the muster day.

29th   *Blank*

30th   The cavalry move farther off in consequence of the forage here being used up.

August

1st   There are disturbances every evening in the gardens of the Tuilleries, under the king's windows and reports of conspiracies. The brigade encamped on the Champs Elysees are subsequently under arms at night. It does not appear that [the] police are sufficiently active in suppressing these disorders or in punishing the culprits when arrested.

Fouche[35] is accused everywhere of conniving at such practises and several of the public journals comment very freely on his conduct and that of his party. The increasing freedom of this class is now very observable. The public are beginning to recover from the depths to which they were thrown by the late extraordinary events and consequently public opinion is beginning to revive. If the current of public censure continues to run against Fouche who is considered as the head of his powerful party, he must retire.

2nd   Went today to the Hospital des Invalides to see the models of French fortresses, they are very fine[36]. The Prussians and Austrians are taking away several, particularly those on the Rhine. Went to the Palais du Corps Logis lately, there are some fine pictures there.

8th   There was a review of Russian troops today in Paris. They are exceedingly fine looking men well equipped, the cavalry & artillery particularly surprised me, the officers are chiefly young men, there were only two to each company. The Russians have not at all the German style of countenance, their language is much softer.

I went today to see the figure of [the] elephant fountain, which Bonaparte intended to erect on the spot where formerly stood the Bastille. It is to be 55 feet high & 45 foot long & it [when] eventually finished which [will] be the most magnificent public monument in Paris.[37]

James enquired of the French farmers regarding the value and productivity of the land and betrayed his business acumen in rapidly calculating the financial yields.

9th   Rode today to Malmaison, it is a pretty country seat. Lord Castlereagh is there. Could not get in and rode home across the country, which is very fine. It is principally vine land. I asked a great many questions about the price of land. The vine land on the hills (it is dearer there than on the flat), sells for from 1200 to 2000 francs per arpent.[38] The arpent contains only 100 perches, the English acre 160. The rent is about 5 percent, an acre in a good year will make 20 pieces per acre, each piece worth 15 francs, so that the rent is about 100 francs and the produce worth 300. One peasant told me that he rents 45 perches (160 in an acre) at the rate of 80 francs per acre which he said contributed last year 30 francs. Meadow land sells for about 1500 francs per acre.

18th   The pictures in the Louvre taken from foreign countries are to be restored as also the statuary and they have commenced taking them down[39].

The commission made by Blucher & Wellington is much blamed, with what degree of justice I know not. Lord Wellington particularly is accused of want of firmness in the cabinet.

27th   The waterworks of Versailles play today. The king will render himself very unpopular to the Parisians if he removes his court to Versailles. It is by several considerations of a country nature, that Bonaparte rendered himself popular in Paris, particularly by keeping his court there and by obliging the public functionaries to reside there.

A dreadful persecution is undertaken in the south of France amongst the protestants by people calling themselves royalist and the peasantry and armed bands of the worst kinds in some of the provinces are committing such outrages that the gentry are obliged to reside in cities[40].

James wrote to Laura indicating that he was now tiring of Paris and had little good to say regarding the French.

Paris 4 September 1815
My dear Laura,
I believe I deserve your charge of laziness. I ought to have written to you before, however tho' not actually busy I have been very much occupied here. You want to know what I think of Paris, I think it extremely well worth seeing, but now that I have seen it I am very anxious to get away from it. As a curiosity it is worth taking a great deal of trouble to see, but is the very last of all the cities I ever was in that I should like to set down for life in. it is not near so handsome as

London but there are more public curiosities, that is to say at the present moment, for they consist entirely of stolen goods and are disappearing very fast. The gallery of the Louvre (which is the greatest curiosity in Paris, and which indeed is the most perfect thing of the kind in Europe, and consequently in the whole world) is made up entirely of plundered pictures. It is delightful to walk through it now and see the Prussians at work, and then to mark the ill concealed rage and wounded pride in the countenances of the Frenchmen. Whenever I see anyone who looks particularly angry I go up with as innocent a look as I can put on and ask why they are moving the pictures. 'Oh I know nothing about it' is the answer and the fellow starts off to avoid any further conversation on so sore a subject.

Those Prussians are exceeding fine fellows and Blucher is the only man who treats Frenchmen as they ought to be treated. Our worthy duke is very much abused for his lenity to the rascals. The Prussians, and indeed all foreign officers do not hesitate to say that he is little better than an old woman; as to winning battles, say they, who would not win battles with such troops as the British. However for my own part giving him credit as I certainly do for being the best general in the world, he is certainly no friend to his own army. I am completely disgusted with the French people. They say that the Emperor of Russia and the Duke of Wellington are the only friends that the Parisians have throughout Europe, and if as we are told the character of our friends reflects credit or discredit on us in proportion to their own, certainly the friendship of the Parisians is not one to boast of. For my own humble part, I cannot walk the streets without losing my temper, I do hate them so. Oh if I were absolute for twenty four hours. What a different people they are from those in the south of France, as a proof of that, there was a letter came the other day, written in the name of the whole of the inhabitants of Castelsarrasin, directed to our regiment saying that they heard that the regiment was engaged at Waterloo, and [that] they were exceedingly anxious to hear from those of their old friends who were fortunate enough to have escaped. I really am sorry to say that it is not the men only that I dislike here. The ladies are more provoking as they are more bitter in argument and talk of things that it is not possible they can know anything about.

One lady told me the other day that Englishmen do not know what patriotism is 'You Englishmen', says she 'love your country as you do everything else, in a cool tranquil way, from principle as you call it, but you can have no conception of the excessive love that a Frenchman bears to his country'. Did you ever hear such stuff? I begged leave with all due deference to assure the lady that she knew nothing at all about it, that she had entirely mistaken the character of Englishmen. An Englishman, said I, whatever he does feel, he feels it deeply, he feels it with all his heart, but he feels quietly. It is the same with the French and English armies. The French army have done very little and made a great noise, the English army have done a great deal and said nothing about it. Her husband who is a French colonel, took a pinch of snuff and grinned horribly. I wish they would move us away from this into cantonments, the country about here is quite exhausted. So General Bonaparte is off at last for St Helena.

It is a pity, poor fellow, that they would not let him live *quietly* in England, I always thought him a coward, now I am convinced of it. He ought to have died like a soldier at Waterloo, then he would have been admired in after times as a hero, his faults would have been forgotten, and nothing would have been remembered but the great achievements which marked the commencement of his career and the glorious death which closed it. But he to whom by his own account agitation is life, and camps, horseback and fatigues are luxury, how will he brook 'the waveless calm and slumber of the dead'[41] which await him at St Helena? Followed moreover by the contempt of that world which he in pride of his greatness, trod on and despised. But leave him to his fate and to that oblivion which is to him the greatest of punishments. I am exceedingly obliged to those ladies who have done me the honour to take an interest in my fate. With respect to that Mr Tully you mention, I have no opportunity at present of ascertaining who he is, as Jock is not here, he is on his way from Brussels, quite recovered. How anxious poor Emily must have been, I shall let him know how she has felt, but I doubt not that she has written. Nancy Mallet's death is a fortunate circumstance as her life was distressing to herself and family. Remember me to all friends. I hope to be with you in the course of the winter, I do not suppose affairs will be settled here for two or three months yet and then in the spring I hope to be in America. By the bye I do not see why you should take it for granted that if I go there you are never to see me again. Remember me to my aunt and all friends and believe me my dear Laura, your affectionate brother, JP Gairdner.

PS Edward Kemp[42] called on me the other day but I have not been able to see him, he is always out.

James' father had sent a letter immediately after the news that Britain and America were finally at peace. It is not clear if this was actually received, as it is not in the preserved papers. However his father wrote again in the September with a clear hope that he would soon see his son again.

James senior had not seen his son for a full ten years and with the end of the Waterloo campaign he was therefore very keen for James either to gain leave to come home or even to sell up his commission and return home permanently.

To Lieutenant J P Gairdner, 95th Regiment

New York, 10th September 1815[43]

My dear James,

I wrote you immediately after the treaty of peace was ratified by Madison[44], desiring you would meet me here, but soon after heard of Bonaparte's arrival in France and saw by the newspapers that your battalion was embarked for Belgium and since by the same, seen that you was wounded at the Battle of Waterloo. From the last return by Lord Wellington I flatter myself that your wound was slight and that you are now recovered. It is surprising your Uncle Gordon did not drop me a line, but I have not heard from him for a long time & still longer from your Aunt Jane who used to write frequently. I had a letter from my mother of 27 March which mentioned she was well. There is a report here that all the officers of Waterloo are to have a step, another that it is only the majors & captains[45]. You have not as yet got that length I suppose, the last battle will bring you nearer it, I have not seen an Army List for some time[46]. Before leaving home I directed a bill for two hundred pounds to be remitted to you. Let me hear from you how money matters are with you. I see parliament voted £800,000 to the army for prize money, but very little of that I suspect will fall to your share[47]. As no doubt the army will be reduced considerably, many who are so, will be wanting to purchase on full pay, you [will] find no difficulty in selling should you be inclined. If not you can easily get leave of absence, therefore expect to see you in Georgia very soon & in the meantime to find another from you by the army [post] which will be in less than a month. I remain, my dear James, your very affectionate father, James Gairdner.

September

19th, 20th, 21st There are many heavy transports now taking away the plundered property from the Louvre, the French therefore are savage, almost to madness and come in crowds to look at their misfortunes. How different would be the behaviour of an English public under such circumstances, they would rather avoid a sight, which must be humiliating, but the French find a vent for their sorrows in talking, they direct it entirely to the English.

24th   Went to see Talma. The play was *'Le genie en Autriche'*. I do not like Talma's style of acting at all, it is too ranty, noisy & declamatory, there are none of these nice touches, none of that strength reading which is so much admired on the British stage, for which Mrs Siddons,[48] Kemble[49] & Kean[50] are so celebrated, in fact the boisterous passions are the only ones studied. The other principal performers were Lannat, [Pria?] & Madame & Madamoiselle Georges[51] both, all these very good.

30th   Fouche and Talleyrand have resigned. It is said that they refused to sign to the terms of peace proposed by the allies. Fouche must have had great influence to have kept in so long. He is the head of the Jacobin party who were always powerful, even under Bonaparte, both who when he was last on the throne were everything. Besides this Jacobin party are two others; the common Royalist party who are for the monarchy and the constitution or charter, at the head of which is the King and the Duke of Orleans. The other, or the Party of the princes, at the head of which are Monsieur, the Duke & Duchess of Angouleme, the Duke of Berri, this party consider the constitutional charter as encroaching too much on the privileges of royalty.

The royalist party it is said gain strength every day. The Duke de Richelieu is the new prime minister.[52]

October
4th   Went to see the Panorama of Amsterdam, I thought it exceedingly good, it represents that city during winter and the effect of light is admirably managed.

7th   The chambers meet today.

11th   We were ordered out to be reviewed today, it was a bad day, we were sent home again.

Finally James got his wish, as the army was marched into cantonments further away from Paris.

29th Marched to St Germain today, the whole army moves into cantonments.

30th Marched to our destination today, the headquarters of the division are at Meulan [en-Yvelines], the division is scattered about in different villages; our regiment occupied the villages of Vaux [sur-Seine] where the headquarters and three companies and a half are. Our company with another company and a half are at Evecquement, the officers are all in the chateau[53] and are exceedingly comfortable. There is a very good library & the house contains every comfort we can wish for. It overlooks the Seine, the country in the neighbourhood is beautiful. It is about 10 leagues from Paris, I hope we may stay here a long time.

Given the extended stay in this neighbourhood and without the lively distractions of Paris, James proceeded to write a long passage with his thoughts on the differences between the French and the English:

The French have certainly a greater flow of animal spirits than the English, they act consequently less upon fixed principles, being more easily carried away by an artificial flow of enthusiasm, hence their great impetuosity at the commencement of an undertaking and the inconstancy with which they abandon it if opposed by calm steadiness. The character of the two nations cannot be better illustrated than by that of their respective armies. The French army at the period of the revolution, fired by the enthusiasm of newly recovered liberty, campaigned under all possible disadvantages, for want of equipment, commissariat &c but they were irresistible because the national impetuosity was at first attended with success & success kept enthusiasm alive. The political chiefs also intoxicated with success knew no end to their projects. To revolutionise the world, to overthrow royalty and all existing institutions, to make the population of the universe a French republic. But in all instances of defeat, how soon a French army has gone to pieces, witness Jourdan's retreat, Bonaparte's different retreats, nothing kept the French soldiers together as an army but the fear of their pursuers. Witness again the late action at Waterloo, with what enthusiasm was the French army inspired at the commencement of the campaign, with what impetuous courage they fought as long as that enthusiasm existed, but baffled by the steady constancy of their enemies, their enthusiasm once destroyed all powers of exertion were paralysed

182

and there was no interval between supporting the cause of Bonaparte with all their energies of mind and body and giving up his cause entirely.

On the other hand mark the conduct of the British army, it like the nation in success or reverse had one fixed object, viz the emancipation of Spain, to conquer; an honourable peace. It never lost sight of this object and when the most complete success had crowned its efforts, its demands did not rise with its success, unlike the French when the first wars after the revolution were successful. There was no thought of extension of dominion, because the nation acted on the same fixed principle on which it set out to establish a balance of power, because they saw that the destruction of that balance was the cause of those evils, it had required so many efforts to remedy. No enthusiasm made them enlarge their views beyond that which on sober reflection they found necessary to their happiness. The French have more fire, animation, quickness, animal spirit, than the British. The British have more steadiness, firmness, perseverance, reflection &c than the French.

What is the cause, I cannot pretend to say, doubtless there are many, both moral & physical, which have concurred to form the characters of the two nations.

The military chamber of the ancient Gauls seems to bear a close resemblance to that of the modern inhabitants of the same country, being [descendants?] of the Gauls who invaded Italy. (*Gallorum quilum corpora labous atque oestus culollerautpensa fuere premaque evorum fivelin plus quam vironum postrema munus quam foemi narum epe.* Lib 10?)[54]

Machiavelli if I recollect might express nearly the same opinion on the French armies which have appeared in Italy under Charles XIII & Francis I.

A Parisian writer on Parisian manners (*L'Hermite de la Chaussee d'Antin*[55]) accuses his countrymen of losing daily that gaiety and lightness which used to be so peculiar to them and attributes it to the lateness of their meals according to the new fashion.

I am of opinion also that their inconsistency or rather inconstancy (the feature of character in which they differ much from the British as their lightness which some have abused and others have called agreeable), arises from a higher flow of animal spirits for vainquer [victorious] people are delicate, more by their feelings than their judgement inconstant.

It is well known that the more violent and impetuous the emotion executed is, whether resentment, love or whatsoever nature it may be, the more violent it is at first the less likely it is to be lasting. The powers of the human mind like those of the body are circumscribed and cannot sustain efforts at once violent and durable. The more violent & excessive then the prolongation whether of the feelings or bodily strength, the greater the lassitude and void which follows.

Moreover the feelings are liable to be put in play and acted upon by all circumstances, however opposite they may be and the higher animal spirits a people are endowed with, the less liable are they to reflect and the more liable to be carried along with the crowd in their opinions, as well as feelings. Among such a people the few who do reflect and whose opinions, from their rank in life or their reputation for ability are most respected, are prone to lead the minds of the many, hence the power of fashion among the French, even in their judgements on literary subjects, they are too light, too gay, too frivole [frivolous] to think for themselves, but are content to take the opinion of a journal, for what they ought to think of this or that book, picture, theatrical representation &c.

There is another difference between the French and English arising partly from the commercial spirit of the one and the anti-commercial spirit of the other, and partly from the greater degree of phlegm in the English or higher flows of animal spirit in the French, the difference I mean is that the society of the Englishman it is generally confined to people of his own profession or pursuit, but of the Frenchman is more general. Another effect arising from the same causes is that there are a greater number of idlers, I mean people living without possession or an annuity, for instance a Frenchman by inheritance or any other cause becomes possessed of a property yielding a moderate annuity, he is content to live in the capital or some other city or large town on that annuity, he becomes an idler & frequents coffee houses & public places, reads the journals, hears and mingles in conversations on all subjects and thus acquires that tact of society for which the French are generally speaking remarkable, above all other nations. The Englishman under the like circumstances whose friends and associates are people engaged in business of some kind, whose habits are formed and who from his phlegmatic nature cannot so easily as the more lively Frenchman acquire new habits and form new acquaintances, then further engages his capital in some new business or employs it to extend that bis[uiness] which he is already engaged, he becomes a richer man but not a man of the world. His associates are people like himself, engaged in some commercial pursuit in which their ideas as well as their time are absorbed, they have no conversations & understand no conversation but such as relates to their own immediate pursuits. The reserve of the Englishman arising from his phlegm or comparative want of animal spirits deters him from entering into conversation with people he does not know, or forming new acquaintances. In this state of isolation from general society, he acquires a shyness, an awkwardness which renders every effort at conversation among strangers painful to him.

On the other hand the liveliness or comparative superabundance of animal spirit in the Frenchman induces him in his hours of relaxation when he goes in public to enter into conversation with the first person he meets, that person is also a Frenchman & is actuated by the same *besoin de coeur* [need of heart] which with the Frenchman as with all reasons possessed of high animal spirits, is like eating and drinking, a want that must be gratified. Raise the spirits of the most phlegmatic by intoxication and his tongue will go. The Frenchman by thus conversing indifferently with people of different professions, habits & characters acquires a kind of superficial knowledge which fits him for general conversation and what is more, he by this habitude of frequenting general society shakes off that shyness which is an insuperable obstacle to being what is called agreeable.

The Englishman coming less into contact with general society retains the peculiar masks which distinguish the profession or circumcised society in which he lives. If on one hand the Frenchman acquires a more easy agreeable manner from the variety of his society; on the other that very variety and the rapidity with which his acquaintances (for they cannot be called friendships) are formed is an obstacle to their being sincere, durable to their being in fact friendships (I must here *per parenthesis* remark that all these observations are to be understood in the most general scene, the better sort of society as in all civilised country nearly the same, there is no general remark to which there are not many, very many exceptions, but the general character however many the exceptions is the national character. To ascertain the national character you must not study the higher circles nor the inhabitants of the country, but those of the large towns and cities and most particularly those of Paris whom the French themselves call 'Les Francois par excellence' [the quintessential French]).

Another natural consequence of the above mentioned peculiarities, is that the English are more domestic than the French, which I attribute to their reserve of character. The society of Englishmen is as I have already said more confined than that of Frenchmen, they have an opportunity of knowing each other thoroughly, they in those societies which in England we call domestic, which admit of less variety are composed always, of nearly the same persons with each of whose names are appreciated in the minds of the rest various agreeable recollections in these societies, there is more heart, more affection than in those of the more volatile Frenchman. The one when he wishes a relaxation dresses himself and goes with his family if he has one, to a coffee house, promenade or other public place, passes there an hour or two in lively animated conversation on general subjects with a person he never saw before & probably will never see again. In such intercourse the mind is employed and improves but the affections are dormant. The family return home with regret because they go there from a place of enjoyment and they look forward to no pleasure there, but perhaps that of recalling to mind and conversing of those that are past.

The Englishman on the other hand instead of going in public to seek his relaxation, goes to the family circle of some relation or friend, or to the fire-side of his own immediate family, the time passes there in an intercourse in which the mental qualities shine less but in which the heart has more part. Thus home to which the Frenchman attaches merely the idea of the place where he eats, drinks and sleeps, the Englishman attaches the idea of the place where he enjoys his dearest pleasures. Doubtless many moral as well as physical causes have contributed to form or model, the French character to what it is and I am rather inclined to think that the peculiar tendency or rather policy of the government of Bonaparte, which by restraining the freedom of the press by purposely discouraging all serious inquiry into the liberal arts and sciences in order to turn the minds of the people & talents of the nation from the contemplation of public liberty and political rights, by encouraging on the stage only such frivolous subjects as form our modern romances; that his government purposely endeavoured and actually succeeded in rendering a light inconstant people still more frivolous than nature intended them to be.

To this anti-domestic spirit of the French we must assign the reason why their country is so little inhabited, (by any but the agricultural classes, the *badauderie* [rubber necking] of the nation is such that they must burrow en masse.

This constant abuse of proprietors from their estates and men of easy fortunes from the country must have a great effect on that part of the nation & must confine the changes and improvements almost entirely to the cities. In England from the frequent intercourse of the inhabitant of the fields with the inhabitant of the city together with the freedom of the press & other causes, there is no novelty of any kind which occurs in the one which is not known to and more or less interests the other. The variations in the character of the nation are in some degree felt throughout the whole the inhabitants of the country of France here entirely among themselves without seeing or scarcely hearing of their gayer countrymen the citizens, and they are nearly the same people now that they were centuries ago the labourer and the farmer, cultivate the fields as their father and grandfather did before them and not having intercourse with any more enlightened than themselves their ideas seldom wander beyond the sphere of their daily occupations.

There is another circumstance which improves French society (that of the towns & cities I mean, from the observation of which society alone the opinion and national character to be found) and gives it an advantage over English, that is that in France the two sexes mingle together which tends certainly to improve both. In England the morning occupations of the two sexes are entirely different and even in the higher ranks the two sexes rarely speak before dinner & if they do it, it is only in short visits of ceremony. At dinner they mingle together, but soon after dinner they again separate and each retiring from the other have their separated occupations, the conversation of the men when thus left to themselves turns on dry political or other such subjects and even these are heated in a manner less delicate & elegant than that of which their nature is susceptible and with which they would be and are heated in the presence of women. The women left to themselves not having those motives to please, which activate them in their intercourse with the other sex, their conversation is reserved and partake of that littleness to which women are subject from the confined nature of their life. The young persons of both sexes not being brought up in the habitual intercourse with each other are shy, diffident & awkward.

In France throughout all ranks the sexes mingle more together, their amusements are more identified with each other. At table or in the salon the conversation is general, the men thus by a continual intercourse with the women have a continual motive for endeavouring to please, their emulation excited, they are always attentive to propriety and acquire a portion of that polish and elegance which are the particular attributes of the sex. The women have the same motive as the men to be agreeable and well informed.

In England general conversation is not expected from a woman especially a young one in the country, she would be blamed as forward if she were to offer a remark or opinion unless somebody addressed her particularly. And there is such a great portion of vanity in all the motives for human actions that few people will be at the trouble of mental application, if they have not the prospect of displaying their *savoir* [knowledge]. In France a certain degree of information is necessary for a woman because she is expected to take a part in the conversation. By being thus constituted a more important part of the society, they acquire a general information and shake off in a great measure that littleness which I am convinced does not belong to the sex but to their manner of education and life.

Women are said to feel everything in extreme, cannot this be accounted for by their secluded manner of life? We know that intercourse with the world generally blunts the feelings which I attribute to the selfish state of society in general to the disappointed and coldness which the warm confident heat of youth meets with in what is called the world. As women from their mode of life are less exposed to this as their occupations are more sedentary and their thoughts consequently less liable to distraction, they are more occupied with their feelings, thus with them it is not only the heart but the imagination which is employed. To the same cause I attribute that littleness and those petty resentments and jealousies which we see in some women, and in travelled men whose ideas like their life & occupations are confined within the small sphere perhaps of a country town.

As the French have great criminal spirits they have very little of what we call feeling or sensibility which are two qualities, perhaps incompatible, they go to the spectacle less to be seduced by the imaginary use of the scene than to criticise in England the feelings of the audience (that part I mean who go to see the play) are intent on the representation, the judgement only wakes to condemn or applaud on curtain, as of gross error or brilliant acting, while the feelings are alone intent on the interest of the drama and after it is over & the emotions excited have subsided, the judgement then and not till then approves or condemns in proportion as the music has more or less powerfully acted on the feelings. If the tragedy does not re-awake the sensibility at all the judgement at once condemns it, because an English audience go to a tragedy to feel. A French audience go to a tragedy to criticise.

Esprits is the maxim of the French people, a witticism will often gain a bad cause and during the representation instead of abandoning themselves to the fictitious woe of the scene, their minds are employed in thinking what they should say when asked their opinion and even if they should happen involuntarily to feel admiration for a play or an actor who is generally condemned, they would not say it for fear of being thought *des gens de mauvais gout*, [people of bad taste]. So much for the sensibility of the French, now for their feeling or their intercourse with each other, as they are inconstant, which I have attributed in a great measure to their high animal spirits, of course they can have no deep or lasting feeling in their affections, I do not think they have even keen feelings or what we call warm passions. In all things which regard the point of honour their first impulse is keen & impetuous but this arises from the influence of society & public opinion which proceeds from society; but on their feelings of love or desire they are cold. Setting aside constancy of attachment I will venture to affirm that the passion (I will not talk of the sentiment) of love is seldomer felt in France than either England or Spain, the one a more northern, the other a more southern climate, that in fact they have less passion than either the English or the Spaniards this may be owing in a great measure to a certain laxity of morals & indecent freedom in French manners. Subjects are heated indifferently in French conversation which are the height of indecency elsewhere and we all know that too much familiarity & knowledge on those subjects vents the feelings. There must be a great deal left to the imagination to keep passion warm, were men & women to go naked, there would be even less of it.

November

22nd The treaty of peace was signed at Paris on the 20th[56]. The French are to maintain 150,000 of the allied troops in their country for five years, those that exceed this manner are to go home immediately.

30th   The regiments who do not form a part of the army of occupation have commenced marching today. Some of them come into our village for this night.

December
9th   Marched today to St Germain [en –Lay], very cold indeed.

The 95th returned to Paris and James enjoyed the opportunities to visit the theatres again.

10th   Marched to Paris our men are in the barracks in the Rue de Clichy, the officers are billeted chiefly in the Rue Mont Blanc[57]. The people are very sulky, they attribute chiefly to [the] English the hard terms of the treaty of peace. The weather is exceedingly cold.

12th   We have got a mess room and are very comfortable, I hope we may remain here some time.

13th   Went this evening to the theatre des varieties. The performance is very pleasing.

20th   To the Italian opera *Semiramide*[58] was performed in which Catalani[59] sung divinely, the orchestra is very good.

23rd   To the Italian opera *Il Fanatico perla Musica*[60] was performed, in which Catalani was still more exquisite & the orchestra shone more than the last time I was there.

24th   To the Theatre Feydeau or Comic opera, the singing is very good. This is a style of acting in which the French excel every other nation. It is a species of composition also in which they write well, but their tragedies though they consider themselves the first dramatic nation in the world appear to me very unnatural. In the first place their choice of subjects do not like our own Shakespeare whom they are pleased to term a barbarian, appearing to me to show a greater knowledge of spirit of dramatic act, viz the exciting of interest. It is more natural to suppose that a modern audience would be interested in subjects drawn from the history of their own country or founded on the popular tales of modern times, such as Romeo and Juliet, Hamlet, Othello & because we can conceive such feelings & such manners but how any modern people & above all how the French can enter into the feelings of

190

Achilles, Agamemnon & Alexander the Great is what I cannot conceive, besides there is a coldness & dignity which characterises all classical stories & writings ill suited to the excitement of either violent passions or tender feelings. I have seen Addison's certainly very elegant tragedy of Cato[61] performed with all Mr Kemble's[62] fine acting and have certainly admired it much, but could not feel it. With such subjects tied down also by the strictest rules and to which all other subjects are also obliged to conform, and a language naturally too light for the dignity of tragedy, French tragedy can never seriously interest, it is not only their tragedy but their manner of performing that I dislike, it is all declamation and the language of the tragic actor like that of the writer is not the language of nature, there [are] none of those sudden bursts of genius, those gestures, glances, that look which express the most inexpressible feelings of the heart, such as you see on the English stage. In French tragedy I never can forget the actor but I have seen Mrs Siddons[63], Miss O'Neill[64] & Mr Kemble without recollecting for the time that there were such people in existence.

27th Marched this morning (our brigade only) our regiment is in four villages, our company and another at Marly, head quarters at Louvre.

29th Went to Paris. Went to the French opera, saw the ballet of *Flore et Zephire*[65]. Very grand indeed.

30th Returned to Marly.

? Ugly old house, I am sick of being divided [up].

Chapter 16

The Army of Occupation

In early 1816 the army marched into the north of France, it was none too soon for James.

January 1816

26th Marched through Gournay [sur-Aronde] to Cuvilly where headquarters stopped, our company went off the road to Ressons [sur-Matz].

27th Through Roye to Liancourt [Fosse] where our company stopped with head quarters.

28th Halt. Fine hard frost.

29th Through Peronne (La Pucelle as it used to be called), which is strong by its nearby situation only. Our company to Allaines.

30th Through Fins to (our company) Gonnelieu.

31st Through Cambrai to our final destination, our company is cantoned at Marquion two leagues from Cambrai & about 5 from Arras. The rest of the regiment are at Inchy [en-Artois], Baralle, Pronville & Cagnicourt. Head quarters of the brigade are at Buissy.

Moeuvres 15 February 1816

My dear Laura,
I have no doubt you will think me unpardonably lazy in not having answered your letter before. A short time after the receipt of it we

again commenced moving, and after various short halts arrived in the cantonments on the first of this month which I suppose will be the cantonments of this army for three or perhaps five years. A pretty prospect. Everybody was delighted at the idea of remaining in France, and those regiments who were not destined to form a part of the army of occupation were thought peculiarly unfortunate; a fortnight's trial however has wrought a wonderful change in the ideas of our citizens of the world, who begin to think now that their own country is the best after all.

The army is woefully disappointed, instead of being as they expected in the large towns, where they could have plenty of society, their regimental mess, and where they would have an opportunity of playing the elegant, we are all scattered about in different villages, which are hereabouts very poor, and in bad weather the roads which are nowhere paved are impassable, so that in bad weather one [is] absolutely a prisoner in one's house. Is this not a brilliant prospect for five years, especially to those who have no resources within themselves, who never read, and who are perfectly dependent on others for their amusement which I am sorry to say is the case with the greater part of the officers of the army. This is very different indeed from the south of France.

I was very sorry to learn by your letter that my aunt is still confined to her room; but I hope that the fine weather which we may expect shortly will give her an opportunity of taking a little exercise now and then which surely would be of advantage to her. But perhaps the winter lasts longer with you than it does in England. The weather has been very cold here lately and I have had an opportunity of skating, an amusement which you know I used to be very fond of and which I have not had in my power since I have been in the army. The people of this country do it in great perfection, and as there are in Flanders and Holland almost as many canals as high roads, one might in winter make a skating tour through the whole country. They tell us however that we may soon expect spring weather here. I had a letter from my father of later date than that you mention written from Shady Grove after his return from the northward. He had then seen all the particulars of the Battle of Waterloo[1]. I am in daily expectation of hearing again, if I do not hear shortly I will apply for leave of absence and will of course see you before I go out [to America].

You mention that Robert Walker is a captain. Do you mean a post captain? He was a commander some time ago. He has no right to complain of his promotion, it has not been bad, but in the rank he now has it is difficult to get employed unless you have very good interests especially in peace time. But we cannot remain very long at peace. It is not in the nature of [Europe?] to be quiet. We shall be quarrelling I suppose next with the [Russians?] or some of those who have hitherto been our friends. I should like very much to see Robert again. I suppose he will be taking a wife now that he has gone to domesticate in Scotland.

I hope to hear from you soon with better accounts from you all. Tell my aunt that I will write to her soon. Remember me to Morisson, love to Jane, Mary and Gordon. And believe me my dear Laura, your affectionate brother, JP Gairdner.

The monotony of garrison duty in northern France meant that James saw no reason to continue his journal and his final notes show that he was successful in gaining an extended leave to sail over to New York and to finally meet up once again with his father:

Embarked onboard the *Montagu* packet[2] for New York by Halifax on the 12th of May [1816]. Landed at Halifax on the 14th of June. It is a small wood built town, the country about it is barren & little cultivated, but not destitute of picturesque beauty. We remained there five days. I rode up the arm of the sea[3] (which forms a basin in the interior) about ten miles the scenery was exceedingly beautiful; there are several straggling Indians here, they miserable, half clothed, dirty looking wretches but I was struck at first sight with the resemblance between them and the Cossacks I had seen in Paris, in their very peculiar cast of countenance.

Anchored in the north River opposite New York on the 30th of June.

It is uncertain how long James stayed in America but it would appear to have been around a year, as the next correspondence we have written from him to his father does not appear until early 1818 when he was back in England. This refers to a letter sent from his father in the previous autumn which would have been written many months after he had left America. It would appear that having sailed to England, he had spent the winter with his family in Scotland and was now back with the regimental depot at Shorncliffe before returning to his battalion, which still remained as part of the Army of Occupation in France.

James now encouraged his father to visit the family in Scotland himself.

194

Shorncliffe 27th March 1818[4]

Annotated: Received 3rd November

To James Gairdner esq, Shady Grove, Augusta, Georgia.

My dear father,
I received your letter of the 27th October about six weeks ago while I was at Wooden[5], where I spent a month on my way to Aberdeen. I should have answered it before, but I have been so continually engaged and occupied during the time of a very hurried visit which I paid to my friends in the north, that I have not had time. I went away for only three months and as I knew that there was no getting a prolongation and I had to pay visits at Wooden and Corsbie *en passant*, I had my time quite occupied. I found my aunt in better health than she has been for some time, but she has suffered a great deal since she has been at Aberdeen. My grandmother I found in good health and spirits and not in the least altered since I last saw her eight years ago. I have been greatly delighted with my visits to, and infinitely gratified by the renewal of the acquaintance with my relations in Roxburghshire, my cousins at Wooden and Corsbie, who have all given up since I (and more especially since you) saw them, have always cherished an affectionate remembrance of us all and I was much pleased with the warmth of heart with which I was received and by the terms in which they all expressed themselves of you and of their wish that you would settle among them, and really my dear father I wish you would think of some such plan. I am sure if you would as you have promised, come to this country on a visit, you would find so many in that part of Scotland where your relatives live, whose attentions and society would please you, that you would be convinced that it is a country more congenial to your tastes and feelings than you at present imagine; certainly more so than the one you now reside in. Mr Murray is an excellent man and speaks of you in terms of most affectionate regard as also Mr Walker and I am sure you need be at no loss for occupation there. Farming on a small scale, enough to give you employment and amusement, without involving interest enough to give you anxiety, would be much more calculated to make you happy, surrounded as you would then be by your friends and relations, than your employments in America, cut off as you are from all who care for you. I do not mean that you should, or that it would be practicable to put such a scheme into effect immediately. I know very well that the property in America must at present be looked after, but some such

plan in perspective, something to look forward to in which we might hope to be all reunited would be a consolation to us all. It would I am sure be so to you, it would be so to me, and really my aunt's mind and spirits require some resting point of that kind. They are all disgusted with Aberdeen and must leave it, it does not agree with the health of any of them and Gordon cannot finish his education there. They have met with some kind friends who have showed them a good deal of attention, but still they are strangers, they have no family connections there and in Aberdeen as in all other parts of Scotland those connections are of such primary importance, families are so large indeed and society runs so much as it were in clans, that strangers must feel themselves in a manner lost, if living in Scotland they have not there ties about them. Besides, there is another consideration, an important one, and which my aunt feels; and that is, that for her family's sake it is a duty to cultivate the good understanding which her children's relations have every disposition to show; if anything were to happen to her in her present situation, what would become of her family? They could not continue to live in Aberdeen, they must seek another residence which would then be done under circumstances peculiarly distressing and disadvantageous.

All these and many other considerations with the most thorough conviction that the life of a country gentleman in that part of the country where your relations live, is the most suited to your tastes and feelings induce me to urge most earnestly the fulfilment on the earliest possible opportunity, of the visit you promised to pay us. You will then see yourself all that which I now attempt to impress you with, and besides the gratification that I am convinced it will afford you to renew your acquaintance with the scenes of your own country and with those who love you. It will be of great service to my aunt, it will be so to your own affairs; that business of Simpson & Davison I think absolutely requires your personal attendance to it. I am sorry to hear such bad accounts of the crops, but I do not give any credit to the story of the *rot* being permanent, the farmers in several districts in England and Scotland had their wheat destroyed for two or three successive years by something of the same kind for which they could not account and which went away in a manner equally inexplicable. I hope it may be the same with what you complain of, I however am always ready to forward any arrangement or second any plan that circumstances may render necessary.

I hope I have said enough my dear father, to induce you to comply with the request in which my aunt and her dear family earnestly join with me, that you will take the earliest possible opportunity of paying us your promised visit. Louisa returned home before I left it, much improved in health by her journey to the south, where I wrote to you she came and spent the winter with my Uncle Gordon. Jane is a nice, a very nice girl, and Gordon a fine gentlemanly boy. My aunt is much at a loss about him and wants to get at my uncle's intention and opinion respecting him. I want to have some conversation with him on the subject. Robert Walker[6] and his sister Rebecca accompanied me to Aberdeen, he is a fine fellow, but is very tired and restless at being so long out of employment. Thomas[7] is a gentlemanly, nice young man, he has polished very much by the two or three years that he was at sea, Mr Walker has opened his eyes with respect to the bad system he pursued with respect to his sons and has sent Hugh[8] away to school. The girls & the family are better brought up and are very ladylike, the Murrays are particularly so.

But I must conclude, I will write again very soon. Remember me to all the Gairdner's and all their friends in your part of the world and believe me my dear father, your most affectionate & dutiful son, James P Gairdner.

By June, James was back in France and writing to Scotland about the rumoured end of the occupation and a possible trip into Switzerland.

To Miss Gairdner, Skene Street, Aberdeen
Cambrai, 9 June 1818

My dear Laura,
I was very happy to learn by Jane's letter that you have been much better lately, I wish her account of my aunt had been as good, however as it appears decided that you are to leave Aberdeen I hope your change of residence will be of advantage to the health of all of you. I wrote to my aunt about a fortnight ago, since which as you will perceive by the date of this we have changed our quarters, it has been the custom every summer to encamp the army near the fortresses. We accordingly a week ago left our winter cantonments and encamped on the glacis of this place, I am very well pleased at the change, for we are all together now, whereas before we were very much divided. Such officers as choose to have lodgings are in the town among which number I am one, having no predilection for stewing in a tent when I can by any means get under a roof. The weather here is intensely hot and everything parched and burnt up for want of rain of which with the exception of about three hours one day there has been none since I landed in the country, now nearly six weeks.

The farmers are grumbling greatly but that is so much the nature of the animal that it generally means nothing; be that as it may it is certainly the most unswerving relaxing weather I ever felt; the time was when I cared no more about the extremes of weather than for the more temporary inconvenience with which it was attended and if I could get into the shade and keep quiet on a hot day I felt light and capable of anything that did not require bodily exertion. But this weather makes me quite lazy, and I perfectly agree with definition of happiness given by I forget what writer (and it is too great an exertion to try to recollect) who however makes out the quintessence of it to be, lolling on sofa and reading novels. Either it has in it something peculiarly inclining to idleness or else the infirmities of age are coming upon me and you may take it as no bad proof of my desire to please you, that I am capable of the exertion of writing to you, having within my reach as I have, the luxuries I have described viz the sofa and novels; for my lodging is at a bookseller's shop and Madamoiselle, one of the belles of Cambrai and a very pretty girl I assure you, has made me free of the library and recommended several which she declares to be '*fort interressantes*' [very interesting].

I think you judge harshly of the Walkers in supposing that Rebecca intends to forget her old connections because about to form new ones, they are certainly queer people and do not do things as other people do and Rebecca is a queer girl and has puzzled me more to comprehend than almost anybody I ever met with, but I do not think they want heart. I have had another Italian epistle from Robert [Walker] since I came out here, he says that his sister has not fixed the time for her marriage yet but that Captain Hood[9] talks of leaving England about the middle of July. He seems to be more pleased with his future brother in law the better he becomes acquainted with him. Has David returned to Scotland yet? I saw [him] when I was in London, I do not imagine that he is likely to shine as a very brilliant luminary anywhere. I mentioned to you I believe the invitation I had through him from Mrs Paton to *renew* my acquaintance with them, an honour however which I did not avail myself of when I was in town. I am very sorry to hear by a note that I had from my Aunt Gordon accompanying a review which she sent me that my uncle has been very unwell, she talks of going out of town this summer for the benefit of a change of air which I hope will set the matter to rights again.

I believe a change in the country seldom fails having a good effect upon his health. We have nothing of interest stirring here, shooting matches are the rage just now, and I have rather to my own surprise become all at once a dead shot. I have been long a shooter and have always been fond of it, but I used formerly to be surprised when I killed, now it is a matter of surprise to me to miss. The report still continues to prevail that the army of occupation will leave the country in autumn, but we know nothing positively. I intend in a week or two to go to Paris, where there are several people I am acquainted with. I have been strongly urged to accompany one party to Italy. That is out of the question but it is not improbable but that I may go with them as far as Geneva. Give my love to all with you, kisses to dear Mary, and thank Jenny for her letter, I will write to her soon and believe me dear Laura, your affectionate brother, James P. Gairdner.

18 June I received your mother's letter this morning.

Three months later both father and son were writing to each other again, his father enquiring[10] what James' plans were if, as widely expected, the Army of Occupation ended soon.

To Lieutenant J P Gairdner, 1st Battalion Rifle Brigade, British Army, France.

New York, 7th September 1818[11]

My dear James,
Some time ago I had the pleasure of receiving your favour of 10th May, the letter written on your return from Scotland has miscarried, as I requested Mr Gardner to forward on here any letters that might arrive after I had left Augusta, but as I have not heard from Aberdeen for a very long time, suspect he has omitted sending them. It now appears certain that the army will be withdrawn from France, there will of course be a great many more regiments reduced, which will make it more difficult to purchase. I therefore hope you will soon get admitted into the military college,[12] what time do they generally remain there? There are a great many people northerly this year from Carolina & Georgia. Thomas Gardner & family are here now, they were at Morristown 30 miles from this all summer. I left Robert Walker there as I came on (I believe shall leave him there at school) and went on to Newport Rhode Island, stayed there better than 3 weeks, then went to Boston & Salem, I meant to have gone farther to the eastward but the weather was very warm & dry which made it disagreeable travelling. It has been very dry in Georgia, at Shady Grove they had only one shower in two months. Corn crops are

mostly ruined, it is now two dollars a bushel and expected to be at 3, the cotton crop is also bad and the rot has got into it again, but I have just received a letter from my overseer, he had got none of it 23rd August, but says it may come yet, it was bad at Walkers, T. Gardner's and others in my neighbourhood.

Charleston & Sava[nnah] has been very healthy the summer, Dart tells me that old Doctor Barron is very ill, not expected to live, he is worn out, Miss Barron is also very unwell. I shall move from this in 2 days & hope to get home by the 10th October, when I hope to find letters from you & our friends in Scotland, if you write to them, say that I am well & will write on getting home. I remain my dear James your most affectionate father, James Gairdner.

James was simultaneously voicing his concerns regarding his future, given that the Army of Occupation was drawing to an end.

To James Gairdner esq, Shady Grove, Augusta, Georgia

Cambrai, 20th September 1818[13]

I have just received yours from Shady Grove of the 5th of June and are glad to find that you are well and about to migrate northward as usual, it appears you have made the old house so sumptuous that I shall hardly recognise it again. I am sorry to hear little Robert has been so unwell, he will no doubt be greatly delighted with his tour, for little fellow he has the world all before him and everything has the charm of novelty for him. You say nothing about Edwin, how does he get on, is he as fond of planting as ever? The exploit of the two young Baylies does not surprise me in the least, one of them who I did not see had already shown himself a confirmed blackguard and I had no great opinion of the other. The young men in that country are for the most part great rips and the old ones great savages. How is General Jackson's business to be settled?[14] His occupation of Florida has excited some interest and a good deal of surprise in Europe and the American government seems by the last accounts we have to be rather at a loss what line of conduct to adopt, but I suppose it will end in the purchase of the territory from the Spanish government it is I believe of little use to anybody but the United States.

I have written to you twice since my visit to Scotland last winter. I spent some time at Wooden & Corsbie & then went to Aberdeen, I gave you an account of all our friends in that quarter, Robert Walker and I have corresponded since and nothing new has occurred there since I left them except the marriage of Rebecca with a Captain Hood of I forget what regiment, he is a gentlemanly good sort of young man, of pretty good property and in short a very desirable match; it was in contemplation when I was there but was not concluded until about two months ago. She and her husband departed immediately after the ceremony for London, from whence they were to proceed to Falmouth to embark for the Mediterranean where his regiment is stationed[15].

Robert is very anxious to get employed and with the rank he holds it would be a capital thing, but I fear he has very little chance, for it must require very great interest indeed to get the command of a vessel now.

I have just returned from a short leave of absence of six weeks which I got for the purpose of going to Paris from whence I intended to have gone to Geneva and have returned by the Rhine to Cambrai, but I met so many people I knew in Paris, both English & French, and found it altogether so fascinating that I lingered there, until I was obliged to give up my excursion to Switzerland, which would have required more leave of absence than I had obtained. I have not heard very lately from Aberdeen, but by the last accounts it appeared that my aunt had been a greater deal better lately than she has been for a long time. She has I am glad to find at last determined to leave Aberdeen as it is a climate that is much too severe for her and does not agree with any of her family, but she will be obliged to spend another winter there, which I wished might have been avoided.

They have been electioneering mad in England all this last summer in consequence of the dissolution of parliament, but we here have interest engaged principally by the approaching congress which is to be held at Aix la Chapelle[16] and where our destination for the next winter is to be decided. The general opinion is that we shall evacuate the French territory this autumn and return to England when there will be great reductions in the army, to the account at least of the strength of what comprises the Army of Occupation and they say that one of our battalions will be among the number, but that will not affect me. I hope we shall be sent out of this country at any rate, for we are all very tired of it, at least of this part of it. I almost give up all hope of promotion until there is another war. We have had a great many reviews here as usual this summer, whenever any acquaintance of the Duke's comes up to head quarters to see him, we are brought out to be shown. Among others who but the American General Harper[17] had the honour of a review on purpose for himself, the man we saw at Ballaton. His niece a Miss Caton is married to Colonel

Hervey[18], the Duke's first aide de camp & military secretary, he did us the honour to express approbation of our corps. It is reported that previous to the breaking up of the Army of Occupation there is to be a grand review of all the contingents of each nation which will I suppose be the finest thing of the kind ever known & it is also said with what probability I know not, that it is to take place on the field of Waterloo.

My Uncle Gordon has been all this summer at the Isle of Wight, I heard from Mrs Gordon lately, who says that he is much better for the change of air, but she seems very tired of her abode there. I am very sorry to learn [of] poor Tunno's death, but it was to be expected, he had been suffering a long time. I hope you will take into consideration the visit to this country we so much wish you could make out. Remember me to all friends with you & believe me my dear father, your dutiful & affectionate son, James Gairdner.

James wrote home at the end of the year to apprise his father of the fact that the Army of Occupation had ended and that the regiment had returned home. The government had immediately ordered a reduction in army numbers as a part of the peace dividend. James was placed on half pay initially, but was soon reinstated. But as the prospects of promotion, even by purchase, in such a reduced army were minimal, and the inherent boredom of garrison life failed to appeal, causing James to consider going on half pay as preferable.

To James Gairdner esq, Shady Grove, Columbia County, Augusta, Georgia.[19]
Undated, written from Aberdeen

Marked 'Sent February 1819'

My dear father,
I wrote to you a short time before I left France saying that we were positively to give up the occupation of that country; which we in fact did and returned to England in November. I delayed writing to you because as soon as the army came home a very sweeping reduction took place in which contrary to every idea I had had I found myself included and I asked to be able to see my way a little before I wrote. I exerted myself in every way to get promotion by purchase but without effect. I then came down here [to] stay some time, but a short time ago learnt that by a new arrangement which had been made with

regard to the establishment of my regiment I was replaced again upon full pay in my old rank. I confess I felt no very great delight at this as during this time there is so little to be done that I had rather be on half pay, master of my own time to go where I please than be confined to a listless regimental quarter, however it has the advantage of making me eligible for purchase though I do not think I have much chance of effecting that at present, when there is so little [of] going on, and if I could ascertain that there was no hope. I think I could voluntarily go on half pay until military life becomes more active for this state of peace cannot last for ever.

By your letter of the 7th September from New York you mention that they were to return home in a few days where you expected to arrive about the middle of October. We have been in hopes of hearing from you after your arrival. I hope the rot from which your crop was free at that time, did not make its appearance afterwards. I was much vexed to learn that the letter I wrote after my return from Scotland last year had not come to hand because I hoped it might induce you to cross the Atlantic the next autumn instead of going northward, it could not I should think make much difference in point of time, it would even be less fatiguing, and would give much gratification to my grandmother and aunt. I think too it might be a means of bringing to a close that business of Sampson and Davidson which seems entirely at a stand-still and I really do not know what can be done on it. Mr Gibbon is still in Ireland and I see no prospect of his return, his wife is about to go over to him. I wish my dear father you would think of this and accomplish this if possible. My aunt has decided on removing from this place to Edinburgh in the spring and has been in treaty for a house occupied at present by a friend of hers.

I have applied since I was replaced on full pay for leave of absence and hope to get it prolonged so as to enable me to be with my aunt and family until they get established in their new abode. I think their plan of removing a very wise one, as Gordon who is really very nice boy, could not stay with any profit much longer at the college here and there is nothing in Aberdeen which renders it desirable for the rest of the family to remain here. By removing to Edinburgh they will be nearer our relations in Roxburgh and Berwickshire, who are very much attached to the family. I passed a few days at Wooden and Corsbie on my way here from the south, my grandmother and all the rest of them were very well. They have heard from Rebecca [Walker] since her arrival at her new destination, she was well and happy. I was sorry to learn by your letter that old Dr. Barron was so ill, Mrs Moodie heard lately from my uncle who wrote in very low spirits on the doctor's account, he was not expected at that time to outlive the day.

James Moodie has been placed by Mr Kinnear, his guardian, in a counting house in Glasgow, to the distress of his mother, who has a very bad opinion of the place. She has decided I believe, upon removing thither, how far this may be of advantage to her son is I think very problematical. I was very glad to learn, that you had left little Robert at school in the state of New York, I think provided there was anybody there you had confidence in who would take the trouble of looking after him, it would be very advantageous to leave him altogether. How is Edwin coming on in his planting? I should think he should be old and skilful enough now for you to trust your overseer under his eye for any time longer than usual you might wish to be away, especially as he could apply to Mr James Gardiner in case he were himself at a loss. How are all that family, is Henry Gardiner still at New York?

I was sorry to hear of poor Mrs Turner's death, but it was to be expected. Mr Mitchell was I understand in England last summer but in very bad health, I do not think he will hold out long. Mr Harvey is I believe doing very well, his son is at St John's Newfoundland, his daughter has now two children. When I go to London I shall try and ascertain whether I have any chance of getting promotion, if not I should not be losing time to get placed on half pay and it would be much more agreeable, as soon as I can form any idea concerning it, I will let you know. My uncle is very anxious to serve me but he allows himself to be put off with any answer by these people.

I do not know whether you will perceive any difference in my hand writing, but I have taken three lessons lately from a man who professes to make a good hand out of a bad one[20]. On that number I think I have improved my hand a little, at least I write with more freedom and I think it will improve yet. My aunt will write in a few days, she is well, as all here unite in affectionate love with my dear father, your affectionate, dutiful son, J P Gairdner.

The problems of transatlantic correspondence are highlighted here. Two months after James wrote home to inform of his reinstatement to full pay, his father was still writing about his prospects on half pay, but also worryingly that the funds for purchasing a captaincy and his allowance from his father were now under threat because of poor harvests.

To Lieutenant J.P. Gairdner[21] care of David Hutcheon[22] Esq, Advocate, Aberdeen

Shady Grove, 16th March 1819

My dear James,

I wrote to you 4th January[23], since then have not had the pleasure of hearing from you, but have from Mr Harvey, informing that you was on the reduced list and that you had been trying to purchase a company without effect at the date of his last 11th December. I am much disappointed at the state of funds in his hands, but I suppose you had received more than he advised of, which was only £300. If the purchase has not been made there will not be funds to pay the allowance to your aunt & self unless the business is settled with Simpson and Davison. I mentioned this in my last & it is on that account you wrote.

We have now very unpleasant weather, colder than January, so much so that I am afraid to put corn in the ground for fear of its rotting. The two last years not half crops & this has a bad beginning, but live in hope it will have a good ending. Remember me to all friends. I remain your most affectionate father, James Gairdner.

Chapter 17

Demob

With few prospects of promotion or active employment, James finally decided to retire from the army on half pay on 1 July 1819 and he went to Scotland for the winter before he planned to do the European tour in the summer.

To James Gairdner Esq, Shady Grove, Augusta, Georgia[1]

Edinburgh, 19th October 1819

My dear father,

I wrote to you about a month ago from Wooden[2], I had hoped before this to have heard I had from you, which I am still looking for. I returned here shortly after, where I propose staying all the winter, and intend to pay attention to some of the winter philosophical classes of the college here and my present intention is to go abroad next summer. I think Edinburgh undoubtedly agrees better with my aunt and her family than Aberdeen did. Herself and Laura[3] are considerably better and though Jane has been confined with a complaint in her leg, that being a constitutional attack would have been the case wherever she might have been, her health is in other respects good and she is mending fast. I am sorry I cannot give so good an account of my grandmother, she was when I left Wooden confined to her bed with a violent inflammation in her leg which gave her great pain, she is I understand, a little better since I came away, but at her time of life such attacks are very enfeebling. Mrs Hood, who has been safely delivered of a daughter is expected home very shortly.

The Murrays with whom I spent some time, are all well, Andrew the eldest one has decided on practising law as an advocate, Gabriel is in a country house at Leith, and John is at home, he had decided on becoming a farmer but has got tired of it and talks now about going out to India. He says the sameness and want of variety disgusts him, and I do not wonder that at Corsbie he finds it so, for my uncle literally graces nobody, they are without neighbours and he has somehow got into solitary habits and does not seek society, this for a very young man must be irksome and indeed I think farming is a bad profession to begin with, if a boy immediately on finishing his education sets down to farm without seeing anything of the world, his mind must become contracted. He does not possess a store of ideas on which he could feast in retirement and fill up with delight and profit that leisure which his profession leaves unoccupied, but to one who has travelled and employed the early part of his life in active avocations it must I think be a delightful profession to a soldier particularly if his passion for his profession is cooled, is in any case there is something so rational and dignified in passing one's youth in camps and cities amidst men and arms and then retiring to domestic enjoyments, and country occupations.

You will perceive that I am now stating my own case and I have considered it seriously, I left the army partly and principally from inclination, because it was changed in its desirableness and is now time thrown away partly because I consider it most likely that the service on which it is more likely to be employed that any other (though I do not think any service is likely) would not be expedient for me. I do not regret the step I have taken nor do I think I am likely to do so. But I must do something, I am young and it neither suits my ideas of propriety nor my inclinations to be idle and I am inclined as well by taste and preference, as because it is the most obvious thing, to turn my thoughts to farming, I really think I should like the occupation extremely. I would not be happy in any profession however lucrative that entirely occupied the time, because I am fond of reading & now farming leaves a great deal of leisure and is at the same time a pleasing occupation. But I believe I have before mentioned that I have long had a passion for a tour in Italy.

I could not sit down satisfied without accomplishing it, which I shall commence next year if nothing occurs to prevent me. If I do undertake the farming plan the most obvious place to settle, would be in the neighbourhood of my relations in Roxburghshire, for besides the advantage of their advice on a career new to me, it is so much more respectable as well as agreeable settling in a place where one has connexions than where one is an entire stranger and probably considered as an intruder. If my plan succeeds so far I may possibly find what I can never be truly happy without, a wife. I have thus given you an account of what I have been thinking seriously about for some time, part because I wish to have your opinion about it, as it cannot consistent with my other views be put into execution, yet awful, it is no use to consider details.

There is nothing of general interest in this country now except the increasing licentiousness of that detestable set who style themselves radical reformers, but who in fact as far as their powers of doing evil enable them are promoting revolution. God knows in what it will all end but something decisive must be done, I think one way or the other before things will subside into a peaceable train.

I mentioned in my last letter what enquiries I had made when in London concerning the suit with Simpson and Davison, that the lawyers think they can do nothing without Mr Gibbon, that I had written to him repeatedly. I have not yet heard a word from him nor do I now expect it. I cannot tell what is to be done, nor can I think of anything so effectual as your presence. I am ready to do anything that you wish. James Moodie mentions in a letter I had the other day that Mr Harvey's son is on his way to Charleston, I do not know what is his object. Perhaps you may see him, he is a fine young man. Mr Moodie has followed his son to Liverpool which will not I think do him any good, but I am glad for my aunt's sake that she has left this, for really she is so tormenting to all those about her that I do not think it good for my aunt's health that they should be in the same place. My aunt desires me to mention that she wrote to you in the beginning of September and will write again soon. All here unite with her in love to you. I heard not long ago from my Aunt Gordon, they have been staying all the summer at Tunbridge Wells, but she does not think she is better, I do not think she ever will be. I have just heard that my grandmother is a great deal better. Let me hear from you soon and believe me my dear father your most affectionate son James P Gairdner.

James wrote to his father again, just before embarking on his European tour. He was worried at the political upheaval with demands for reforms and where it might all end.

To James Gairdner Esq, Shady Grove, Augusta,[4] Georgia.

London 31st July 1820

My dear father,
I wrote to you shortly before I left Edinburgh for Roxburghshire

where I went to pay a short visit before coming south. I brought Jane with me who has come to stay with my Uncle Gordon, poor thing she has had a tedious tantalising illness for the last twelve months which however I hope change of air and of medical advice will get the better of. Indeed I think my aunt and Laura as well as herself require a milder climate and I am glad to find that my aunt thinks of moving to England after next winter when Gordon's education will be completed as far at least as Edinburgh can do it. His uncle wishes him then to pass a year in France for the purpose of making himself master of the language &c which plan I think is a very good one. What my uncle has then in view for him I cannot tell, nor do I suppose he himself knows exactly. My aunt is about to proceed in a day or two on a visit to Wooden. I left them all well in Roxburghshire though my Uncle Walker has been very ill since I left it with severe bilious attack, of which however Robert says he is much the better now that he has got over it. My grandmother has got wonderfully well over a severe attack of encephalus[5] which alarmed them very much and is now looking as well as I recollect ever to have seen her. There is a young man of the name of Walker, a relation (cousin) of my uncles, who was staying there at the time and who I gave a letter of introduction to you. He is about to proceed to the southern states for the purpose of planting, if he finds it likely to succeed, for it seems that just now nothing is to be done in the farming way in this country, entirely owing to the unnatural state to which the rents of land rose during the war, and which the land holders are not inclined to lower. Things cannot always continue in that state I should think, if they become settled on a fairer footing I should think I might do something in that way, however at present it would be a bad business.

When I return from my tour I will join you in Georgia and it will be then time to talk over these things, but really the state of this country just now gets every day so much worse, the degree of irritation to which the public mind is excited and which this affair of the queen who is merely a tool in the hands of a party continues to exasperate. The openness with which appeals to the worst feelings of the worst part of the people are made, by herself in her answers to the addresses sent to her, and by the party who pretend to be her advocates. All these present a picture of fearful demoralisation and may I think excite in the friends of order fears of the worst consequences. It is impossible to foresee how all this may end.

I fear it cannot end quietly, if this country is to be revolutionised. America bids fair to be the only haven of tranquillity, for all other European countries seem to be even in a worse state than this. By the bye when I was at Corsbie Mr Murray was talking of sending out his second son Gabriel to the United States to make a tour of the country, in order to judge for himself whether he would like to settle there for he was thinking of farming in Scotland but his father cannot find any opening for establishing him to his satisfaction. In short there never, I suppose, was a period in which there was such a difficulty in finding an opening for a young man in all professions in this country as the present. Mr Gibbon who has been so long in Ireland is now in London but I am afraid this will be of no more use towards forwarding the business with Simpson & Davison than if he had remained where he was There is no seeing him at all, Mrs Mallet his mother in law has not seen him since he came over. He says that he is so occupied that he has not time to call. There is something strange in all this, I have attempted in vain to find him out. Mr Harvey does not give any hope that through his means anything can be effected. I perceive by your letter to my aunt of May 20th which (she sent me together with the bill for £400 drawn on William Mitchell and which has been duly honoured) that you have expected that I should have departed on my tour. I was obliged at any rate to wait until the arrival of the bill which you said in your letter you was to send me and am now writing for my friend Felix[6] who is well as his brother a Captain[7] in the navy are going to Italy & we are to travel together. I am afraid the funds in Mr Harvey's hands are not so large as you mention in your letter. I myself have received no money from him since I wrote to you in March, which made the amount of all I have received as I then mentioned £1,000 since the period of my leaving Georgia and yet there appears to be from the account he sent me less than you suppose. However, he says he wrote to you in May which I suppose will explain it. I must ascertain however that my aunt is not likely to be exposed to any inconvenience before I make my arrangements for my departure, for my plan is to place in Coutt's[8] hands the sum at my disposal to get letter of credit from him available on the continent.

I shall request Mr Harvey to send all your letters for me to my Uncle Gordon whilst I am abroad, who will know how to forward them. My Aunt Gordon with Laura are by this time at Wooden, I hope she will receive much benefit from the country air. You will have heard that young Adam Walker who married Katherine Murray, has had a son and heir. Mrs Moodie and her son are still at Liverpool, she has an unquiet speech that will not I suppose allow her to rest there long. I will write to you from the first place I make any stop on the other side of the water. We talk of Pisa as a winter residence. Pray do not give up writing to me, although I may be a little longer getting your letters and believe me my dear father your most affectionate son, James P Gairdner.

Having arrived at Paris, James wrote to Laura of his adventures to date, next stop was Italy.

To Miss Gairdner, 140 Princes Street, Edinburgh.

Paris, 3rd October 1820

My dear Laura,

I had hoped to have been able to have answered before I left England your letter which I found at Dover, but I found the travelling along the coast to Portsmouth more tedious than I expected. I only arrived there on Saturday evening and as I had to sail on Tuesday, I could not make it out. In passing through Hastings where I only stopped a night, I found on entering the public room of the inn Captain Robertson[9] who was making one of a whist party which had been obliged on account of the house being so full to hold its session in the room the travellers were shown into, a circumstance without which I should not have met with him.

It was too late in the evening to call and see any of the ladies of the family and I could not stay the next day which he very kindly pressed me to do. His daughter Isabella he says he has no hope of whatever. It must be bad indeed when he can so express himself to an almost stranger. Long before this gets to hand you will I suppose have returned to Edinburgh. I wrote a letter to my aunt which I directed to Corsbie (when I was at Dover) supposing that she would be there by that time. I hope if she had not arrived, as I think by the date of one I received from her two days ago she had not, they will not send it travelling about the country for they are very careless about those things. I am really sorry that she has not derived more benefit from her visit to the country. I wish the next winter and spring may not be severe upon her but in Edinburgh it is very trying and I do not think your situation in Princes Street a warm one. I really do not think that your non appearance in London can give any offence to our friends there whose kindness to Jane I can never forget even though they had no other claims on our grateful remembrance and I should feel very uneasy at the idea of my aunt being left alone at the time she is so frequently unable to make exertion. On my journey from Dover to Portsmouth I met Orlando Felix as I expected at Brighton, but he there made another change in his plans. He had found himself so much fatigued with the travelling from London that he preferred sailing from Brighton to Dieppe, but as the captain had been appointed to meet us at Portsmouth and he did not know where to write to him he wanted me to proceed there with positive directions to sail on Tuesday on which same day he was to leave Brighton and we were all to meet at Rouen, which we did accordingly on the Friday. I found the Strachans as I left them except Mr S[trachan] who had returned home in the meantime poor man. He does not seem to feel himself much at home there. The business of the Grove is as unlikely in appearance to be brought to a satisfactory termination, as ever Mrs S[trachan] takes special care of her precious health. Magdalen who was not well when I was there first was looking much better. Emmy and Pattie in high preservation.

The Churches had left the Isle of Wight for some place, I forget the name of it, not far from Portsmouth. They have it seems given up the idea of going to Hastings. By the bye when you write to Bessie Church I wish you would tell her that I wrote to her from Havre de Grace to tell her what I had done with the parcel I took charge of from her to Captain Evans[10] at Caen, but it is very likely she might not get my note. The following was the substance of it, I made enquiries at the Havre about Captain Evans and the best means of forwarding the books to him. Mrs Wilkinson or Wilkins the landlady of the Hotel de Londres informed me that she was in the constant habit of forwarding things to Caen and that she was almost certain that Captain Evans had left it but that if I chose to leave the parcel with her she would send it safe to him if he is still there, if not she would keep it until she received further directions about it, so that should Captain E[vans] not have received it any of the captains of the packets sailing from Portsmouth or Southampton will enquire about it. We all met as I mentioned at Rouen, that is the captain and myself who travelled together and Orlando who travelled from Dieppe to that place alone. He suffered dreadfully he says from sea sickness but was looking I think all the better for it and has borne his journey here much better than I expected. We stayed a day at Rouen which is a most interesting old city, the cathedral and several of the churches are among the finest specimens of gothic architecture in France and the commodore who has a good deal of the antiquarian mania and is really a very intellectual companion was in raptures. We have been here about ten days, and will set off for Italy I believe about Monday next, for as the autumn is advancing we cannot afford to make a long stay here, indeed nothing detains us now but the ceremonial of getting our passports countersigned by the different ambassadors. Orlando and myself having seen the lions[11] here and Robert Felix intending to return this way. Pisa is the first place we intend to make any long stay at, so that you had better direct your letters there until you hear further from me. I received a packet of letters the other day enclosed by Jenny containing my aunt's of the 11th September written at Wooden, also one from my father and Robert Walker.

My father I am very sorry to learn was suffering at that time from the Erysipelas in his foot,[12] I trust it will not prevent him from going to the westward in the fall of the year, though it is fortunate it did not come on while he was travelling. I hope we shall soon hear farther and better accounts of him. Jane's letter is more cheering. She writes in good spirits and gives a very satisfactory account of herself. Paris is much as when I was last there, except that the birth of the little Duc de Bordeaux[13] has given rise to a great deal of rejoicing and fetes, illuminations etc.

They are obliged to exhibit the poor infant at the windows of the palace three or four times a day to gratify the loyal curiosity or whatever it may be of the Parisian gossips. I do not think that I ever in London in the same space of time met with so many acquaintances as I have since I have been here and it is really a most fascinating place to spend a short time in. On looking at my letter of credit I find no banker at Pisa so you had better direct to me at Florence, to the c/o Donat Orsi & co[14]. I shall stay a fortnight or three weeks there and will leave directions for the forwarding of any that may arrive after we leave it. If we do not travel all the way there together, we shall meet there. I have not time to look this over so pray excuse blunders. Best of love to all with you and believe me dear Laura yours most affectionately J. P Gairdner

I am writing Jenny by this post and will write from Florence.

James duly kept his promise to write again from Florence.

To Miss Gairdner, 140 Princes Street, Edinburgh

Florence, 2nd December 1820

My dear Laura,
I wrote to my aunt from Milan which I hope got to hand and as in my letter to yourself from Paris I gave my address to this place, vis., to Donat Orsi & co. I fully expected on my arrival here to find letters from your part of the world as also from some of the folks at Dover who by the bye are I suppose before this in town again. One from

Patrick Thackery was however the only dispatch I found at my bankers, which was doubly welcome as giving me later accounts than I had of my friends in England and Scotland, both too, favourable. I left Milan a day or two after I wrote for Genoa. I travelled with two Italians and an Englishman of the name of Heyer a gentlemanly fellow. We lived together at Genoa and have travelled together from thence to this place stopping at different places on the route which presented anything of interest, of which there were very many.

I mentioned that I had separated from the Felix's at Lyons for the sake of passing through Switzerland and crossing the Alps and that I expected to hear about them at Genoa, which I did. They had arrived at Nice having been detained on the road longer than they expected and a physician to whom Orlando had letters advised him to stay there at all events until the end of this month as there were sometimes heavy rains until that period which it would be very imprudent in him to expose himself to the risk of travelling in. As my going to Nice would be only retrograding I decided on coming here to wait their arrival. If they come on to Pisa to pass the rest of the winter I can go to them in a day, if they go on at once to Rome to which at all events they will go in February they must pass through here. In the meantime, instead of passing four or five weeks in such an unprofitable place as Nice, I am in the centre of the purest Italian dialect and in one of the most delightful cities in the world. I am in very comfortable lodgings in the same house with [an] old brother officer of mine who like myself has gone on half pay for the purpose of free locomotion.

The number of English people in Italy particularly Florence is astonishing. I was at a ball the other evening at the house of Madame Orsi, my banker's wife, at which all the young ladies, at least all the dancing ones were English, which is rather a nuisance as one does not travel abroad to see the manners of one's own country, indeed it is the only fault I find with Florence which is a delightful place to abode. I walked about the first days after my arrival quite bewildered with delight and I am only now though I have been here nearly a week beginning to get a little sober upon it, indeed I have been pleased hitherto with my tour in this country far beyond my expectation and I have yet the object of greatest interest viz [torn-Rome?] to see. My travelling companion from Milan Mr Heyer is a gentlemanly man, clever and well informed but desperately argumentative.

That you will say I would not quarrel with, but it is on subjects on which I feel no interest that he is fondest of getting into, viz politics on which we cannot at all agree as he is a zealous advocate of the queen's and a little of a radical. However he is mild and always the gentleman, never like our Uncle Murray, suffering himself to be carried away by the heat of argument. After battling for two entire days on the subject of parliamentary reform and the queen's case, both of which I am heartily disgusted with, together with occasional digressions on the most inscrutable points of theology, viz free will and fore knowledge, I proposed that we were passing constantly through most beautiful country without observing it, we should come to the agreement that whenever either of us hold up his finger the other should hold his tongue and moreover that we should not argue on any subject that was not in some manner connected with Italy, a tolerably wide field and indeed we have discoursed with considerable profundity. We were much pleased with Genoa where we stayed a fortnight and with the country between it and Pisa, at least that part of it which we travelled through, for we left Genoa in a felucca[15] for Lerici[16] about half way to avoid the almost unpassable roads in the neighbourhood of Genoa to the south, which passes through the most rugged parts of the Argentines and is only to be travelled on mules at a very tedious rate. We got to Lerici in about twenty hours and had most delightful weather, from hence through Carrara, Massa and Lucca to Pisa. The country is among the most beautiful even in Italy. As my companion was anxious to get on to Florence, to join a friend from whom he had parted at Milan for the purpose of making the excursion to Genoa we only stayed a day at Pisa but I shall certainly go to that part of the country again even if the Felix's do not come to stay there, and shall from Leghorn visit Elba and return to Florence by Piombino and Sienna which will enable me to take a different route to Rome for Sienna is a place to see though not on the most interesting route. However I shall be stationary here for some time and shall also wait until I know something positive about the movements of the Felix's. I must defer saying anything about the wonders of Florence until another opportunity.

I shall write again soon and hope it will not be long ere I hear from you. I am very anxious to hear of or from my father who mentioned in the letter I received from him at Paris that he was then suffering much pain from an attack in the foot of the Erysipalus. I am anxious to know whether my aunt has formed any plan yet with respect to her removal from Scotland, Patrick mentions in his letter that she was keeping her health wonderfully well since her return from the country, I hope that the winter will be less severe upon her than the last which indeed was a very hard winter and I think the house in

Union Street was by no means a healthy one, at least I never suffered so much inconvenient health without actually being unwell. Pray when you write be particular in mentioning whatever you know about everybody. Tell me has Captain Robertson's daughter got my letter or is it as he told me he thought past all hope. How is our Aunt Crosbie and in what part of the world is she now? I should not be much surprised at meeting her at the corner of the street some morning. Give my love to her when you write, also to Miss Robertson. Remember me to the Murrays, to Mrs Miller and all who may care about my dear Laura, yours most affectionately, James P Gairdner.

Kiss Mary for me and tell her I do not forget that I am in her debt a letter, I have written to Jenny by this post.

The tour continued to the Eternal City.

To Miss Gairdner, 140 Princes Street, Edinburgh, Scotland
Rome, 12th March 1821

My dear Laura,
I wrote to my aunt about a month ago shortly after my arrival here which I hope she received for I find that letters frequently miscarry. I heard from Orlando Felix a short time since, the first account I had received after an interval of nearly three months. He mentioned having written several letters none of which I got. I have been expecting daily to hear from some of you, I had a letter from Jenny shortly after my arrival here, the only account I have received since I left Florence. She mentioned having heard from you a short time before and that you were getting the better of bad colds. I fancy such things are inevitable in Edinburgh, it is a bitter place to winter in. This climate is as delightful at this season of the year as it [is] severe with you.

Now and then there is [a] wind from the mountains and as they are covered with snow all the winter it is rather piercing, but it never lasts above a day or two, and I have never seen it rain here two days running. We have just made an end here of a very curious ceremony, the Roman Carnival. The Carnival, properly so called, is the whole period between Christmas and Lent, but every principal city has some particular period of it which is appointed for being more than usually ridiculous, the Romans fix on the last ten days (excepting the Sunday and Friday which are within that term) if I were to describe all the absurdities of that time you would say that the nation that could be so amused must be superlatively children. But what would you say if I were to confess that I was as much delighted as any child among them, and I could not deny it. I did indeed at first think that it was unbecoming the descendants of the Brutuses, Catos and Caesars, and as it interrupted occupations of a very different cast I suspected it was not altogether worthy of those who came with the purpose of externally observing the monuments associated with such names, but by degrees I entered into the spirit of the thing and felt quite sorry when it was over. However the Romans have resumed their gravity and I have returned to ruined arches, broken columns and the materials of that magnificence which once overshadowed the world. It is impossible that any written description can give any idea of the deeply melancholy fascination, the very peculiar interest that this place inspires. It happens fortunately that the modern city extends over that part which in the early period was occupied by meadows, while the Forum, the greater part of the seven hills and the scenes most remarkable for the interesting events of their history are left in that imaginative solitude which accords so well with the mood with which we wish to view them.

To stand within the Coliseum by moonlight is a thing never to be forgotten. I believe I have always been singular in my feelings towards the Romans, even as a schoolboy I scarcely ever sympathised with them, they appeared to me so arrogant and over bearing, they made such an ungenerous use of victory, that my wishes were almost always for the success of those enemies, and independent of any of my admiration for Hanibal's talents I loved him for that very success. In such detestation do I hold the desire of conquest, whether in nations or individuals, so execrable do I think the crime of ambition, that selfish and ferocious passion, misnamed the vice of noble minds, that I never think upon the long years of suffering and the present humiliation of Rome without feeling that the hand of God is there. With those sentiments, though I could not experience all that enthusiastic veneration for the past greatness of Roman character, though I did not find my heart overflow with that worship towards the buried dead in whose foot steps I then trod which some feel, and more affect, however I did feel a deep and intense interest excited by the scene around me. The history of Rome proves that bravery and cold blooded cruelty can co-exist. This very building (the Coliseum) is a monument that records the most disgusting trait in the character of that people, it was built by two of the best of their emperors one of them was named 'the delight of Rome and of the human race'. In the construction were employed prisoners of war whose only crime against Rome was in having tried to defend their country and their religion, and here in this spot an hundred thousand Romans, senators, priests, women and rabble, sat to glut their eyes with the agonies of men who had never offended them. And yet there are many who believe they are expressing liberal sentiments when they point to Rome as the standard of all that is great in human character. It is an inconsistency to me the most incomprehensible and yet I have observed those people who are the most zealous declaimers against everything that looks like an arbitrary proceeding in modern politics, are those who refer to the Roman character and government as the beau-ideal of a national system. For my own part I detest arbitrary power wherever it exists, and with whatever fictitious splendour it be surrounded, whether in a Louis 14th or Henry 8th, an Augustus or a Napoleon, a Roman Senate or a Parisian Directory. I would wish to see liberty, national regulated liberty, everywhere, and national independence where ever it can maintain itself. And notwithstanding that I look upon the centuries of calamity that have weighed down this beautiful and interesting Italy during which she has been made the contests of those whom she formerly scarce deigned to consider as of the same nature with herself, during which she has seen her own blood poured forth in quarrels not hers and whose only possible result to her could be a change of masters.

Notwithstanding I consider this as a retribution whose measure does not equal that of her crimes, there is no one who wishes more sincerely than I do to see her rise once more to the dignity of a nation. No one who execrates more than I do the arbitrary measures which are now taking [place] to force on again those degrading fetters which she has made an effort to cast aside. And though I cannot always in viewing the magnificent ruins scattered in beautiful decay around me cast back a sigh of affection and unmixed admiration to the memory of the men who raised them, there are few I am persuaded who view them with greater admiration as surpassing specimens of art, or who feel more deeply, though they may express it better, that sad yet pleasingly melancholy interest excited by the wrecks of that power which once issued its proud commands to a subject world, the monuments of a nation that with all its faults, that in spite of its enemies, was great. But enough at Rome for the present. I mentioned that I had heard from the Felixes. Orlando wrote in very good spirits and gives a good account of his health. He mentioned that they were to set off in a few days for this place so that I expect now every day to see them. Orlando has been appointed extra aide de camp to the Lord Lieutenant of Ireland so that I suppose he will find no difficulty in obtaining his leave of absence extended as much as he may wish.

I do not know what their plans are and they may perhaps make an alteration in mine, but my intention at present is to stay here until after Easter and then go to Naples, however it is impossible in the unsettled state of affairs in this country just now to decide anything positively. At present there is no obstacle to private travellers passing to and fro from this to Naples though the frontier is the seat of war.

I long to hear from you and to know if my aunt has formed any plans with regard to her removal from Edinburgh, and what Gordon is to do after the close of the college session. James mentioned I think that Mr Strachan was likely at last to settle the business of his house near Gosport. I have not received any answer to a letter I wrote to Patrick from Florence. Remember me to them all, and to the Walkers, by the bye Robert owes me a letter too. I am much obliged to Dr Jamerson for his *love,* you may give my remembrance. Love to all with you and believe me dear Laura yours most affectionately. James P Gairdner.

The next letter was written at Sienna on 21 July 1821:

Marked – received 6th August 1821

My dear little Mary,
A thousand pardons I beg for having left your letter from Wooden so long unanswered. Indeed I do not know what better cause I can plead than that with which you began the said letter, namely that 'I have been riding about so much that I quite forget it' but in this I am better than you for indeed I did not forget either you or the debt I owed you. I suppose long before this you will have left Scotland and see Jenny again. Tell me when you write if you find her any tamer than she used to be. Lallys[17] too I hope behaved herself better after I left you. She is a sadly wild young lady as you well know.

You must recollect how all my exhortations and discreet example were thrown away upon her. I am sorry it is not in my power yet to give you any account of the clock at Basle about which you seem so interested, but as I shall pass through Switzerland on my way home I shall take that road and will not fail to make every research necessary for your satisfaction and if you have any other questions to ask that I can satisfy I shall not think that I have travelled in vain. Your mama asked about my voice. Tell her that it is beautiful, but that it always was, tell her that it sometimes astonishes even the Italians themselves, who when I occasionally in the streets pour it forth in song turn round and look at me with amusement, which of course proceeds from admiration. I have not yet got a guitar and am in some doubt whether any accompaniment can add to the charm of so fine a voice. I suppose you are now a great proficient on the pianoforte.

Tell Gordon I hope he still continues to play the flute. I sometimes find it a great consolation particularly when I feel anything like *flutiness*. I never however have since felt anything like that particular attack that Lallys seems to recollect with so much horror, for we have not in this fine climate say of the kind of weather which produces that disagreeable complaint in Scotland. Mr Felix of whom you have heard is quite well and desires me to say that though he has not the happiness of her acquaintance he nevertheless sends his love to Mary.

Is he not an impudent fellow? He is learning to play the guitar and sing but poor young man, his voice is not just like mine. I hope you found Aunt Gordon better than she has been and uncle and Mammy Bell quite well. Give my love to them all, also to Mr Crosby and our aunt when you see him which will of course be seen. I was very sorry to hear of my aunt's illness but I hope it will prove nothing serious. And now dear Mary adieu. Write to me and tell me all about your travels and adventures. Love to all with you and believe me dearest [Mary] your most affectionate J P Gairdner.

James remained in Italy into the following spring.

To Miss Gairdner, 7 Durnford Street, Stonehouse, Plymouth, Devon. Florence, 1st March 1822

My dear Lallys,
I was thinking very long to hear from some of you when I received my aunt's letter of the 22nd of January. But I have no right to complain I know for I have been very remiss myself. This last carnival, that is the period between Christmas and Lent, which is the prescriptive season for gaiety in this country, has been very gay in Florence, and somehow I got more involved in the bother of it than I intended, for one can go to balls and parties at home. But when one is travelling to see a country all the time so spent is a loss of opportunities which will never recur; and as this society consists more of the English than the natives, I look back upon as nearly a dead loss. However I forgot the caution by which I have been hitherto guided since I came to the country, to avoid English visiting acquaintances and having gone to Mrs Higgins' ball I could not help going to Mrs Wiggins' and so on, the long and short of the matter is that I have passed two months very idly and very pleasantly but if I had them to come over again I would

spend them very differently; no uncommon case with many who like myself can be wise enough when it is all too late.

However the close of the carnival was the breaking up of the society here. The Italians go into the country, and the English go to Rome and Naples. Most of my acquaintances and all my friends have left this. I was greatly tempted to go to Rome too with two sailor men who have been great allies of mine but I resisted for the present. Perhaps I may go down for a fortnight or three weeks, but at any rate I wish to be moving northward towards the middle of April before which the travelling is not pleasant in the north of Italy. The Felixes left this about a fortnight ago for Naples which they have not yet seen as they stayed so long at Nice and arrived so late at Rome that they were not able to go when I did last year.

Whether we shall meet again in Italy I do not know. The reinforcement to their party has altered their plans and not a little spoiled them, in fact they do not know themselves what they will do. I never much liked this cousin, and the egotism and selfishness she has shown on this occasion has not raised her in my estimation, and yet I think it is rather silliness than calculating selfishness. Orlando is now off the staff in consequence of Lord Talbot's recall from Ireland[18]. His leave of absence is consequently definite and he must be back in the summer. He asked me if I did not think it very hard upon her that he should be recalled just as she came out. I said I had no doubt it was very annoying but I could bring myself to confess I thought it a legitimate grievance. Orlando is her sheet anchor for the commodore is so absent and careless that during their journey from Chambery here he left her in some awkward predicaments. If he saw a fine view he would jump out of the carriage, scramble over rocks and leave her who did not understand a word of any language but her own to proceed perhaps to the next town alone, and join her an hour or two after in raptures at the beauty of the country and find her perhaps surrounded by police officers demanding passports, innkeepers and *laquais de place*[19] offering their services, not one of whom she could understand or make herself understood by. These escapades of the gallant commander (at the accounts of which I laughed to a degree that did not at all please her) have given her such a dread of being left under his convoy that I fancy she will not lose sight of Orlando again. I am sorry for them both, for Orlando because the care falls principally on him, for Robert because he was so happy, enjoyed himself so much before this new burthen was thrown upon them, and I may add for them all for they must feel that the appearance of the thing is not respectable.

My aunt gives me in her letter a great deal of domestic news all of which is really news for me, for until that letter I had not heard for a long time from any of you. My Aunt Gordon has not written since August. I am sincerely sorry to learn the death of Captain Robertson, it must be a terrible blow to his family, I suppose they will return to Scotland as they will be more among their friends there. How our friends in that part of the world are getting on I do not know. Robert Walker has not written to me for ages, I do not suppose he considers the marriage of Agnes with the Minister of [Noumarkle?] an affair of sufficient magnitude to call forth his epistolary powers.

I am happy to find that you all continue to be pleased with your new quarters. I wish you had given me some account of your neighbours, at least those with whom you have made or expect to make acquaintance. My aunt mentions the names of two or three but enters into no detail. Now all this as an important concern to you must be interesting to me. The Strachans I think at one time talked of trying Devonshire, is it likely to come to anything? William Church I think was put on half pay, what is he about now?[20] Having once got his commission which is the great difficulty he cannot find much on getting on full pay again, at least it is to be done for money which the other was not. What is our Aunt Crosbie about, has she gone on any fresh voyage of discovery. I positively should not be surprised to meet her in my wanderings. I hope you have heard from my father since my aunt wrote, it is a long time since I have had a letter from him. I trust he has not been prevented by ill health from writing, however he is not fond of it at any time. Some of you of course will let me know should he write to you without writing to me. I heard a short time ago from Henry who you saw I believe in Edinburgh. He is in the eighth regiment stationed in the Ionian Islands[21] and near the scene of the present struggle between the Greeks and Turks[22]. He gives a terrible account of the barbarities exercised by both parties and represents the Greeks whom our English patriots exalt to the skies, as by far the greatest savages of the two, and that is precisely the opinion I have always heard of them by those who had had personal opportunities of judging. It is all very fine to talk of the descendants of Themistocles and Aristides, but the modern Greeks no more resemble Themistocles and Aristides than the modern Jews do Saul and David. I am sorry to say that the modern Italians are equally degenerate, I feel however a great interest in the fate of this beautiful country, and though the inhabitants taken collectively are as bad as need be I cannot think that is proof that they might not be better if they had fair play. But things cannot go on long as they are now, and in the struggle once fairly commences between the Italians and their Austrian masters, woe to the vanquished. The last explosion took place at the wrong extremity of the country. It is from the inhabitants of the north not the south of Italy that she must expect her redemption.

I am in daily expectation of hearing from you, if you should write very soon after the receipt of this you may still direct to Florence as I shall not finally leave this until after Easter, i.e. about the middle of April, but should you write later so that there may be any doubt of your letter reaching this before that time, direct to Venice to the care of Siri and Willhalm bankers there, and if you be writing to my Uncle Gordon or aunt, will you tell them this, and dear Laura adieu. Love to all with you and believe me yours most affectionately. J P Gairdner.

The Grand Tour came to an end and James decided to throw up his commission completely, retiring from the half pay list on 30 December 1826[23]. It would appear that by this date, James had sailed permanently to America to start a new life. Here James married Mary Macintosh Gardner on 1st March 1827 in Richmond, and settled down as a plantation owner and trader.

Few letters remain of this period but it is likely that James continued to write to the family in England although less frequently than previously.

The next letter we have, sent to his uncle, announced the death of his father who had died on 24 August 1830. He also told of both his marriage and the birth of his second son Adam. His first son James Gordon was born on 10 July 1828 and tragically died 30 August 1829, at just over one year old; Adam Gordon was born 30 October 1831. James also wrote of early signs of the breakup of the American union.

To Adam Gordon Esq, Secretary of State's Office, Downing Street, London.
Postmarked 'Ship Letter Liverpool'
Post dated New York 1831 [November?]

Though few and far between have been the direct instances by letter my dear uncle, since circumstances have cast my lot in a land which though to me a *natale solum* [latin- native soil], is less connected with my early associations than many parts of Europe. Yet I am sure this arises as little from estrangement or failing on your part as on mine. I should be ungrateful indeed were either time or distance, capable of effacing from my recollection the impression of the many kindnesses I have received from one, who for so many years stood towards me in *loco parentis*.

That you have sympathised with me in the loss of my dear father I am well assured for you know his worth and loved him as a brother. Time, and sincere endeavour, to resign myself with fortitude to a disposition, in which even our imperfect views can discern much of mercy mingled in the cup of bitterness; have soothed the first keen sense of anguish, the bereavement and the recollection of his many kind and endearing qualities has become a feeling, it is now sweet to dwell upon. I am grateful that this sorrow did not come upon me the lone being I was a few years before. I have found in the sympathy of my wife all the gentleness, the kindness, and soothing manner which take from the weight of one half it had, by taking away all its sense of badness, I wish I could make you acquainted with my gentle wife and my fine manly little son, however I do not live without the hope of some day accomplishing this.

I am much gratified at hearing from time to time, through Gordon and the different members of the domestic colony that you and my aunt continue to enjoy at best as much health as when I last saw you. I have not heard from G[ordon] since you had a Whig administration, they seem determined to make a root and branch work of their parliamentary reform. We are anxious here to see how the new system will work. I greatly fear that it is but le commencement de la fire. As somebody said of the new constitution promulgated by the French reformers, though I sincerely hope otherwise and that old England will come out of this crisis as she has out of every previous one in renovated strength, augmented.

We are not very quiet here tho' there is nothing which indicates a very speedy change in the existing order of things, but the principle of disunion is I fear deeply held in the very nature of our institutions. Some of the states have already begun to talk of a separation from the federal union and their motto is 'Peaceably if we can, forcibly if we must'. That such separation must take place and at no very remote period is what no one can doubt and then will our children's children (if indeed the consumation be deferred so long) smile at the complacent boast of their forefathers of having set the world an example of liberal institutes, so happily formed as to be exempt from all the inherent principles of decay which have undermined all previous systems. I will not inflict a crossed letter on you[24], pray give my best love to my Aunt G[ordon] and write to me when convenient and believe me my dear uncle, yours ever most affectionately J P Gairdner.

No further letters survive until 1849, when he wrote again to Laura.

To Miss Gairdner, 17 Hamilton Terrace, St John's Wood, London.

Moreland[25], 23rd February 1849

My dear Laura,

When yours of the 27th December was received a few days ago it was so long since I had heard I was feeling anxious for tidings. The usual fatality seems to have attended our correspondence however, for you mention a former letter written by yourself which never reached me. I was probably saved some suspense an uneasiness as you write that you had then given me such an indifferent account of dear Jane. I rejoice to learn that you are relieved from the fear of all consequences whatever those might be which Dr Blackmore apprehended. Still the account you give of her is sufficiently distressing. Asthma is a visitation which I believe is rarely if ever entirely eradicated. However I am glad to hear that you have good reason to expect that she will be restored to a tolerable degree of health. You tell me that Edward B[lackmore] is in a position to do well and with a friend who acts a kind part by him. I should like to be more particularly informed on that subject. When I remember that it will be thirteen years this coming summer since I last saw you all and Jane's (then) little flock, it reminds me that her other boys must be fast coming forward.

You remark that my boys must give me something to think about now that they require to go out into this strange world. It does indeed, many an anxious thought, they are good boys though and there is nothing in their characters or dispositions as far as yet developed to cause uneasiness as to their future course in life. Edwin, the next to be launched is with us here pursuing his studies under my tuition. The two elder boys are as you know in business and live during our absence from Augusta with their Uncle and Aunt Gould. The two eldest girls accompanied their grandmother who went to pass the winter with her daughter Elizabeth, where there is a very good female school. Down here there is a lamentable deficiency of anything of the kind. The rest are with us for we spend the whole of our winters at the plantation, a place in some respects not altogether desirable as it involves the necessity of separation from so many of our children for half the year, but unavoidable for economical considerations. We in this country ought if only on selfish considerations to pray that there might be peace throughout the world and that wars and fighting might cease, for there is no revolutionary outbreak in Europe, no disturbance in Ireland that does not affect us here in purse if not in person. Previous to the revolution in France which sent Louis Philipe[26] on his travels everything looked prosperous, here we were anticipating a fair remunerating price for our agricultural produce, but the panic produced in the mercantile world by these events produced disappointment again, and then to mend matters and not be out of fashion we get up a little war of our own to plunder our weaker neighbour Mexico of one third of her territory to pay the expenses[27].

However that matter is settled, you seem to be getting quieter in Europe and we again hope for better times. And by the way, talking of wars reminds me of a matter on which I wished to communicate with Gordon. I saw it stated some time ago in an English newspaper that an act of parliament of some kind has passed for the creation of a number of medals to be issued the officers and soldiers engaged in the Peninsular wars. It stated that a medal was to be granted for every military service, battle, siege etc which is borne on the colours of the regiment or, which is the same thing, which appears at the head of the regiment in the army list. According to this I would be entitled to nine medals for I was present in every action in which the regiment was engaged commencing with Ciudad Rodrigo to the end of the war. Will you ask Gordon to see into the matter for me for I have enough of the old leaven in me to set a value on these things. It is an act of tardy justice to the Peninsular army which ought to have been done when the Waterloo medals were issued upwards of thirty years ago.[28]

You say you would be glad to know something of James Moodie and his family. I hear directly from himself nearly as seldom as you do. I have not been at Charleston for five or six years though it is only an eight hours journey by the railroad. In that interval he has been once or twice in Augusta for a day on business connected with his office where we always see him. I hear of him however on enquiring of persons from Charleston more frequently. His family consists of two daughters, Caroline and Blanche now nearly grown up, three sons Adam Gordon, Clarence and Joseph Payne and I think there is a baby but I am not sure. His office is that of clerk in one of the banks with a very good salary and his circumstances are altogether very comfortable. His wife's health which for three or four years was very bad is I understand nearly re-established.

We are all well and are expecting a visit from our sister Elizabeth next week[29]. She is now a widow. The death of her husband Colonel Foster took place last summer and was an event which neither his or her friends could consider in any other light than in happy release to him or to her. He was a helpless paralytic for the last eighteen months of his life. The paralysis too affected his whole frame, he could scarcely cross a room without stumbling, sometimes falling. He was unable to make his wants known either by speaking or writing and yet they say his mental faculties were not impaired, he was moreover perfectly prepared and anxious to die, an incessant reader and his Bible his favourite book; Elizabeth has come to Augusta for a few weeks on business connected with the winding up of his affairs leaving her children and our two girls with her mother. It is six years since I have seen her. Mary[30] made her a visit two years ago. She returns home this way. She came to Augusta by one rail road and can return by another which passes ten miles from where I live.

Our sister Margaret has never recovered from the affliction she sustained in the loss of her eldest child last fall. He was a very lovely boy though his health was never strong and her remaining child a little boy not quite a year old is very delicate. There was an epidemic among children through this section of the country last summer and fall, they called it malignant scarlet fever, its worst symptoms were sore throat accompanied with cough and it proved in many instances fatal. Our little Crawford was, our doctor said, the worst case he saw to recover and when the first symptoms appeared in the little Gould I requested the doctor to see him, he remarked if that child has the prevailing epidemic it will go very hard with him, for he is not one to be easily managed and I attribute your little Crawford's recovery under God mainly to his perfect docility and the prompt obedience with which he submitted to every remedy. But I must conclude and have left myself brief space. I rejoice to hear that my dear aunt as far bore the winter well.

Mary desires much love to you all and particularly to be remembered to the Murrays when you write. Remember me also to the Gibbons and any old friends you may meet with though I suppose there are not many now. Do beg Gordon to enquire about those Peninsular medals[31] and if the account I read is correct to secure mine and contrive some way of sending them to me. Adieu dear Laura yours ever most affectionately, J. P. Gairdner.

Chapter 18

Aftermath

Mary and James seem to have had nine children in total. James Gordon born 10 July 1828 but died 30 August 1829, just over one year old; Adam Gordon was born 30 October 1831 and died 27 July 1906; Edwin was born 23 June 1833 and died 8 May 1902; Anna McKinne was born 1 May 1835 and died 2 October 1894; Joseph William born 11 May 1837 became a doctor and died 5 May 1860; Mary Gordon was born 14 February 1839 and died 23 July 1907; Henry born 16 July 1841 who became a merchant, cotton buyer and guano manufacturer and enlisted in a company of the 5th Georgia Regiment Volunteers during the Civil War and died 12 October 1897[1]; George Crawford was born 20 January 1843 became a lieutenant in the Confederate Army and was killed at the Battle of Missionary Ridge 25 November 1863; and Harford Montgomery was born 25 March 1847 and died 1 June 1854 aged 7 years.[2]

His strong connection to his church is also evident. Indeed in 1847 he is listed as a lay delegate from St. Paul's Church in Augusta at the 25th Annual Convention of the Protestant Episcopal Church of Georgia.

James moved to a plantation he bought in Jefferson County, Alabama for twenty years before eventually moving to Augusta. Whilst there, he provided detailed evidence of the treatment of his slaves at his plantation.

As a historian I never make the mistake of judging people, their circumstances or opinions by modern standards. By the standards of the time, James was quite normal in possessing slaves in the Southern states of America and he seems to have treated them humanely and with great kindness, but this cannot hide the fact that he did not see anything against this, despite the growing campaigns to end the slave trade in America as had already been achieved in the European states and their colonies.

A book entitled *The Slaveholder Abroad, or, Billy Buck's Visit with His Master, to England,* with a clear anti-slavery slant was published in 1860 but which also included a number of replies from estate holders regarding their slaves and their conditions. One such reply was received from James regarding his estate.

The following letter is from a gentleman of Jefferson County who was formerly in the British Army, served with distinction under Wellington in the Peninsula and in the campaign which terminated at Waterloo, and has received from the Sovereign of Great Britain the usual decorative rewards in such cases, in the shape of medals, clasps, &c.

Dear Sir,

I have received from you a paper containing twenty queries with regard to the treatment and condition of slaves. I would remark that I was born in a slaveholding community, which I left in early childhood for Europe, where I was educated and lived some years. I have, however, lived in Georgia for the last thirty years, the last twenty three of which I have been the owner and superintendent of slaves.

I now proceed to answer the questions seriatim as far as my knowledge and experience enable me to do.

1st Answer. [Number of Slaves] Sixty five, of which there are

Males, grown (i.e. above 16)	19
Women	21
Children under ten	17
Children between 10 and 16	8
	65

2nd Food – They receive three pounds of bacon per week. When fresh meat is given, as occasionally in winter and spring, they receive more. One peck of corn-meal per week, besides which, potatoes are given occasionally and as long as they last. A piece of cow-penned land is sown in the fall in turnips, which they are permitted to use *ad libitum.* They all have gardens, in which they raise cabbage &c. I have offered to increase the allowance of meat, if they wished it, but have always been informed by them that they had enough.

3rd Clothing – To each of the men and boys, a winter suit of factory plains (without wool), consisting of a sack and pair of pantaloons: a shirt, a hat, and pair of shoes. In the summer, the same, of lighter factory cloth, except the hat and shoes.

To the women, in winter, of factory plains, a frock and petticoat; a shift, pair of shoes, and head handkerchief. In the summer, the same of summer cloth, except the petticoat. All the above-mentioned clothing is given to them made up. For the young children, their cloth is given to their mothers. Each negro of every age receives a blanket every second year.

4th. [House Room.] Each family has a house 16 by 20 feet, with a fireplace. This they divide into two rooms. Some of the families have an additional house or room adjoining, in which the larger children sleep.

5th. [Winter Fuel.] The woods are convenient to the quarters, where they procure whatever fuel they want to use.

6th. [Medical Attendance.] The same physician that attends my own family. Lying-in women are allowed one month in all cases. If delicate, they are kept in from regular work longer. Sewing and other light work is given to them.

7th. [Suckling.] All infants are suckled by their mothers, who in almost all cases have a sufficient supply of breast-milk.

8th. [Milk to Young Children.] The young children are allowed milk generally. There are three old women whose sole business is to take care of the children during their mother's absence. Also, to attend the sick, receiving their instructions from myself or the overseer.

9th. [Still born and child losses in 1st, 2nd, 3rd years.] Still born children in the last ten years. Answer one. With respect to the proportion of deaths in the first, second, and third years, I am not able to answer, but believe it to be less than in any white population which I have known. In connection with this subject, I may remark that eleven years after the death of my father, the slaves that I inherited from him had more than doubled.

10th. [What age put to work.] At about twelve years old, they begin to make themselves useful in the field as water-carriers to the labouring hands; after which, with a light hoe, they are put to work with their parents, and are not tasked.

11th. Aged and infirm – Six. They have the same food, clothing, &c, that they always have had. As to work, three women attend, as I have said, on the sick and children. Of two old men, one is a carpenter, and does light work of that kind; the other shells corn to send to mill, and attends about the stables. One woman, aged 85, the oldest person on the plantation, does nothing.

12th. [Hours of Work.] All field hands go out to work at good daylight. The plough-hands come in at 12 o'clock, and stay in two hours. They then return to plough until near dusk. The hoe-hands work by task, which some finish between three and four o'clock.

13th. [Lunatics.] One idiot, a woman of about 28. Food, clothing &c, the same as the rest. She is able to take care of herself. Can understand everything she is told, and is perfectly harmless.

14th. [No. of negroes charged with serious crime against the person in last ten years.] I have not known among my negroes of any instances of the crimes stated in this question.

15th. [No. of negroes charged with theft in last ten years.] No such cases have occurred.

16th. If so, how many were women. None.

17th. Petty thefts among themselves. I do not often hear complaints of such things.

18th. Suicide. I have never had such a case, nor have I ever heard of one. I have stated that I have lived in a slaveholding community the last thirty years, twenty-seven years as owner and manager of slaves.

19th. [Religious Opportunities] They have free access to all opportunities of religious worship in the neighbourhood, with occasional meetings for that purpose on the plantation. Many of them are members of the Baptist, and some of the Methodist Church.

20th. Separation of families by sale. I never have either by sale or purchase. The practise in the county, I believe, is never to separate husband and wife, or young children (viz. under 12 years of age) from their parents.

I am not aware that it is in my power to furnish you with any further information on the subject of your inquiries. Dear Sir, yours respectfully, J.P. Gairdner.

In 1861 he is recorded in his tax return as still owning twenty-two slaves whose value was assessed at $13,200, he owned $5,000 in cash, furniture worth $2,000 and the sum total of all his property was $17,750.[3]

The Augusta city directory for 1862 lists a Major [?] Gairdner who had an office and house on the corner of Bay[4] and Lincoln in Augusta.

James died suddenly at Augusta on 21 April 1862 aged 69 years. He was buried at Summerville Cemetery, Augusta, Richmond, Georgia, where his wife and most of his children were also eventually buried.

References and Notes

Chapter 1: The Gairdner Family

1. It is recorded that in 1802 James Gairdner was treasurer of the South Carolina Golf Club; reference the article *Scottish Merchants and Aiken's Ladies: Golf's Evolution in South Carolina*, by Dr Faye Jensen.

2. James Gairdner was born in Edinburgh in 1761 and died at Charleston on 24 August 1830; reference Summerville Cemetery Records.

3. Gordon Gairdner had been joint owner of a number of ships with his brother James, including *Thetis (1797)*, *Harmony (1799)* and *Nymph*, which were captured by French privateers. He also claimed for goods shipped on the *Leeds* packet ship. All these insurance claims were for nearly £5,000 each; reference *The French Assault on American shipping, 1793-1813 by* Greg Williams.

4. For further details on this complicated and unique case, see *Reports of Cases Argued and determined in the Court of Chancery of the State of South Carolina from the Revolution to December 1813* volume 3, pages 498-513, published by Henry Williams of Desaussure 1817.

5. Caroline Gordon, Mary Gordon's sister, married James Moodie British Consul in Charleston.

6. Mary's sister Jane actually married James' brother Edwin.

7. Reference Burial records of Circular Congregational Church Burying ground, Charleston.

8. Family tradition states that he was at both Eton then Harrow schools, but he does not appear in the records at Eton. The tradition that he attended Harrow and was under Lord Byron has some possibility of being true. Lord Byron attended the school from 1801-5 and there is a record of a 'Gardiner' with no forenames attending from 1804. Therefore he could have been associated with Lord Byron in his last year of attendance.

9. 1st Lieutenant Donald Macleod died at the Action on the Coa, 24 July 1810. According to George Simmons, he was shot through the heart.

10. Reference *The London Gazette* Issue 16398 page 1262 dated 21 October 1810.

Chapter 2: Enlistment and Training

1. The 'purchase system' may seem an anathema to modern readers but it continued in the British Army until 1871. The ability for the wealthy to purchase

high rank for their children had previously caused huge problems, with even colonels of regiments still at school! However by the time of the Napoleonic wars, the Duke of York, as Commander in Chief, had abolished most of the extreme abuses and although 'purchase' was still allowed, minimum terms in each rank ensured that the system did provide experienced officers. There is no evidence that James' first appointment was purchased as the records show he was given a death vacancy, which were usually filled without purchase, the deceased losing the value of his rank from his estate. But the fact that James and his father discussed purchasing further steps in rank would indicate that even if it was not purchased, that they had at least planned to do so if necessary.

2. His father James Gairdner.
3. National Army Museum (NAM) reference 7011-21-1.
4. James Penman was gazetted a 2nd Lieutenant in the 95th on 23 August 1810 vice Joseph Austin who had become a 1st Lieutenant. He however seems to have had the entire month of September to prepare his equipment and kit.
5. This would appear to be Caroline Moodie (née Gordon) who had married Benjamin Moodie the British Consul at Charleston and had a son named James Gairdner Moodie.
6. 'Town' was of course London.
7. Regulation pay for an Ensign or equivalent in the line regiments. Reference *The British Military 1803-15* by S.J. Park and G.F. Nafziger.
8. The lands sold actually covered the territory that forms Arkansas, Missouri, Iowa, Oklahoma, Kansas, and Nebraska; the portion of Minnesota west of the Mississippi River; a large portion of North Dakota; a large portion of South Dakota; the northeastern section of New Mexico; the northern portion of Texas; the area of Montana, Wyoming, and Colorado east of the Continental Divide; Louisiana west of the Mississippi River (plus New Orleans); and small portions of land within the present Canadian provinces of Alberta and Saskatchewan.
9. This payment equates in modern terms to approximately $240 million, a snip at the price.
10. National Army Museum Reference 7011-21-2.
11. It was quite normal for junior officers to require an additional income from their parents or benefactor to maintain themselves.
12. Robert Walker one of nine children of Alexander Walker and Helen Eleanor (née White).
13. Adam Walker (1788-1867), Robert's brother had been born in South Carolina and married Mary Anne Wylie there.
14. NAM Reference 7011-21-3
15. Lieutenant Colonel Hamlet Wade had originally joined the army as an ensign in the 25th Foot in 1791, rising to Captain by 1795. He served at Gibraltar, the West Indies, then the Helder in 1799. In 1800 he became a major in the 95th and became a Lieutenant Colonel in 1805. He served at Copenhagen and the Peninsular, seeing action at Vitoria, Orthes and Toulouse. He later became a Colonel, retiring in 1815 and died in 1821.
16. Major General Sir John Murray. He had joined the 3rd Foot Guards as an Ensign in 1788 and became a lieutenant in 1793. He served in Holland as aide de camp to the Duke of York. In 1795 he became lieutenant colonel of the 84th Foot and served at the Cape of Good Hope, Egypt and India before being put on the Staff

of the Eastern District of England. In 1813 he served on the East coast of Spain with Lord William Bentinck and became embroiled in the debacle of the lifting of the siege of Tarragona, abandoning his siege artillery. He was court martialled but the Prince Regent cancelled his admonishment and he continued to serve.

17. Shorncliffe Redoubt is seen as the birthplace of the Light Division and is currently being preserved by a trust.

18. As the third battalion had already been raised in 1809, was there an idea of raising a fourth battalion?

19. The house at Wooden, Roxburghshire, was in the hands of the Walker family from 1757. Robert Walker inherited the estate in 1787 and he probably rebuilt the house in its present form about 1820. It was advertised for sale in 1826 and was bought the following year by Robert Haldane Scott of Kinloss. Several years later Scott left Scotland for Jamaica and passed the estate to his brother George Scott who was a captain in the Royal Navy. It passed to a third brother in the early 1860s and thereafter to his three unmarried sisters.

Chapter 3: Journey Out to the Battalion

1. First entry in his *Journal commencing from my embarkation at Portsmouth 14th November 1811 for Lisbon* reference National Army Museum 1969-02-5.

2. Eight companies of the 1/95th were currently serving in the peninsula.

3. Captain John Phillimore, Royal Navy.

4. The convoy was escorted by at least HMS *Diadem, Leopard* and *Endymion.*

5. James was particularly fortunate. Storms in the North Sea and Baltic led to the loss of a great number of ships during this period.

6. This is one of the few occasions where it appears that James has revisited his diary in later years.

7. Figueira da Foz at the mouth of the Mondego River.

8. Captain William Percival 9th Foot who served at Roliça, Vimiero, Salamanca, Vitoria and San Sebastian. The Challis list however has him absent from Spain from June 1809 until December 1812. This is clearly a mistake as James proves that he returned to the Peninsula in December 1811.

9. The league did vary in length depending on the country, but the English league measured 3 miles (all but 5km).

10. 1st Lieutenant James Stokes had served previously with the 2nd Battalion at Walcheren and Cadiz before transferring to the 1st Battalion, he then participated in the battle of Fuentes d'Oñoro, the siege of Ciudad Rodrigo and was later killed at the Storming of Badajoz on 6 April 1812.

11. 1st Lieutenant Alexander Coane had served with the 95th in the peninsula since July 1809, seeing action in numerous small affairs, besides the battles of Corunna and Fuentes d'Oñoro. He had been severely wounded at the Coa in 1810, but died on 14 February 1812 at Lisbon of an unknown illness, where he had presumably been transferred to hospital after James saw him.

12. 'On command' indicates that he was there on official business.

13. A small village one mile west of Lamas and twelve miles south of Coimbra.

14. The Royal Waggon Train provided, for the first time, the army with wagons and professional drivers to move stores etc. Commissary General John Bissett oversaw its work in the peninsula.

15. The 9th Foot were then at Fuenteguinaldo, see the letters of Lieutenant Colonel

Sir John Campbell by the editor. The troops for this division would therefore march east via Vide, whilst the remainder marched north east.

16. Lieutenant James Fraser who after arriving in the peninsula in November 1811, remained with the army until the end of the war in 1814, served at Salamanca, Burgos, the Pyrenees, Nivelle, Nive and was severely wounded at Toulouse. He later fought in the Waterloo campaign.
17. One mile west of Seia.
18. The Cameronian Highlanders.
19. The Cameronian Regiment of Foot.
20. On the road from Guarda to Sabugal.
21. Lieutenant Thomas Smith had just returned to Spain having been severely wounded at the Coa. He served at Corunna, the Coa, Ciudad Rodrigo, Badajoz, Salamanca, Vitoria, the Pyrenees, Nivelles, Nive, Orthes and Toulouse.
22. Lieutenant Charles Grey 52nd Foot whose regiment was in the light division with the 95th, he served at Fuentes d'Oñoro, Ciudad Rodrigo, Badajoz, and Nivelles, Nive and Bayonne as a captain in the 85th Foot. He was killed at New Orleans.
23. Captain John Uniacke had fought at Corunna, the Coa, Bussaco, Fuentes d'Oñoro where he was severely wounded. He was blown up by a mine at the siege of Ciudad Rodrigo.

Chapter 4: Two Sieges in Four Months
1. The breach being formed, the riflemen were positioned to fire on the breach to prevent the French from repairs or preparing new defences.
2. A small group of volunteers would attack first in the hope of causing the defenders to set off any mines etc. before the main storming party arrived. This dangerous job, with little prospect of survival, was always oversubscribed with volunteers as surviving officers received a step in rank and the ordinary soldiers gained great prestige and the opportunity to be first for plunder.
3. Harry Smith records that he 'ran on with poor Uniacke's company to meet the 3rd Division, or rather clear the ramparts to aid them, when the horrid explosion took place which killed General Mackinnon of the 3rd Division on the spot, and many soldiers, awfully scorching others. I and Uniacke were much scorched, but some splinters of an ammunition chest lacerated him and caused his death three days after the storm.
4. General Craufurd died of his wounds and was subsequently buried in the breach with full military honours.
5. Major General John Ormsby Vandeleur is perhaps most famous as a cavalryman at Waterloo. He had served previously in India and served in the Peninsula commanding a brigade of infantry in the Light Brigade. He fought at Ciudad Rodrigo where he was slightly wounded, and subsequently at Salamanca, Vitoria and the Nive.
6. Edward Costello p.147.
7. The 5th Division were tasked with repairing the breaches in case of a French attack.
8. Privates William Mills, Miles Hodgson and Malcolm McInnes of the 95th, Corporal Robert Fuller, Privates James Cummins, William Robinson, Patrick O'Neil and John Maloney of the 52nd and Private Thomas Price 43rd were found

guilty of desertion. Nine others from other divisions were also tried and found guilty. Costello records that two deserters were pardoned before the execution, one being 'Hodgson of the 95th ... The other was a corporal of the 52nd Regiment, called Cummins.'

9. Brevet Colonel Thomas Beckwith had previously served in Ceylon, India and Copenhagen before serving in the Peninsula. He saw service at Vimiero, Corunna, the Coa, Bussaco, and Fuentes d'Oñoro. He commanded a brigade of the Light Division before returning home in July 1811.

10. 1st Lieutenant Joseph Austin served at Walcheren and then at Badajoz, but strangely, although he then served throughout the remainder of the Peninsular War, he did not serve at any other action.

11. 1st Lieutenant Thomas Bell served in the 3rd Battalion 95th at Cadiz and Barossa then joined the 1st Battalion and served at Badajoz where he was wounded. Following his wound he retired in June 1812.

12. The writing is unclear and would appear to be either Jas or Jos for James or John. Despite the best efforts of the editor and Ron McGuigan, we have been unable to identify this officer with certainty. Ron has suggested 2nd Lieutenant John Fry of 2/95th, but Challis shows him in the Peninsula only from May 1812.

13. Three miles north-west of Sabugal.

14. Others describe traditional burials as short affairs with little if any religious involvement; one describes the burial of an infant below the flagstones of a chapel being laid in a simple cloth and then being virtually pummelled flat before the flagstone was replaced to ensure that the floor remained level. See *An Eloquent Soldier,* by the editor.

15. A large country house or estate.

16. About two miles south east of Castelo de Vide.

17. Mark Urban has him as Almond, but the minutes of his court martial agree with Allman.

18. Lieutenant General Sir Thomas Graham had been an aide de camp to Sir John Moore and had then commanded the British forces at Cadiz, gaining a significant success at the Battle of Barossa.

19. Major General Sir Rowland Hill had seen great service Toulouse, Egypt and Hanover, before arriving in the Peninsula. He was probably Wellington's ablest and most trusted general who was one of only a few given independent commands. He regularly commanded forces in the south of Spain whilst Wellington's forces fought in the north.

20. Captain William Balvaird had served at Corunna, Bussaco, Fuentes d'Oñoro and Ciudad Rodrigo. He was severely wounded at Badajoz but served at Salamanca, the Pyrenees, the Bidassoa, Nivelle and the Nive.

21. Lieutenant Colonel Sir Andrew Barnard had transferred from 1st Foot to the 95th in March 1810. He had previously served in the West Indies and Helder. Whilst in the Peninsula, he served at Cadiz, Barossa, Ciudad Rodrigo, Badajoz, Salamanca, Vitoria, the Pyrenees, Bidassoa, Nivelle, Orthes and Toulouse. He also fought at Waterloo where he was wounded.

22. Captain Peter O'Hare had previously served at Buenos Aries before the peninsula, where he served at Corunna, Fuentes d'Oñoro, Ciudad Rodrigo and Badajoz where he was killed.

23. 1st Lieutenant Richard Freer, had served at Walcheren before the Peninsula,

where he served at Cadiz, Fuentes d'Oñoro, Badajoz where he was wounded and Toulouse. He also served at Waterloo.

24. Lieutenant Richard Ellwood was not actually present, he served at Talavera, Bussaco and Albuera where he was wounded and made a prisoner of war, only gaining his release in 1814.
25. Kincaid p.66.
26. Lieutenant Colonel Sir George Elder served in the Portuguese Army commanding the 3rd Cacadores.
27. George Simmons records that Lieutenant Gardiner was wounded at Badajoz, this is a clear misidentification of our James Gairdner. These two officers are constantly confused.

Chapter 5: Recovery
1. Volunteer John Fitzmaurice gained a commission as a 2nd Lieutenant in April 1811. He served at Fuentes d'Oñoro, Ciudad Rodrigo, Badajoz, Vitoria, the Pyrenees, Bidassoa, Nivelle, Nive and Toulouse. He was slightly wounded at Badajoz, he captured a gun at Vitoria and served at Waterloo where he was wounded.
2. 1st Lieutenant William Johnston served at Rolica, Vimiero, Bussaco, Fuentes d'Oñoro, Ciudad Rodrigo, Badajoz and Toulouse. He was wounded at Badajoz as a volunteer on the storming party.
3. It is only on entering this fort that we become aware of its strength, for though ... a fortified square, there is so much more of solidity and strength, and so many obstructions to surmount, that we wonder how so simple a figure could be rendered so strong. At the back there is a horn-work, which takes in the entire summit. ... the ditches are traversed in every direction by loopholes and casemates, while the ramparts are crowded with artillery. There is a reservoir constantly supplied with water sufficient for the garrison of 2,000 men for two years, and stores of corn and provisions for that time are also laid up. There is a mill within the walls for grinding corn, and an oven for baking sufficient bread, so that as there are no means for taking the fort but by treachery, surprise, or famine, the siege of La Lippe must be a work of patience, not to mention the loss; for as the besieged will be perfectly safe within their walls, so will the besiegers be completely exposed to the fire of the garrison: though surrounded on three sides by hills, they are all too low and too well commanded by the fort to admit of any annoyance from them. *The Penny Magazine*, 9 September 1837.
4. Major General Victoria, governor of Elvas.
5. 2nd Lieutenant Thomas Worsley had been severely wounded at Badajoz. He had previously served at Ciudad Rodrigo and saw further service at Vitoria, the Pyrenees, Bidassoa, Nivelle, Nive, Orthes and Toulouse. He served at Waterloo where he was wounded.
6. Ebenezer Gairdner & Sons Ltd was declared bankrupt on 17 August 1810, reference *The London Gazette* of 28 May 1816 page 1028. He was a brother of James Penman's father and therefore his uncle.
7. Gordon, the son of Edwin Gairdner was born in 1803.
8. Rebecca Walker was a sister of Adam Walker and later married her cousin David McDougal of Caverton Mill.

9. Emily and Jane were daughters of Edwin Gairdner and Jane (née Gordon), therefore were James' cousins. Emily married Mr Mallet but died in Old Aberdeen in 1815. Jane who was born in 1799 married Dr. Edward Blackmore who emigrated from Cornwall to New Zealand in 1834.
10. 1st Lieutenant Henry Manners, who had seen service at Walcheren, Rolica, Vimiero, Ciudad Rodrigo and Badajoz (where he was severely wounded).
11. Captain Jonathan Leach who had served in the West Indies before fighting in virtually every major action in the Peninsula. He later served at Waterloo where he was wounded. They seem to have been quite close colleagues in the battalion and often billeted together.
12. Almost certainly the village of Donas.
13. 1st Lieutenant Christopher Croudace, 3/95th was killed 6 April 1812 at the storming of Badajoz.
14. Reference, *The London Gazette* Issue 16604, page 931, dated 16 May 1812.
15. Vila Boa is a small village some five miles north east of Sabugal.
16. The main house in this village was often used by the Duke of Wellington as his headquarters.
17. 1st Lieutenant Nicholas Travers returned to the Peninsula in May 1812 and served at Walcheren, Salamanca, Vitoria, the Pyrenees and New Orleans with the 2nd Battalion 95th.
18. 1st Lieutenant Duncan Stewart who served with the 3rd Battalion at Cadiz, Barossa, Ciudad Rodrigo, Badajoz (where he was severely wounded), Salamanca, Vitoria, the Pyrenees, Bidassoa, Nivelle, Nive and Orthes.
19. Lieutenant Thomas Wilkinson 43rd Foot served at Ciudad Rodrigo, Badajoz (wounded), Salamanca, and having transferred to the 85th Foot, Nivelle, Nive, Bayonne and Bladensburg before being mortally wounded at New Orleans.
20. A tiny village 3 miles north east of Calzada.
21. The French had actually prepared three separate convents as makeshift fortresses in Salamanca named St Vincent, La Merced and St Cayetano.
22. Charles Alten served with the Hanoverian Army, rising by 1802 to Lieutenant Colonel of the Hanoverian Guards. He joined the King's German Legion in 1803 became a Major General in 1810. He served at Copenhagen, Sweden, and in the Peninsula he commanded a brigade. He commanded a division at Waterloo.

Chapter 6: Salamanca
1. 1st Lieutenant William Lister served at Walcheren, Salamanca, Vitoria (slightly wounded), the Pyrenees, Bidassoa, Nivelle, Nive and Toulouse. He was killed at Quatre Bras.
2. The Portuguese Douro River is actually called the Duero in Spain.
3. The Light Dragoon brigades were reorganised on 1 July with the arrival of the King's German Legion cavalry. Anson's Brigade consisted of 11th, 12th and 16th Light Dragoons and Victor Alten's Brigade consisting of 14th Light Dragoons and 1st Hussars KGL.
4. The French general officer, one General Carrie commanding a brigade of French dragoons, was actually captured in an action with the 1st Hussars KGL.
5. *Costello, the True Story of a Peninsular War Rifleman* p.189. Eileen Hathaway has understandably misidentified him as Lieutenant John Gardiner, but he did not arrive in Spain until January 1813. Our James Gairdner however <u>was</u> present.

The confusion between these two persons with similar surnames in the same battalion often leads to misidentification and has challenged the editor on many occasions.

6. Captain John Mc Dermid served at Corunna, Bussaco, Fuentes d'Oñoro, Ciudad Rodrigo, Badajoz, he was slightly wounded at Badajoz.
7. Captain Charles Smyth originally served in the peninsula with the 11th Foot but joined the 3/95th then 1/95th in 1812. He was severely wounded at the Nivelle and died of wounds on 18th June 1815, from a wound received at Quatre Bras.
8. Captain Jeremiah Crampton who served at Rolica, Vimiero, Bussaco, Fuentes d'Oñoro, Ciudad Rodrigo and Badajoz where he was severely wounded.
9. Marmont had been severely wounded in the right arm, but it was not amputated.
10. Montejo de Arevalo?
11. General de Division Claude Francois Ferey had been mortally wounded at the Battle of Salamanca.
12. 1st Lieutenant John Hopwood served at Bussaco, Ciudad Rodrigo, Badajoz, Salamanca, Vitoria, the Pyrenees, Bidassoa and Nivelle. Hopwood was severely wounded at Vitoria and was killed at the Battle of the Nive.
13. 1st Lieutenant Jonathan Layton served at Corunna, Fuentes d'Oñoro, Ciudad Rodrigo, Badajoz, Salamanca and Waterloo where he was wounded.
14. Leach believes there were about a thousand sick.
15. Assistant Surgeon William Jones served virtually throughout the entire Peninsular War, initially with the 95th, transferring as a surgeon to the 40th Foot in September 1812.
16. A flogging.
17. I have not been able to identify this village.
18. I have not been able to identify this village.
19. Gairdner mixes two incidents in Chapter 15 of Cervantes' *Don Quixote*, the knight and his faithful companion Sancho Panza get into an altercation with a number of goatherds from Yanguas and are severely beaten. Moving on they arrive at an inn which Don Quixote mistakes for a castle and it is here that Sancho Panza gets rolled in a blanket.
20. In the novel *'L'Histoire de Gil Blas de Santillane'* by Alain-Rene Lesage, the hero is imprisoned in the tower of Segovia.
21. Lieutenant James Fraser 79th Foot who saw service at Salamanca, Burgos, the Pyrenees, Nivelle, Nive and Toulouse. He was severely wounded at Toulouse and again at Quatre Bras.
22. 1st Lieutenant Andrew Pemberton who had served at Walcheren, Corunna, Bussaco, Fuentes d'Oñoro, Salamanca, Vitoria and the Pyrenees where he was severely wounded.
23. This former china manufactory was transformed into a major fortification and when captured was found to house a huge amount of military stores including two eagles.
24. Brevet Lieutenant Colonel Lord Fitzroy Somerset, Wellington's Military Secretary served through the Peninsular War and lost his arm at Waterloo. Later as Lord Raglan he commanded the army in the Crimea, where he died of dysentery.

Chapter 7: Retreat

1. This information was inaccurate as after his defeat at Fuentes de Oñoro in May 1811, Masséna was not actively employed again by Napoleon.
2. 1st Lieutenant John Budgeon served at Walcheren, Corunna, Cadiz, Tarifa, Barrosa, Vitoria, Pyrenees, Bidassoa (slightly wounded), Nivelle, Nive, Orthes and Toulouse. He also served at Waterloo.
3. Captain George Watts 3rd Dragoon Guards, served at Albuera, Usagre and Toulouse.
4. The Spanish General Don Carlos de Espana, there is no evidence of him being a traitor.
5. Established in 1574 to train Irish priests, the college closed in 1951.
6. Gairdner is slightly in error here. Captain Jeremiah Crampton served at Rolica, Vimiero, Bussaco, Fuentes d'Oñoro, Ciudad Rodrigo and Badajoz where he was severely wounded and died of these wounds in September 1812.
7. The New Cathedral of Salamanca was consecrated in 1733.
8. The impressive Plaza Maior was completed in 1755.
9. 2nd Lieutenant Walter Firman served at Badajoz and Salamanca.
10. *A British Rifleman*, p.255.
11. Brevet Lieutenant Colonel Alexander Cameron served at the Helder, Egypt, Baltic, Vimiero, Corunna, Bussaco, Fuentes d'Oñoro, Ciudad Rodrigo, Badajoz, Salamanca, Vitoria (severely wounded) and Waterloo (wounded).
12. 1st Lieutenant Thomas Macnamara, served at Buenos Aries, Rolica, Vimiero, Ciudad Rodrigo, Badajoz, Salamanca, Vitoria, the Pyrenees, Bidassoa, Nivelle, Nive, Orthes Toulouse and Waterloo.
13. 1st Lieutenant John Molloy served at Rolica, Vimiero, Salamanca, Vitoria, the Pyrenees, Nivelle, Nive, Toulouse and Waterloo. He was wounded at the latter.
14. Captain Harry Smith who was Brigade Major, served at Buenos Aries, almost the entire Peninsular War, Bladensburg, Washington, New Orleans and Waterloo. He wrote his own very entertaining memoirs.
15. These men had been arrested by the provost for stealing foodstuffs; it is hard to condemn them, however, given that they were literally starving.
16. 1st Lieutenant Dugald Cameron served at Salamanca, Vitoria, the Pyrenees, Orthes, Toulouse & Waterloo.
17. Lieutenant General Sir Edward Paget was renowned for being very short sighted. He had served in Flanders, the naval action of St Vincent, Minorca, Egypt, Corunna and was severely wounded at the Douro. After his capture here, he was held captive for eighteen months until the end of the war.
18. Lieutenant General Sir William Erskine committed suicide at Lisbon in May 1813.
19. Lieutenant Thomas Macnamara served at Buenos Aries, Rolica, Vimiero, Ciudad Rodrigo, Badajoz, Salamanca, Vitoria, Pyrenees, Bidassoa, Nivelle, Nive, Orthes, Toulouse & Waterloo.
20. Captain Henry Dawson 52nd Foot served at Corunna, Bussaco, Fuentes d'Oñoro, Ciudad Rodrigo, Badajoz and Salamanca, before dying at San Milan.
21. Lieutenant George Ridout 43rd Foot served at Bussaco, Fuentes d'Oñoro, Ciudad Rodrigo, Badajoz (severely wounded). He was severely wounded again at San Milan and died of his wounds in November 1812.

22. Leach p.94.
23. This would appear to be Villar de Arganan.

Chapter 8: Winter Quarters

1. 2nd Lieutenant John Doyle joined the 95th having originally been a volunteer with the 5th Foot. He served at Ciudad Rodrigo, Badajoz, Salamanca, Vitoria, Pyrenees and Nivelle where he was mortally wounded.
2. The fortress of Real Fuerte de la Concepcion is a star fortress found half a mile west of Aldea del Obispo.
3. Now known as Puerto Seguro.
4. 'A Val is a certain written form signed by the commissary of the division, and given to the quarter master of a regiment, who inserts therein the number of officers of each rank present with the corps, requiring their regulated quota of forage, and countersigns it, and delivers it to the officer of the foraging party to give to the owner of the crop of corn, from which the forage is taken. This Val is paid on demand by the Paymaster or Commissary General. Many, very many of these Vals were never presented for payment, the owners not troubling themselves. Some were sold to the camp followers for a mere trifle; the sutlers were said to be the chief purchasers and to make a good market thereby'. Reference Charles Crowe *An Eloquent Soldier*, p.93.
5. The 29th Foot formed part of this battalion for a very short period, before returning to Britain.
6. 2nd Foot or Queens Regiment.
7. 1st Lieutenant John Gardiner served at Walcheren, Vitoria, the Pyrenees, Bidassoa, Nivelle, Nive, Orthes, Toulouse and Waterloo, where he was wounded. Because of his similar surname to our James he is often confused with him by historians.
8. 1st Lieutenant James Percival served at Vitoria, Pyrenees and San Sebastian where he was severely wounded.
9. 1st Lieutenant John Cox served at Rolica, Vimiero (wounded), Bussaco, Fuentes d'Oñoro, Ciudad Rodrigo (severely wounded), San Millan, Vitoria (severely wounded), Pyrenees, Bidassoa, Nivelle, Nive, Orthes & Tarbes (severely wounded). The editor has been seeking permission to publish the Cox brother's diaries for many years without success.
10. General Francisco Ballesteros commanded Spanish divisions in the South of Spain, fighting stubbornly at Albuera. Unwilling to accept a foreigner as supreme commander of the Spanish army, he mutinied and was imprisoned at Ceuta.
11. The glorious news was the retreat of Napoleon's army from Moscow. His army of over half a million men emerged from the snows of Russia counting less than 50,000.
12. Fought over three days 3-5 May 1811.
13. *She stoops to Conquer*, a comedy by Oliver Goldsmith was first performed in 1773.
14. Lieutenant General Thomas Maitland commanded the army that had landed on the East coast of Spain in 1812, but found that he could do little against overwhelming numbers of French troops and he requested to be relieved of his position. This drew criticism which obviously caused him to call for a court martial to look into his actions. He was appointed Governor of Malta and he

became well known for his autocratic but reforming zeal, being known locally as 'King Tom'.

15. *The Rivals*, a comedy by Richard Sheridan was first performed in 1775.
16. It was true that Napoleon had ordered a significant reduction of the army in Spain to form a nucleus on which to form new regiments following the Russian disaster.
17. A farce produced in 1803 by James Kenney.
18. A farce produced in 1800 by John Allingham.
19. A comedy written in 1653 by James Shirley.
20. A farce written in 1783 by John O'Keefe.
21. Major General Sir Galbraith Lowry Cole was invested as a Knight of the most Honourable Military Order of the Bath.
22. Major General James Kempt served in the Helder, Egypt, Calabria, Maida, Badajoz, Vitoria, Bidassoa, Nivelle, Nive, Orthes, Toulouse and Waterloo
23. Napoleon's brother had been placed on the Spanish throne by Napoleon but was not given command of his armies, leading to poor coordination of the French efforts in Spain.
24. Marshal Louis Gabriel Suchet, 1st Duc of Albufera, was one of Napoleon's most reliable marshals and one of only a few he could trust in independent command.
25. Marshal Jean de Dieu Soult was a very able general and was probably Wellington's most formidable opponent amongst Napoleon's marshals.
26. Lieutenant General Sir John Murray had extensive service in Flanders, Cape of Good Hope, Egypt, India, Oporto and Talavera, before being given the command of the army in Eastern Spain. He had initial success in defeating Marshal Suchet at the Battle of Castalla, but he failed to follow up his victory. His force was then landed near Tarragona to lay siege to this important post. But frightened by rumours of French relief columns caused Murray to re-embark, spiking and abandoning his siege train in the rush. He was later court-martialled and found guilty of abandoning the guns without reason, but it does not seem to have harmed his new chosen career in politics.
27. General de Division Marie-Francois Auguste de Caffarelli du Falga had spent much of his career as an aide de camp of Napoleon but now commanded a division in Northern Spain.
28. General de Division Jean Baptiste Drouet, Comte d'Erlon was later to become a major player in the Battle of Waterloo.
29. General de Division Joseph Souham.
30. Paymaster John McKenzie served at the Coa, Bussaco and Fuentes d'Oñoro. He went home in May 1813 but served again at Waterloo.
31. A play written in 1756 by Arthur Murphy.
32. General Francisco Castanos 1st Duke of Bailen, who forced a French army under Dupont to surrender and later played a significant part at the Battle of Albuera.
33. 2nd Lieutenant Allen Stewart served at Vitoria, Pyrenees, Bidassoa, Nivelle, Nive, Toulouse and Waterloo where he was wounded.
34. The Blues are the Royal Horse Guards.
35. The combat on the Coa occurred on 24 July 1810. General Craufurd held his brigade in front of a steep valley with only one narrow bridge behind him over the Coa River and when attacked by Ney's entire corps only escaped annihilation by the narrowest of margins.

Chapter 9: The Great Advance
1. I have been unable to identify this village.
2. This could well be Private Michael Clements of the 95th who subsequently received a General Service Medal for the Nive, Orthes and Toulouse. As a servant with the baggage, he would not have been eligible for a bar for those battles he was present at but in the rear.
3. General de Division Antoine Louis Popon de Maucune.
4. British soldiers were routinely vaccinated for smallpox before being sent on foreign service, hence they were better equipped than the Portuguese to use the village to rest in.
5. General de Division Eugène-Casimir Villatte, Comte d'Oultremont.
6. Major General Victor Baron Alten was the elder brother of Major General Charles Baron Alten. He was a Hanoverian in the British army and commanded a brigade of cavalry in the Peninsula.
7. This refers to the Action of Morales where a rearguard of French dragoons under General Digeon was surprised and Major George Robarts immediately charged bringing on a short and sharp clash. As many as 212 of the French 16th Dragoons and ten horses were cut off and captured. The cost: Lieutenant John Cottin, one trooper and four horses killed, with Captain James Lloyd wounded and captured along with regimental Quarter Master Cowley and seventeen men and twenty-three horses wounded or missing.
8. Captain Charles Lennox Earl of March 52nd Foot was an extra aide de camp to the Duke of Wellington. He was sent home with despatches following the actions of Salamanca, Astorga and the Pyrenees. He was severely wounded at Orthes. He served at Waterloo as an extra ADC to the Prince of Orange.
9. Marshal Jean Baptiste Jourdan, 1st Comte Jourdan.
10. Gairdner's note – this is false, for he commands a part of the Russian Army.
11. Lieutenant General Lord George Dalhousie who commanded the 7th Division at Vitoria, the Pyrenees & Bidassoa.
12. Captain the honourable Arthur John De Ros 1st Foot Guards who served as an extra aide de camp to General Graham.

Chapter 10: San Millan
1. Private Costello records a very odd incident here, when a German Hussar of the King's German Legion recognised his brother amongst the wounded French cavalrymen brought in.
2. It was the 5th Division that attacked them here.
3. The gap in the extant journals would indicate that a small pocket diary used perhaps to record any incidents during his recuperation and certainly to resume his narrative on his return to the battalion unfortunately appears to be lost. The fact that the subsequent journal simply continues mid discussion shows that he did maintain another journal during this period, even if with some difficulty because of his wounded arm.
4. He was issued a bar for the Pyrenees on his General Service Medal when issued in 1848.

Chapter 11: Into France
1. Pedro Agustín Girón, 4th Marquis de las Amarilas, Duque de Ahumada (1778–

1842) was a Spanish military officer and politician. Francisco Tomás de Anchia Longa (1783 – 1831) was a Spanish guerrilla whose troops formed a brigade in 1813 and he became a general.
2. 2nd Lieutenants Alexander Campbell and John Hill were both killed in the attack on Vera.
3. NAM Reference 6902-5 (2)
4. Note by Gairdner - Several straggling farm houses that go by the name of Sarla.
5. Lieutenant Mackay Baillie 43rd Foot was killed and Captain Samuel Hobkirk 43rd was wounded and made a prisoner of war until the end of the war in April 1814.
6. Probably news of the defeat of Napoleon by the allies at Leipzig 16-18 October 1813.
7. French: A defensive obstruction made of felled trees.
8. A Board of Survey was organised to assess the quality and state of equipment or foodstuffs supplied to the army.

Chapter 12: The Battle of the Nive
1. Lieutenant General Sir John Hope commanded 1st Division.
2. Lieutenant General Galbraith Lowry Cole commanded 4th Division.
3. Second Lieutenant James Church was surrounded with a group of men in a hollow and remained a prisoner of war until April 1814. He did however serve at Waterloo the following year.
4. *Adventures in the Rifle Brigade* p.136.
5. Captain Henry Lee served at Corunna, the Coa, Bussaco, Vitoria, Pyrenees, Bidassoa, Nivelle, Nive, Toulouse and Waterloo.
6. 1st Lieutenant John Cox.
7. I have been unable to identify this place.
8. Barbette – A protective mound of earth for artillery, over the parapet of which cannon may fire.
9. Costello, p.257.
10. General Sir William Schaw Cathcart 1st Earl Cathcart, had previously served as Commander in Chief Ireland and led an expedition to Hanover in 1806 and Copenhagen the following year. He became Ambassador and Military commissioner to the Russians and served at the allied headquarters during 1813-14 receiving his earldom for this service.
11. Charles William Stewart, 3rd Marquess of Londonderry was Envoy Extraordinary to the Prussian court.
12. Major General Lord Matthew Aylmer commanded an independent brigade.
13. Wellington's army was regularly many months in arrears with its pay.
14. The Austrian Field Marshal Karl Philipp, Prince of Schwarzenberg, had overall command of the Grand Army of Bohemia.
15. Russian Field Marshal, Count Michael Barclay de Tolly commanded the Russian forces that entered France.
16. Russian General Peter Wittgenstein.
17. Fort Louis is an Alsace.
18. French Marshal Jean Baptiste Bernadotte had been elected heir presumptive to the Swedish throne in 1810 as King Charles XIII had no heir. Bernadotte took the opportunity of the collapse of the French Empire to force Denmark to cede

Norway and to participate in the siege of Hamburg. These matters caused the Swedish contingent to be severely delayed and led to criticisms from the other allies.

19. Prussian General Friedrich Wilhelm von Bulow.
20. General de Division Charles Decaen.
21. Two troops of Royal Horse Artillery were equipped with Congreve rockets in 1813, one of which fought at the Battle of Leipzig, the other in Southern France and at Waterloo.
22. i.e. French rather than Basque.
23. Major General Sir William Pringle.
24. The 39th (Dorsetshire) Regiment of Foot.
25. 79th (Cameron Highlanders) Regiment of Foot.
26. 74th (Highland) Regiment of Foot.
27. The Battle of Orthez was fought on 27 February 1814. It seems incredible that news of the battle took a week to reach them.
28. Lieutenant Colonel Sir William Ponsonby commanded the 2nd cavalry brigade.
29. Wellington suffered a minor wound when a musket ball or canister shot struck his sheathed sword and severely bruised his hip.
30. Requests were made from the city officials of Bordeaux for Wellington to send troops to the city, which would then allow them to openly declare for King Louis XVIII. He detached two divisions of infantry under Marshal Beresford which entered the city in triumph on 12 March 1814.
31. Spanish General Manuel Freire de Andrade y Armijo.
32. The Chateau de Viella is near the village of Viella a few miles to the south of Saint Mont.
33. 1st Lieutenant John Cox was severely wounded at Tarbes.
34. *Maison de Plaisance* – A weekend retreat or second home.
35. i.e. reprimanded him severely.
36. Lieutenant Colonel Victor von Arentschildt who was serving with the Portuguese army.
37. The beautiful Capitole building constructed in 1750 is the home of the Toulouse municipal administration.
38. The local civil guard.
39. Napoleon signed his abdication on 6 April, but a treaty formally agreeing to peace was not signed with the allies until 11 April and ratified by Napoleon on 13 April.
40. Napoleon was to reside on Elba. One of the reasons given for Napoleon's return to France in 1815 was the failure of King Louis XVIII's government to pay the 6 Million livres.
41. Lieutenant Colonel Robert Coghlan 61st Foot was killed at Toulouse. He had served at Talavera (where he was severely wounded and became a prisoner of war for a few months), Bussaco, Pyrenees, Nivelle, Nive and Orthes.
42. General d'Armagnac commanded a division at Toulouse.
43. General Bertrand Clausel, Comte.
44. General Eloi Taupin was mortally wounded during the Battle of Toulouse and died later that day.
45. General Jean Isidore d'Harispe had his leg shattered by a cannonball which had to be amputated. He survived and became a Marshal of France in 1851.

46. General Honore Gazan, Comte de la Peyriere.
47. Brigadier General Nicolas de Loverdo was actually of Greek origin.
48. General Jean Etienne Bartier Baron Saint Hilaire remained at Toulouse after the army left and was arrested by the British but soon released.
49. The 82nd Regiment of Foot (Prince of Wales's Volunteers).
50. General Louis Emmanuel Rey is most famous for his defence of San Sebastian.
51. General Honore Charles Reille.
52. The Abbey de Belleperche.
53. The 94th Regiment of Foot.
54. This refers to the Place Royale, now more commonly known as the Place de la Bourse.
55. The 13th Century Cathedral Saint-Andre is still tightly enclosed by houses.
56. The *Concord* brig was built at Boston in 1772 and owned by the company Weighill & Bell.
57. Off Le Verdon sur Mer in the mouth of the Dourdogne.

Chapter 13: Napoleon Returns
1. NAM Reference 7011-21-4.
2. It is unclear whether the battalion all travelled on one ship, but George Simmons records that he sailed on the *Wensleydale* packet.
3. King Louis XVIII resided at the Hotel d'Hane Steenhuyse at Ghent which can still be viewed today.
4. The Cathedral of St Bavo was completed in the 16th Century. It is no longer entirely enclosed by houses as described by James.
5. Mr Huet was an actor who regularly played on the Paris stage, but on Napoleon's return he retired into Belgium with Louis XVIII.
6. Charles Ferdinand d'Artois, Duc d'Berri was a nephew of King Louis XVIII.
7. NAM Reference 7011-21-5. Although dated 23 April it was continued until 3 May before posting.
8. This is quite possibly Samuel Moody of Liberty County Georgia, if so James had a lucky escape as he was lost at sea in 1815.
9. His aunt and her family had moved to Aberdeen.
10. King William I of Orange had recently been made sovereign over the Netherlands, which covered modern Belgium, Luxembourg and Holland together.
11. Sint Michielskirk
12. This would appear to be a painting known as *Christ on the Cross* painted in 1627 and now in the Koningklijk Museum voor Schone Kunsten.
13. Note by Gairdner- M. Paelinck is a native of this neighbourhood, the gentry of this city subscribed to defray his expenses to Rome for the purpose of studying there.
14. Joseph Paelinck 1781-1839. His painting of the King is now in the Rijksmuseum, Amsterdam.
15. A Parisian theatre company founded in 1789.
16. *Le tableau parlant* (The Talking Picture) is a comic opera in one act by André Grétry.
17. Angelica Catalani a famous opera singer, 1780-1849.
18. The Academy of Music in Meire Street, Ghent.

19. Aalst in Dutch.
20. Welle is 3 miles south of Aalst.
21. Marshal Marmont had remained loyal to the king.
22. Asse.
23. The church of Sint Jacob op Koudenberg had only been finished in 1786.
24. Just east of Namur.
25. The Royal Academy Exhibitions took place at Somerset House each year.
26. This letter has not been found.
27. Ensign George Thomson Jacobs 1st Foot Guards, he survived Waterloo unscathed.
28. 'There are three things a wise man will not trust, the wind, the sunshine of an April day and a woman's plighted faith' from Southey's *Madoc*.
29. This would appear to be a Lieutenant Colonel Thomas Edwards of the 2nd Bengal European Regiment who had retired in 1799. He is recorded as having died in a shipwreck off Ostend on 15 November 1815 on his way to rejoin his family in Brussels.
30. James' cousin Emily died aged only 17 years in 1815.

Chapter 14: The Waterloo Campaign

1. Costello p.279. The small rise is now difficult to identify, but the wood mentioned is believed to have been the Bois des Censes.
2. He of course means the crossroads at Quatre Bras.
3. This is a good indication of how knowledge of events was patchy in the immediate aftermath. The Prussians were actually centred around the village of Ligny some eight miles to the south-east and Napoleon was actually there, rather than facing Wellington's forces in person.
4. Reference William Siborne p.530.
5. One mile west of Nivelles.
6. The official residence of the Belgian Royal family which is found five kilometres north of Brussels centre.
7. Jerome Bonaparte, Napoleon's younger brother had previously been King of Westphalia and had commanded a division at Waterloo.
8. Note by James - In one of the notes found in Bonaparte's portfolio since published is a note to Davout. 'Send me an officer of the Belgian Staff, you know how useful these people may be'. He also in another place desires that so many stand of arms may be sent to a place named, to be at his disposal to arm the peasants when he became victorious.
9. Fought on 11 September 1709, during the War of the Spanish Succession.
10. The Canal du Saint Quentin was constructed in a number of parts starting in 1738, but it took Napoleon to order its completion in 1801 and he officially opened it in April 1810.
11. A toise measures two metres.
12. The Battle of St Quentin 10 August 1557.
13. Grand Marshal of the Palace, Armand Augustin Louis, Marquis de Caulaincourt, Duke of Vicenza, who led Napoleon's diplomatic attempts to gain a peace with Europe.
14. Ham fortress surrendered to the Prussian army, but the French garrison were allowed to stay within.

15. Peronne actually surrendered after a short cannonade.
16. Napoleon abdicated as early as 22 June 1815.
17. Chateau d'Orville.
18. Note by James - Fouche has since declared that he and his party had a revolution in contemplation previous to the landing of Bonaparte from Elba, which had no reference to him. He hearing of it however determined to take advantage of it.
19. Marshal Louis Nicolas Davout who remained at Paris as the Minister of War during the 100 days commanded the French army at Paris after the abdication of Napoleon.
20. It is interesting to note that the heights of Montmartre had so few cannon mounted upon them so soon after the peace treaty. It is true that the army would have removed their field pieces, but the numerous heavier cannon and naval pieces could not be removed so quickly. It would therefore appear that the heights were not as impregnable as some describe them at the time.

Chapter 15: Paris in Peace Time
1. Colborne's Light Brigade had the honour of heading the march into Paris, an honour granted by the Duke of Wellington, which signified their significant role in the victory at Waterloo.
2. A prism.
3. The *Gazette Nationale ou le Moniteur Universel* or more commonly known as *Le Moniteur* was a French newspaper founded in 1789 which became the official newspaper of government in 1799.
4. Although bourse usually signifies a stock market, it here denotes a covered market.
5. The fortress of Vincennes commanded by General Pierre Daumesnil held out until 14 November 1815.
6. Marshall Nicolas Charles Oudinot, 1st Duc de Reggio.
7. Marshal Jean-Mathieu-Philibert Sérurier, 1st Comte Sérurier.
8. Jean Baptiste Huet (1745 – 1811).
9. Augustin Pajou (1730 - 1809) *Psyche Abandoned* 1790, Musée du Louvre.
10. A Hellenistic marble sculpture depicting the Greek goddess of love, Aphrodite, which can today be found in the Uffizi Gallery in Florence.
11. François-Nicolas Delaistre (1746 – 1836) *Cupid and Psyche,* Musée du Louvre.
12. Probably *Fountain of Diana,* a 16th Century Sculpture.
13. Christophe-Gabriel Allegrain (1710 - 1795) *Bather,* also called *Venus* 1767.
14. *La Baigneuse* by Pierre Julien (1731-1804).
15. The Academy formed in 1669 is now the Paris Opera.
16. *Iphigénie en Tauride* (Iphigenia in Tauris) is an opera of 1779 by Christoph Willibald Gluk in four acts.
17. *The Dansomanie* is a ballet-pantomime in 2 acts by Pierre Gardel , first performed at the Paris Opera on 14 June 1800.
18. General Baptiste Kleber assumed command of the army in Egypt when Napoleon left them and was assassinated by a student in Cairo in 1800.
19. Eustache Lesueur (1617-55).
20. Francois-Andre Vincent (1746-1816).
21. Francois Gerard (1770-1837).
22. Jean Baptiste Regnault (1754-1829).

23. The church of Saint Sulpice has an imposing western façade based on St Paul's in London.
24. The dome of St Sulpice contains a fresco by Francois Lemoyne depicting the Assumption of Mary, which dates from 1734.
25. Dominique Georges Frederic Dufour de Pradt, Archbishop of Mechelen became Secretary to Napoleon in 1804.
26. Robert Stewart, 2nd Marquess of Londonderry, more usually known as Lord Castlereagh was Foreign Secretary from 1812 to 1822 when he committed suicide.
27. Painted in 1806, it is now held at the Palace of Versailles.
28. Painted in 1782, it is now held at the Louvre.
29. Pierre Henri de Valenciennes (1750-1819).
30. Jean-Joseph-Xavier Bidauld (1758-1846).
31. Pierre Narcisse, Baron Guerin (1774-1833).
32. Flemish painter Simon Joseph Denis.
33. George Haguette.
34. Antoine Berjon (1754-1843).
35. Joseph Fouche, 1st Duc d'Otrante changed his allegiance with the wind and was again Minister of Police during the Hundred Days.
36. The Musee des plans-reliefs is part of the Hotel des Invalides.
37. The elephant monument was conceived by Napoleon in 1808. It was intended to construct the huge monument, which would have stood some twenty-four metres high, in brass, but only a full scale plaster cast model was ever built which stood on the Bastille site from 1813 till 1846.
38. The arpent would be well known to him, as the land divisions of the Southern states of America were measured in arpents, which measured 0.85 acres (3,400 metres^2).
39. The repatriation of the great art works of Europe which Napoleon had plundered during his conquests and given to the Louvre was very unpopular with the Paris crowds and it was found necessary to provide troops to guard the operation.
40. The Second White Terror (the First had occurred during the Revolution in 1795-5) occurred after the restoration of King Louis XVIII. The civil administration of France was purged of Napoleonists and up to a thousand lost their lives in revenge attacks by those who had lost loved ones to Napoleon's wars.
41. A line from *The Pleasure of Hope; with other Poems,* published by Thomas Campbell in 1799.
42. I have been unable to identify Edward Kemp, he was not in the Army.
43. NAM Reference 7011-21-6.
44. The war with America ended with the signing of the treaty of Ghent on 24 December 1814 and was ratified by President Madison in mid-February 1815.
45. This suggestion that every officer, or at least every major and captain who served
46. James was not to receive a step in rank due to the losses of the regiment at Waterloo.
47. Subalterns eventually received £34 each as their share of the Waterloo Prize Money.
48. Sarah Siddons was a renowned tragedian actress.
49. John Philip Kemble (1757-1823).

50. Edmund Kean (1787-1833) a renowned Shakespearean actor.
51. Both Napoleon and Wellington are thought to have had affairs with Mademoiselle Georges.
52. Armand Emmanuel du Plessis Duke of Richelieu.
53. This would appear to be the neighbouring Château de Vaux sur Seine.
54. I have been unable to identify the original source for this.
55. *L'Hermite de la Chaussee d'Antin, ou observations sur les moeurs et les usages Francais au commencement du XIX siècle [The Hermit of the Chaussee d'Antin, or observations on the manners and customs of the French at the beginning of XIXth century]* by Etienne de Jouy published 1812-14 in 5 volumes.
56. The Treaty of Paris agreed the indemnities France was required to pay for the war. France was to pay 700,000,000 Francs in damages, and France would be partially occupied by an allied army of 150,000 men for five years until France paid up in full.
57. This is in the north of Paris.
58. The opera *Semiramide* is attributed to Rossini but is stated as having been performed for the first time in 1823. The statement that it was performed in Paris in 1815 is hard to reconcile with these facts, but Rossini was writing operas from 1812 and it is quite possible that it was written earlier than thought.
59. The Italian opera singer Angelica Catalani (1780-1849).
60. Written by Gaetano Rossi and first performed in 1815.
61. Written by Joseph Addison in 1712.
62. John Philip Kemble (1757-1823), his sister was Sarah Siddons.
63. The tragedian Sarah Siddons (1755-1831).
64. The Irish actress Eliza O'Neill (1791-1872).
65. A one act ballet by Charles-Louis Didelot first performed in 1796.

Chapter 16: The Army of Occupation
1. This letter is no longer extant.
2. The *Montague* Post Office Packet was famous for two successful fights against American privateers in 1811 and 1813.
3. The Bay of Fundy.
4. NAM Reference 7011-21-7.
5. Wooden was an estate owned by Robert Walker and his wife Mary Gairdner and nearby Mellendean was owned by his brother Adam Walker, both lay just south of Kelso. Adam Walker of Muirhouselaw married Katherine Gairdner in 1787, their son Adam was born in 1788 and then they had a further eight sons and six daughters. Adam Walker junior married Catherine Murray at Corsbie on 3 August in 1819, 3rd daughter of John Murray of Uplaw and residing at Mainhouse. Adam Walker died at his house Rocky Branch in Georgia on 15 October 1812, his estate at Muirhouselaw was divided between David Haliburton and Adam Walker. Reference *Annals of a Border Club 1899* by George Tancred Weens. Wooden House is a Georgian house with 5 reception rooms, 7/8 bedrooms with 5 bathrooms and stands in 11.7 acres.
6. Robert, Robert Walker's third son was a Captain in the Royal Navy.
7. Thomas was the seventh son of Robert.
8. Hugh, Robert's eighth son became a Major in the 14th Madras Native Infantry. James, the 4th son was a lieutenant in the 20th Foot and was killed after

Roncesvalles in 1813.

9. Captain Thomas Hood 75th Foot married Rebecca Hood at Wooden on 8 June 1818 but unfortunately he died at Santa Maura, (modern day Lefkada), on 14 May 1819. On 2 August that year Rebecca gave birth to their child.
10. This letter is no longer extant.
11. NAM Reference 7011-21-9
12. Sandhurst had started operating as the army's military college in 1812.
13. NAM Reference 7011-21-8.
14. General Andrew Jackson reacted to the numerous attacks by Seminole Indians on white settlers by attacking them in their main base despite the fact that they were in Spanish Pensacola. This breach of national boundaries became a moot point when Spain ceded Florida to the United States in February 1819.
15. The 75th Foot was then stationed in the Ionian Islands.
16. The Congress held at modern day Aachen in October 1818 was essentially a meeting of the four great powers (Britain, Prussia, Russia and Austria) to deal with the end of the occupation of France and how France itself would be dealt with in the international arena in future.
17. Major General Robert Goodloe Harper (1765-1825) served in the War of 1812 and commanded the Third Division of the Maryland Militia.
18. Louisa Catherine Caton, Marchioness of Carmarthen, married Colonel Sir Felton Hervey 14th Light Dragoons.
19. NAM Reference 7011-21-10.
20. The editor failed to find a major improvement!
21. Reference NAM 7011-21-11.
22. Hutcheon, David, son of the Reverend John Hutcheon, sometime in partnership with Francis Edmond (1829), firm being Hutcheon & Edmond; Procurator Fiscal of Commissary Court; Justice of the Peace for Aberdeenshire. Died, unmarried, 10 December 1832, aged 67. Reference: *History of the Society of Advocates in Aberdeen* edited by John Alexander Henderson. Aberdeen 1912.
23. This letter is no longer extant.

Chapter 17: Demob
1. Reference NAM 7011-21-12.
2. This letter is no longer extant.
3. Laura Rebecca was the oldest child of Edwin and Jane Gairdner, she was born in 1790. She was also known affectionately as 'Lallys' and sometimes 'Old Maid'.
4. NAM Reference 7011-21-13.
5. Inflamation of the brain.
6. First Lieutenant Orlando Felix of the 95th had served with James in the 1st Battalion and remained in the regiment on full pay.
7. Robert Felix was actually a Commander in the Royal Navy.
8. Thomas Coutts of the private bank Coutts & Co.
9. I cannot identify this officer with any certainty.
10. It is impossible to be certain of this officer's identity.
11. The lions – the sights.
12. A red rash also known as St Anthony's fire.
13. Henri d'Artois, Duc de Bordeaux was the first born son of the Duc de Berri.

14. Donat, Orsi & Co. were bankers in Florence from 1800-1830.
15. A small traditional boat rigged with a lateen sail.
16. Near La Spezia.
17. Laura.
18. Charles Chetwynd Chetwynd-Talbot, 2nd Earl Talbot was Lord Lieutenant of Ireland from 1817-21.
19. Laquais de place – A local man servant engaged when in a foreign city.
20. 2nd Lieutenant James Church (he is mistaken calling him William) went on half pay in 1816 and was wrecked off Holyhead on 5 February 1824.
21. Lieutenant Henry Palmer Hill 8th Foot.
22. The Greek War of Independence from the Turks started in 1822.
23. Reference *The London Gazette* Issue 18326, page 133, dated 19 January 1827.
24. When short of paper, writers often wrote over the previous text at right angles. The editor can confirm that reading such text is extremely difficult.
25. Moreland is now a suburb of Charleston.
26. Louis Philipe I was forced to abdicate in 1848 and was exiled to England.
27. The US – Mexican war of 1846-8.
28. This had been a rancorous issue for many years. The Waterloo Medal had caused great upset with veterans of the Peninsular War who had to wait until 1848 to claim the new General Service Medal which was supplied with bars for claimants back to 1800. James did receive his medal with nine bars as he expected (Ciudad Rodrigo, Badajoz, Salamanca, Vitoria, Pyrenees, Nivelle, Nive, Orthes & Toulouse).
29. Elizabeth was actually James' sister-in- law, she married Colonel Thomas Flournoy Foster who died in 1848.
30. Mary Macintosh Gairdner, James' wife.
31. He did receive one General Service Medal with nine clasps, a faded picture of which is shown in the illustrations in this book, however its current whereabouts are unknown. His Waterloo medal was apparently sold at auction in July 1990 by Christies to an unknown collector.

Chapter 18: Aftermath
1. Reference Elmhurst Cemetery, Georgia. The dates of his birth makes it likely that he is related although it is not certain. James Penman, grandson of our James, is also buried in this cemetery.
2. Reference, Summerville Cemetery, Augusta, Richmond, Georgia.
3. Reference, *Georgia, Property Tax Digests, 1793-1892*.
4. Bay Street faces onto the Savannah River.

Selected Bibliography

Anon, *Army Lists Various*.

Bell, Sir G., *Soldier's Glory* (Tunbridge Wells, 1991).

Bromley, J. and D., *Wellington's Men Remembered*, 2 volumes (Barnsley, 2012-15).

Burnham, R., and McGuigan, R., *The British Army Against Napoleon* (Barnsley, 2010).

Dalton, C., *The Waterloo Roll Call* (London, 1971).

Desaussure, H.W., *Report of Cases Assayed and Determined in the Court of Chancery of the State of South Carolina from Foundation to December 1813*, Vol. 3 (1817).

Hall, J., *A History of the Peninsular War*, Vol. VIII (London, 1998).

Hathaway, E., *Costello, The True story of a Peninsular War Rifleman* (Swanage, 1991).

Hayter, A., *The Backbone, Diaries of a Military Family in the Napoleonic Wars* (Edinburgh, 1993).

Kincaid, Captain Sir J., *Adventures in the Rifle Brigade* (Glasgow, 1981).

Leach, Lieutenant Colonel J., *Rough Sketches of the Life of an Old Soldier* (London, 1831).

Oman, Sir C., *Wellington's Army 1809-14* (London, 1986).

Park, S.J. and Nafziger, G.F., *The British Military Its System and Organisation 1803-15* (Cambridge, Canada, 1983).

Simmons, Major G., *A British Rifleman* (London, 1986).

Smith, G.C. Moore, *The Autobiography of Lt Gen Sir Harry Smith* (London, 1902).

Starnes, E., *The Slaveholder Abroad, or, Billy Buck's Visit with His Master, to England* (1860).

Syrett and DiNardo, *The Commissioned Sea Officers of the Royal Navy 1660-1815* (Navy Records Society, 1994).

Surtees, W., *Twenty Five Years in the Rifle Brigade* (London, 1996).

Urban, M., *Rifles* (London, 2003).

Verner, W., *History and Campaign of the Rifle Brigade 1800-13* (London, 1912).

Whyte, D., *Dictionary of Scottish Emigrants to the USA* (Baltimore, 1972).

Williams, Greg H., *The French Assault on American Shipping 1793-1813* (Jefferson, North Carolina, 2009).

Index

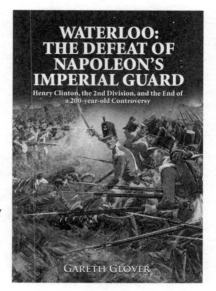

WATERLOO: THE DEFEAT OF NAPOLEON'S IMPERIAL GUARD

Henry Clinton, the 2nd Division, and the End of a 200-year-old Controversy

Gareth Glover

It was called the 'Crisis' of the battle. It was the moment when the infantry of Napoleon's Imperial Guard was pitched at the weakened Anglo-Allied centre. The first French column was beaten back but a second column pushed on, driving the British Guards before them. All seemed lost until Colonel Colborne ordered the 52nd Foot, in line formation, to wheel its face to the left. Suddenly, through the smoke, the menacing column of French Imperial guardsmen became visible directly to their front and still marching inexorably for the crest of the ridge ahead, seemingly oblivious to Colborne's men, now facing its vulnerable flank at short musket range.

The volley of a thousand lead musket balls struck the French column with such venom that it halted in its tracks, and those fortunate to escape injury turned to offer a confused but firm response. Colborne's men did not hesitate to reload, but gave one lusty cheer and advanced immediately towards the shattered column in a determined bayonet charge

The light infantry brigade, led by Colborne's men swept across the field, destroying all semblance of order and any attempts to rally to offer further resistance. Defeat rapidly turned into inglorious rout.

Truly the Light Brigade had swept the field clear of the enemy and had won the battle for Wellington. Or so some historians would claim. But is it all true?

This book uses a mass of previously unpublished material regarding the exploits of the Light Brigade and indeed the entire Second Division of which it was one of three brigades under the command of Sir Henry Clinton to examine this most controversial episode of the most famous battle of the nineteenth century.

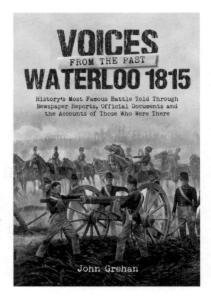

WATERLOO 1815

History's Most Famous Battle
Told Through Newspaper
Reports, Official Documents and
the Accounts of Those Who Were
There

John Grehan

Composed of more than 300 eye-witness accounts, official documents, parliamentary debates and newspaper reports, *Waterloo 1815* tells the story of Napoleon's last battles as they were experienced and reported by the men and women involved.

Heroic cavalry charges, devastating artillery bombardments, terrible injuries, heart-breaking encounters, and amusing anecdotes, written by aristocratic officers and humble privates alike, fill the pages of this book, the latest in the *Voices from the Past* series. Many of these reports have not been reproduced for almost 200 years.

Read of the teeth extracted from the dead on the battlefield, to be used for dentures in Britain. Learn what books Napoleon took with him on campaign; of the gunner who tripped as his cannon was discharged, blowing off his arms and legs, yet who lived out the day; of the soldier whose head was taken off by a cannon ball, as described by the man stood talking to him; of the children born as their fathers fought, and died, at Waterloo who were named after the famous battle; discover why a British soldier was worth more alive and dead; and what Wellington considered a good 'bottom'!